Dr. Natalie Weaver's *Marriage and Family* establishes a solid theological foundation that surely will inspire and challenge students and married couples to think deeply about the meaning of marriage as a holy union and a sacrament. She develops the virtues essential to marriage and family—love, justice, and forgiveness—which mutually enrich the spouses, their children, the church, and society. In order to discover deeper dimensions of marriage and family, she first gives the reader tools to interpret Scripture, history, ethics, and personal experience, then offers a discerning application. Not deterred by the pitfalls of marriage (physical and sexual abuse and high divorce rates), Dr. Weaver emphasizes marriage's prophetic stance against society's evils and strongly affirms its creative possibilities.

Thomas L. Schubeck, SJ
John Carroll University
University Heights, OH

The introductory nature of this book would be especially useful where its combination of foundational theology and theology of marriage could be the course focus. It is a foil for doing fundamental theology with strong material on marriage.

Daniel J. Finucane
Saint Louis University

AUTHOR ACKNOWLEDGMENTS

Many people over many years have contributed to the development of this book. At every turn I have been blessed with personal and professional friends, mentors, and guides whose insights and influences have helped to form my thoughts and words about theology, family, and marriage. Among my foremost contributors, I gratefully acknowledge:

- My wonderful teachers, who have guided and inspired me throughout my years of education
- My colleagues and administrators at Ursuline College, whose support and friendship are invaluable to me
- My students, from whom I learn and grow every term
- Jerry Ruff, Paul Peterson, and the editorial team of Anselm Academic, for their experienced guidance in seeing this project to completion
- My husband, for being the first one always to read and critique my work
- My mother, for thinking my work is good
- My sons, for sharing me
- Joseph Schell, SJ, and Frank Lihvar, SJ, of blessed memory

PUBLISHER ACKNOWLEDGMENTS

Thank you to the following individuals who reviewed this work in progress:

- Professor Jennifer Beste, Xavier University, Cincinnati
- Doctor Daniel J. Finucane, Saint Louis University, Missouri
- Professor Bridget Burke Ravizza, Saint Norbert College, De Pere, Wisconsin
- Professor Gail S. Risch, Creighton University, Omaha

Marriage and Family

A CHRISTIAN THEOLOGICAL FOUNDATION

Natalie Kertes Weaver, PhD

ANSELM ACADEMIC

Created by the publishing team of Anselm Academic.

Cover image © Images.com/Corbis

Printed in the United States of America

7024

ISBN 978-0-88489-977-8

Library of Congress Cataloging-in-Publication Data
Kertes Weaver, Natalie.
  Marriage and family : a Christian theological foundation / Natalie Kertes Weaver.
      p. cm.
Includes bibliographical references.
  ISBN 978-0-88489-977-8 (pbk.)
    1. Marriage—Religious aspects—Catholic Church. 2. Family—Religious aspects—
    Catholic Church. I. Title.
BX2250.K43 2009
234'.165—dc22

                                                                    2009020213

CONTENTS

1   INTRODUCTION: THEOLOGY OF MARRIAGE AND FAMILY—
WHAT IS IT AND HOW DO WE DO IT?   1

2   MARRIAGE AS COVENANT   6

3   JESUS' LOVE AND MARITAL CHARITY   19

4   HISTORICAL DEVELOPMENT AND MARRIAGE   34

5   MARRIAGE AS SACRAMENT   47

6   MODERN MARRIAGE AND HOW WE GOT HERE   59

7   DIGNITY AND HUMAN SEXUALITY WITHIN MARRIAGE   74

8   CONVERSION, CHARACTER, COMMITMENT   88

9   JUSTICE AND MARRIAGE   101

10   DOMESTIC CHURCH   113

11   DIVORCE AND FORGIVENESS   126

12   MARRIAGE AND THE FUTURE   140

Dedication

———

For my boys
William, Valentine, and Nathan

CHAPTER 1

INTRODUCTION: THEOLOGY OF MARRIAGE AND FAMILY—WHAT IS IT AND HOW DO WE DO IT?

Today when we think of marriage we probably think of the elaborate trappings that surround a wedding. In the opening decade of the twenty-first century in North America, people invested on average $20,000 to $30,000 on flowers, clothing, cakes, champagne, photographers, favors, rings, invitations, and musicians in order to celebrate their marriages in high style. The quest for a glamorous wedding is fostered by industry advertising, bridal expos, celebrity wedding coverage, and popular television programs that follow brides and grooms as they prepare elaborate festivities. Other "reality" shows attempt to match men and women romantically through a series of challenges and eliminations. The popularity of wedding-related entertainment reveals that most of us are at the very least fascinated by love, marriage, and family life.[1]

Most Americans will marry at some point in their lives. Despite the enormous investment of time and money that people put into weddings, however, nearly half of all marriages will end in divorce. An odd disconnect lies at the heart of what people want from marriage and what we are willing to do for marriage. I believe that this disconnect comes from an underdeveloped recognition of how much intimate relationships between spouses, parents, and children define our total life's meaning and experience. Can you remember even once a TV host, guest, or celebrity discussing the spiritual meaning of marriage or the role God plays in family life? Probably not—and that helps explain why popular conceptions of love and marriage are failing to create a lasting foundation for lifelong union and harmony between people.

Marriage and family life involve the whole person. Everything we wish to do, achieve, and become affects and is affected by the choice to marry and to have children. As religious values

---

1. To explore the breadth of contemporary attitudes toward marriage and family life, consider Barbara Dafoe Whitehead's documentary, *Marriage: Just a Piece of Paper?* produced and directed by Brian Boyer (Chicago: University of Chicago and WTTW-TV, 2002).

help to orient our lives in general, they absolutely should orient our understanding of marriage. Our era needs a more meaningful foundation for understanding marriage, and this book attempts to explore what such a foundation might be through a discussion of the religious meaning of intimate relationships between spouses, parents, and children. While recognizing and respecting the religious diversity of our audience, we discuss here the historical and contemporary understandings and practice of marriage and family from a Christian and at times specifically Roman Catholic perspective.

THINKING THEOLOGICALLY

Before turning to the theology of family and marriage, one must understand what it means to think theologically. The word *theology* means "logic about God" or "words about God" or simply "God-talk." But why reason about God at all? Why not just believe in God—or not—and let it go at that? The answer is that in life people experience things—both individually and collectively—that defy easy or immediate explanation. The popular Christian author C. S. Lewis notes that there is a numinous quality to our existence that informs our experiences and makes them, at times, seem extraordinary or blessed by a sacred other outside ourselves.[2] As a result, we will at some point or another ask questions about the meaning of our existence. Why am I here? Why did this happen? Is there something more out there than what I immediately perceive with my eyes and ears? Is love real or imagined? How should I live in relationship to others?

Throughout history human beings have felt and believed that there is something beyond themselves that grounds their lives and gives them meaning. Our effort to communicate or talk about what we seek to understand about God and God's relation to the world is called "theo-logia" or "God-talk." Humans experience a fundamental need to engage in God-talk.[3] As with all aspects of life, human beings are drawn to consider the meaning of human union and procreation. When we think about marriage in this sense, we are theologizing about marriage.

Throughout human history, not only have human beings asked questions about existence, they have believed that the source of their being—God—has supplied answers to their questions. In other words, people of many faiths have believed that a "God" or "Creator" has answered these questions about life's meaning in the form of divine revelation or self-disclosure. They have believed that God, who is ineffable and beyond the intellectual grasp of human beings, has made Godself intelligible through divine revelation or self-disclosure. Like a parent accommodating to the limited language and knowledge of a toddler, the indescribable God has communicated intelligibly his very Being to humanity.

What is more, many people have believed that God intended human life for fellowship and friendship with God. They have interpreted their personal histories as directed, touched, influenced, and made sensible by God. Divine self-disclosure is thus believed to occur within history, that is, within human experience. Perhaps more importantly, communities of people, not just individuals, have these experiences. When these collective histories and experiences are codified, passed down, and ritualized, they become religions.

Religions are characterized by a number of elements, including rituals, sacred places,

---

2. C. S. Lewis, *The Problem of Pain* (1940; repr., New York: HarperCollins, 2001), 6.

3. See, for instance, Karl Rahner, "Meditation on the Word God," in *Foundations of Christian Faith* (New York: Crossroad, 1978), 44–51, where he considers the fundamental human need to quest after the transcendent ground of being.

sacred books, sacred holidays, creeds, and prayers. Religions bring together a community of believers around a common set of beliefs and practices. The word *religion* comes from a root meaning "to bind together." Events in history in which groups of people perceive God as present or self-revealing become the cornerstones of religion and are thereafter preserved and passed down in traditions and writing.[4] Among the many important moments in life regularly recognized and ritualized by religions is marriage. This fact reveals the connection people have always perceived between marriage and children and the deepest purposes of human life.[5]

As religions become systematized and practiced over time, they often accumulate numerous writings reflecting their key beliefs. Here we find a communal effort at theologizing, in which groups of people over time reappropriate their beliefs in each new era. This legacy invites each new generation to seek out answers to their own personal and collective questioning. If people were simply to repeat old formulas handed down, the practice of religion in any era would be inauthentic mimicry. But when each generation appropriates religious traditions for itself, faith becomes vital and living. New contexts pose new questions and challenges, and ongoing theological investigation is critical for people to understand their faith and its meaning in the unique circumstances of their lives.[6] Theology thus has the task of asking perennial, fundamental questions, such as: [7]

- How is it possible for human beings to receive information about God?
- How do I know when God is communicating with me?
- Under what circumstances can I encounter God (such as in a place of worship or in daily life)?
- How should I read the sacred literature of my religious tradition?
- How do I understand religious authority?
- What guarantees the authenticity of my tradition?
- What does my tradition say about marriage?

Theology also has the task of asking questions generated by contemporary realities, such as:

- What does my faith have to say about justice and human rights?
- What is my faith's relationship to secular society or politics?
- Do I need to reconcile my faith with modern science?
- How do I address the reality of multiple religions and their competing truth claims?
- What does my faith have to do with economics or my choice of careers?
- How does my religious tradition deal with issues of sexuality and marriage?

Contemporary Brazilian theologians Leonardo and Clodovis Boff said of theology, "All

---

4. For a fine introduction to world religions and the nature of religious communities, consider Huston Smith, *The World's Religions: Our Great Wisdom Traditions* (San Francisco: HarperSanFrancisco, 1991).

5. A comparative study of marriage in world religions is found in Arun Roy, *Marriage Customs and Ceremonies in World Religions* (Victoria, BC, Canada: Trafford, 2005).

6. A number of contemporary Christian theologians, including Paul Tillich and David Tracy, have pointed out the necessity of a critical correlation between tradition and culture.

7. Majella Franzmann offers a friendly introduction to the study of religion, with particular attention to women's issues, in *Women and Religion* (Oxford and New York: Oxford University Press, 2000).

who believe want to understand something of their faith. As soon as you think about faith, you are already doing theology. So all Christians are in a sense theologians, and become more so the more they think about their faith."[8]

Of course, there are those who do theology professionally: pastors, teachers, religious writers, and so on. But any person actively engaged in thinking about his or her religious tradition—or even about human existence—can be said to be doing theology. Contemporary people who strive to relate their faith traditions to their lived experiences regarding marriage may be said to be doing a theology of the family.

WHAT IS A THEOLOGY OF THE FAMILY?

The phrase "theology of the family" may sound like an odd way to express the idea of talking about God and talking about families. When we "do" a theology of the family, however, what we are trying to understand is how the claims and beliefs of a faith tradition relate to the experience of family life and marriage. This relationship is twofold. On the one hand, a religious tradition teaches us to regard the family in a certain way. Part of this book will explore what Christianity and specifically the Roman Catholic Church have held to be true about marriage and family. On the other hand, a faith tradition also has important lessons to learn from contemporary family life—the lived experience of people.

We have already noted that for a faith tradition to be vital and authentic one must bring to the tradition the concerns, questions, and issues that people presently face. The reality of family life in the twenty-first century challenges many

traditional religious expectations and assumptions about what a family is and ought to be, particularly as it is understood from the perspective of the Christian faith. In order to develop an authentic Christian theology as it applies to contemporary family life, there are some things we must do:

* Evaluate the central teachings of the tradition as they relate to family and marriage
* Evaluate the impact of the biblical teachings on the question of family and marriage
* Evaluate the present realities of family and marriage
* Determine the adequacy of traditional teaching on family and marriage in light of present realities
* Choose how we, as contemporary people, will relate religious faith to the reality of families and marriages

As finite and limited human beings, our knowledge of God can only be tentative and approximate. All statements made about God are human statements. We struggle to put into words our beliefs about God, and we do so within the limits of a particular time and place, a particular level of experience and education, a particular language, and a particular bias or predisposition. Therefore, what we say about God reflects as much about what we think about ourselves as it does the reality of God. The Catholic Church teaches that theology true to the teaching of the Church is not mere human construct but rather discernment of God's self-disclosure to human beings, protected and guided by the Holy Spirit. However, the Catholic Church also teaches that God is transcendent, which means that God is bigger than human words, solutions, and contradictions.

---

8. Leonardo and Clodovis Boff, *Introducing Liberation Theology* (Maryknoll, NY: Orbis, 1987), 16.

As the sciences of human biology, psychology, anatomy, and sociology advance, new questions will arise about human life, love, sexuality, and marriage. As medical technologies continue to develop, new debates regarding reproduction and human generativity will emerge. Theologians will have to engage in a mutually critical two-way dialogue between these new questions and their religious traditions. Although perfect answers will evade us, we can reasonably hope to lead more responsible, informed, and reflective lives as a result of this dialogue.

WHO IS THIS TEXT FOR?

This book contains some specific content about the history and development of ideas on family and marriage, primarily from a Roman Catholic theological point of view. Much of the material, however, is not quantifiable data but rather the unquantifiable content of theological investigation and discussion. Be sensitive to the different types of information and knowledge.

You are encouraged to draw from personal experiences and insights as you read through this material. Indeed, as many contemporary theologians have argued, all theological reflection must begin in human experience. It is in and through our experiences that we have the ability to determine the meaning and validity of religious truth claims.

Truth is not always transparent. Through the sharing of multiple perspectives, different conceptions of truth can be clarified and corrected, broadened and humbled. This textbook does not presuppose a faith base or prior theological training on the part of the reader. However, it does seek to provide a thorough theological

foundation for thinking about marriage and family life from a Christian perspective. It also assumes that readers will be open to personal reflection and group dialogue. By sharing your understanding, you will help to illuminate others and to clarify your own ideas.

HOW DO I USE THIS TEXT?

Having taught college courses on the theology of marriage and family for several years, I have discovered that many undergraduate students have difficulty delving into this subject matter because it presupposes a certain background knowledge. It is a challenge, for instance, to discuss marriage as we find it in the Bible when students feel uncomfortable about their basic familiarity with Scripture. To address this issue, this text provides an introduction to systematic theology by looking at theological themes through the specific lens of marriage and family life. Each chapter provides discussions of theological themes, explores scholarly tools necessary for considering each theme responsibly, and concludes with the application of those themes to contemporary marriage and family life. My goal is to provide a foundational knowledge of Christian theology in general as well as its specific applications to marriage and family life.

Reflection questions are provided at the conclusion of each chapter to help prompt discussion and class reflection. While this book builds a framework for thinking theologically from one chapter to the next, the chapters may still be meaningfully assigned or read independently. Suggested readings for further investigation into each of the themes conclude each chapter.

CHAPTER 2

MARRIAGE AS COVENANT

Christians typically discuss marriage as a covenant. The notion of marriage as covenant resembles the covenant relationship between God and the Israelites as recounted in the Old Testament. In fact, the comparison of marriage to the biblical covenant is absolutely central to a Christian theology of marriage.

The Old Testament is a collection of writings developed, collected, and edited by the Israelites between two thousand and three thousand years ago. To the Jews, this collection is simply the Hebrew Bible, also called the Tanak. Christians call it the Old Testament, while the later, Christian writings constitute the New Testament. Both Jews and Christians consider the Old Testament/Hebrew Bible to be sacred literature that reveals God's being and action in history. For Christians, the Old Testament provides the basic framework and context for understanding the distinctive experience of Jesus of Nazareth. The Old Testament then is the best place to begin a contemporary discussion of the theology of family and marriage from a Christian perspective.

TOOLS

Have you ever heard anyone claim that they should do something or believe something "because the Bible says so"? In fact, many widely held assumptions about men, women, children, and family life are shaped by what the Bible has to say about such matters. Christians hold the Bible in such high regard because they believe it reveals God's intentions for human beings. For this reason, the Bible constitutes the first and primary source upon which the Christian faith tradition is built. But the Bible must be used intelligently and responsibly. Without a responsible reading of Scripture, we risk making binding claims about marriage that are either unsupported by Scripture or are biased by our personal interpretations.

At first blush it may seem self-evident what we mean when we use the word *revelation* or claim that the Bible is the Word of God. However, defining *revelation* proves more difficult than we might expect. To some, it may imply that the words of the biblical text are the exact words

DIFFERENT TAKES ON SCRIPTURE

People of Jewish faith refer to their sacred literature as the *Tanak*, an acronym made from the first letters of the Hebrew words *Torah*, *Nevi'im*, and *Kethuvim*, respectively Law, Prophets, and Writings, the major divisions by which the Hebrew Scriptures are organized. Christians call this same body of literature the Old Testament. When the books were canonized (accepted as sacred scripture) in the first century, the rabbis selected those books originally composed in Hebrew, authored by people with recognized religious authority, and mostly completed by the time of Ezra in 425 BCE.

By the time of Christ, a Greek translation of the Hebrew Scriptures, known as the *Septuagint*, was read more widely. The Septuagint also included seven additional books that were originally authored in Greek. The Christian Old Testament preserved these additional seven books, and they remained part of the Christian Bible until the Protestant Reformation in the sixteenth century. The Reformers eliminated these seven books from their canon, while the books remained part of the Catholic Bible. Despite some differences in the arrangement and number of books, today both Christians and Jews accept the Old Testament/Tanak as divine revelation.

chosen by God and miraculously communicated to the Bible's authors. To others *revelation* may refer to a new insight: "Today I had a revelation about what I am supposed to do with my life." Or *revelation* might mean a general sense of God's self-disclosure, not unlike someone revealing a personal secret to a close friend.

When we try to understand what we mean by the term *revelation* in Scripture, we need to consider several realities. First, the Scriptures span several thousand years. The earliest sources underlying the present-day texts were oral stories that date from as far back as 2000 BCE. If you think about how much can change even in one hundred years, it becomes immediately clear how many different cultures and contexts influenced the outlook and perspective of the Bible's authors. Second, because the texts span such a long history, they were written and edited by many different people who lived and worked in many different eras. As a result, the Scriptures tell and retell events in ways that speak specifically to the social situations of their authors. Ideas and attitudes changed throughout this long history,

making it difficult at times to interpret what the Bible is saying.

Let me give you an example of how thoughts about marriage in the Old Testament can change from one era to the next. In the year 587 BCE, the Israelites living in Judah were conquered and exiled to Babylon. The Israelites' cities were destroyed, their Temple lay in ruins, and many people were brutalized and murdered. The devastation the Israelites must have felt is nearly unimaginable. In order to comfort the exiles in Babylon, the prophet Jeremiah sent them a letter from Jerusalem encouraging them to go on with their lives, to seek work, to pray for the welfare of their new city, and to marry and have children (Jer 29:1–7). They did all of these things, with the hope that one day they would be allowed to return home. That hope was realized a few decades later when Persian forces conquered the Babylonians and allowed the exiled Jews to return to their homeland. Although Jeremiah did not instruct the Israelites to intermarry with the Babylonians, by the time of the restoration of Jerusalem many had in fact married and started families with foreign spouses. Upon their return, they were told by their leaders Ezra and Nehemiah to divorce their foreign spouses (Ezra 9–10; Neh 13:23–31).

Conflict over whether it was appropriate for the restored Israelites to retain spouses and other cultural influences acquired while in exile can be detected in many biblical passages and stories. One of the most striking examples is the story of Ruth, which may have been written during the restoration period to counter objections to foreign spouses. Ruth was a Moabite woman married to an Israelite man. After his death, instead of joining her kinsfolk, she stayed with her Israelite mother-in-law, Naomi. Because she stayed with her mother-in-law, she was ultimately rewarded by marriage to another Israelite man, Boaz, on the basis of the levirate marriage custom (Deut 25:5–10). This marriage custom required the nearest relative of a deceased man to marry the man's widow, in the event that she was childless, for the purpose of producing a male heir. Because Ruth was faithful to her mother-in-law, she was joyfully redeemed and socially secured by marriage and maternity. In this story, Ruth's foreignness is mitigated by her faithfulness.

Since both perspectives on marriage to foreign spouses occur in the Bible, one might ask which is right. The key to understanding conflicting points of view is to recognize that the authors and editors of the Bible neither held nor put forth a singular or undisputed teaching. When Jeremiah was written, the people were simply trying to survive their terrible cultural upheaval. When Ezra and Nehemiah were composed, they were trying to reclaim their identity as a people with as little foreign influence as possible. When Ruth was written (or at least edited into its current form), people were likely dealing with the question of whether and how a foreign person might also embody faithfulness to Israel's laws and covenant with God. The fact that multiple perspectives are preserved in the Bible

shows us that reading the Bible for instruction on any given issue (marriage to people of different cultures, in this case) is seldom straightforward, unproblematic, or without debate.

Beyond questions of authorship and context, readers of Scripture encounter issues of literary genre. The many authors of Scripture wrote various types of literature, just as today we have many genres serving a variety of audiences and purposes (textbooks, newspapers, poetry anthologies, biographies, text messages, science fiction short stories, and so on). We cannot expect these literary types or genres each to "reveal" truth in the same fashion. The "truth" of a poem is different from the "truth" of a scientific lab report. Readers of Scripture need to appreciate different types of truth found in different genres of literature within the Bible as well.

The actual manuscripts that have survived the ages pose difficulties for modern readers as well. While mostly in agreement with one another, these manuscripts do differ, often significantly. This stems from the fact that the ancient texts were copied by hand by scribes who occasionally made mistakes. Texts thus changed as they were transmitted from one generation to the next. When manuscripts disagree, the biblical scholar must attempt to ascertain which variant represents the original reading.

There is also the difficulty involved in arriving at the best possible interpretation of a passage of Scripture. Once again, we might think that the meaning of a sentence or a story is self-evident, but it soon appears that there are nearly as many possible interpretations as there are readers. This is especially true when we recognize how much our historical, social, and religious context influences how we understand the world. For example, imagine it is Valentine's Day, and you open a greeting card from your beloved. The card reads, "Your teeth are like a flock of ewes to be shorn. . . . Your neck is like David's tower girt with battlements." Should you be insulted? Not if you understand the imagery as it was originally intended. These images from the Song of Solomon (4:2–4) are part of a wedding poem, whereby the bridegroom woos his beloved. A woman in that time would have heard in these lines praise of her lovely, strong neck and shoulders and beautiful white teeth. Historical context is key to reading Scripture!

Much has changed in the four thousand years since the story of the biblical Israelites began. Today technologies make information and interconnection with people all over the globe literally keystrokes away. We travel with relative ease and speed, and we often live, study, and work far away from the places where we grew up. In the ancient world, not only did the majority of people have no access to written materials, but they rarely traveled great distances from their birthplaces. Twenty-first-century life is markedly different from life even one hundred years ago. It differs much more from life at the times various authors composed the Scriptures. Aware of the issues of context and social location, scholars have developed a number of critical-analytical tools for responsibly interpreting sacred literature. These tools include study of ancient manuscripts, culture, literary forms, editing histories, and ancient source material.

When we combine the findings of Scripture scholarship in all of these fields, we can reasonably conclude that "revelation" in the Old Testament refers to the Israelites' interpretation of their experience of history as an experience of God working within and directing that history.[1] When they thought about and reflected on why and how certain events occurred, they believed that their experiences were only possible by the hand of God. What is revealed through many different authors, time periods, and types of literature is the people's experience of God in their midst. What is the particular nature of that experience? The primary and central theme of the Israelite's identity is their sense of sharing a covenant with God. To put it simply, the covenant between the people and God is the foremost revelation of the Hebrew Bible. This covenant revealed in the myriad and diverse texts of the Hebrew Bible is the foundation for both Jewish and Christian understandings of marriage, and its significance as a result cannot be overstated.[2]

ISRAELITE LIFE AND COVENANT WITH GOD IN THE BIBLE

What is the covenant? The covenant is the relationship between God and the Israelites. The story of the covenant is told throughout many historical eras, by many authors, and in a number of genres in the Hebrew Bible. Sometimes the Israelites wrote about their covenant from a historical perspective while at other times they wrote from a prayerful or contemplative perspective. Sometimes they wrote about their covenant from the perspective of the prophets, or from the perspective of myth and legend. In all cases the covenant is the theme that binds the Scriptures together as a cohesive whole, because the covenant is how the Israelites defined their identity and understood the relationship they shared with their God. Let us consider the covenant as it appears in key books and historical events of the Hebrew Bible.

---

1. For an excellent and thorough discussion of ways of thinking about revelation, consult Richard McBrien, "Revelation: God's Self-Disclosure to Us," in *Catholicism* (New York: HarperSanFrancisco, 1994), 227–272.

2. Good introductions to the study of the Hebrew Scriptures include Lawrence Boadt, *Reading the Old Testament: An Introduction* (Mahwah, NJ, 1984) and Corrine Carvalho, *Encountering Ancient Voices* (Saint Paul: Anselm Academic, 2006).

MAJOR PERIODS IN ISRAEL'S HISTORY

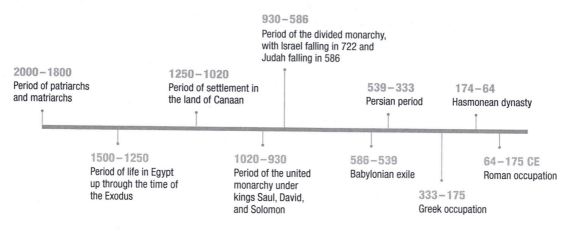

930–586
Period of the divided monarchy, with Israel falling in 722 and Judah falling in 586

2000–1800
Period of patriarchs and matriarchs

1250–1020
Period of settlement in the land of Canaan

539–333
Persian period

174–64
Hasmonean dynasty

1500–1250
Period of life in Egypt up through the time of the Exodus

1020–930
Period of the united monarchy under kings Saul, David, and Solomon

586–539
Babylonian exile

64–175 CE
Roman occupation

333–175
Greek occupation

IN THE BEGINNING

Genesis, the first book of the Bible, begins with the story of God's creation. This book details the birth of humankind; their fall from grace; God's protection of the people in their fallen state; the great flood that devastated the earth; God's renewed relationship with the people; the establishment of the covenant with the hero of the flood, Noah; God's promise of covenant carried on through the great patriarchs Abraham, Isaac, and Jacob; and the descendants of Jacob, who become the heads of the twelve tribes of Israel. Throughout Genesis, we see God establishing and renewing his special relationship with humankind. First, God creates the world, including Adam and Eve (1–2). Then God protects Noah and humankind from future natural disasters, and sees that the human race spreads over the whole earth (5:5–11:26). God then establishes a relationship with Abraham (11:27–12:9; 15:1–21). Finally God renews his covenant with Abraham through the patriarchs Isaac, Jacob, and Joseph (25:19–50:26). The covenant God establishes with these patriarchs is the promise that if they obey and trust in God, God will protect them and see that they and their descendents grow and flourish.

Marriage and family life play a big part in Genesis, beginning with the creation accounts. In Genesis 1:27 the human male and female are created simultaneously, suggesting that the male and female are indissolubly linked in their humanness and common purpose in creation. This idea is ratified in Genesis 2:4–25, where the human male is created first, and the creation of the human female is the culminating act of God's creative work. In this second, more folksy tale, the female is created as the only one who can provide proper companionship for her male counterpart. Upon seeing the woman, the man proclaims, "This one, at last, is bone of my bones and flesh of my flesh" (2:23). They will now cleave to one another, leaving behind even mother and father, because in their union "the two of them become one body" (2:24). These passages become a powerful statement about the mutuality and interdependence of husbands and wives, located at the very beginning of God's work in creation.

Although the couple is subsequently banished from paradise (a common motif in ancient literature of the region), the Hebrew Bible continues to portray God as a loving provider who takes care of the basic needs of human beings.

Indeed, God is portrayed as blessing human beings precisely through their fertility and off-spring. Fertility is the heart of God's covenant promise to Abraham, as we read in the following passage (17:1–7):

1. When Abram was ninety-nine years old, the Lord appeared to him and said: "I am God the Almighty. Walk in my presence and be blameless.

2. Between you and me I will establish my covenant, and I will multiply you exceedingly."

3. When Abram prostrated himself, God continued to speak to him:

4. "My covenant with you is this: you are to become the father of a host of nations.

5. No longer shall you be called Abram; your name shall be Abraham, for I am making you the father of a host of nations.

6. I will render you exceedingly fertile; I will make nations of you; kings shall stem from you.

7. I will maintain my covenant with you and your descendents after you throughout the ages as an everlasting pact, to be your God and the God of your descendents after you."

The idea that God demonstrates his covenantal blessing on human beings is reinforced through the motif of the barren woman conceiving a child through God's miraculous intervention, as in the cases of Sarah, wife of Abraham (Gen 16:1–2; 21:1–2), Rebecca, wife of Isaac (25:21), and Rachel, wife of Jacob (30:1; 30:22–23). Through these interventions, God continues the covenant he began with human beings in creation, while demonstrating that through human union God's providential promise can be fulfilled.

IN THE LAW

At the beginning of the Book of Exodus, we find that the tribes of Israel have migrated to the delta region of the Nile because of famine. They have become a successful and numerous people, who enjoy good status with the Egyptians. However, the goodwill that they shared with the Egyptian pharaoh on account of Joseph, Jacob's son by Rachel, has long been forgotten (Exod 1:8). The Israelites are drafted into servitude by the pharaoh for his building projects, and their burdens are tremendous, dangerous, and difficult (1:9–14). They are a persecuted people and the firstborn male children of the Israelites are targeted for murder (1:15–16). Just when the people of Israel are most oppressed, Exodus

COVENANT IN GENESIS

Mention of the covenant occurs throughout Genesis. Compare the discussion of covenant in the following passages: Genesis 9:1–17, in which God makes a covenant with Noah, and Genesis 28:10–22, in which God speaks to Jacob in a dream.

After reading these passages, answer the following questions:

- What do these passages have in common, and how do they differ?
- In what ways, implicitly or explicitly, do they relate to marriage and family?
- How do these passages characterize the relationship between God and human beings?

relates that God remembers his covenant with Abraham, Isaac, and Jacob (2:24).

In order to deliver the Israelites from their hardships, God raises up the prophet Moses, who will guide them out of slavery in Egypt to another home in the promised land of Canaan. Moses is called by a vision of God in a burning bush and charged with the task of delivering the Israelites from slavery (3:1–10). In this dramatic event, the audacious claim is made that God actually tells Moses God's name: YHWH, which we are told means "I am who am" (3:14). This encounter, complete with God's self-revelation of his name, is an incredibly bold statement about how the Israelites perceived the close relationship between God and humankind.

Numerous miracles in Exodus reveal God's providential relationship with the people. Among the most memorable are the plagues that persuade Pharaoh to release the Hebrews from captivity (7:14–10:29), the Passover in which the children of Israel are spared from death (11:1–12:28), the destruction of the Egyptian forces that pursue the Israelites at the parting of the sea (14:23–31), and the provision of food and water in the desert as the Israelites journeyed to Canaan (16:4–15). All of these miracles show that God has a special purpose in mind for this people.

As Scripture scholars have pointed out, it can be argued that most of the miracles that occurred were actually natural phenomena of the region. However, the fact that the events occurred in such a way as to benefit the people toward the end of their ultimate liberation is where the real meaning of the miracles lies. Just as a person today who survives a deadly accident or recovers from a terrible disease might interpret the hand of God in his life, so also the Israelites saw God at work in their history.

God's work in history did not end with the mere event of the liberation from slavery. Indeed, the story of the liberation from slavery is prologue to the central event of Exodus, God's giving of the covenant law to Moses on Mount Sinai (Exod 19–24). Here, in this face-to-face meeting with God, a God who even reveals his name to his prophet, the meaning of the covenant becomes most clear. The people are not freed to just any end or purpose. Rather, they are freed to become God's people. This involves the twofold commandments to reverence and worship God and to establish just and wholesome relationships with one another. A review of the numerous laws cited in Exodus, Leviticus, Numbers, and Deuteronomy will show that God is as concerned about just relationships between people as with proper worship and sacrifice. The covenant established with God on Mount Sinai is to be lived out in the land of Canaan.

The laws recounted in these books are often difficult for modern readers, because they represent a variety of types of law that are no longer observed. Some of these laws have to do with marriage. This is an area where readers of Scripture need to be critical and discerning both about the meaning of "revelation" and the application of biblical teachings to our present-day lives.

Consider these sets of laws. In Exodus 21:1–11 we find a series of laws pertaining to Hebrew slaves and their families. Although the Israelites were themselves delivered from slavery in Egypt, they continued to keep slaves. Moreover, it was possible for fathers to sell their daughters into servitude. Sometimes slaves were married or were taken as wives by their masters. The laws recounted here describe how slaves, their spouses, and their offspring should be treated in the event that the slave was freed.

In Leviticus 20–21 we find laws that treat, respectively, punishments for sin and rules that govern priests. Many of the issues covered in these chapters relate to marriage and sexual relationships. Some of the topics include sexual contact with animals, homosexuality, incest, intercourse during menstruation, adultery, and proper sexual and marital conduct for priests.

Some of the punishments for sexual or priestly misconduct cited in these chapters are shocking to modern readers. For instance, death is the punishment for adultery (20:10) and male homosexual contact (20:13). Ostracism is the punishment for a couple having sexual contact during the woman's menses (20:18). Immolation is the punishment for the daughter of a priest who becomes a prostitute (21:9).

What are modern readers to make of these laws? I suggest that they should neither be loosely dismissed nor taken as normative. Rather, they should be read in light of the whole covenant law, which helps to explain why such laws would be included in the first place. The covenant law includes a number of different types of law codes, including: the Ten Commandments, the covenant law codes, and the priestly law codes.[3] All of these laws, compiled over centuries, intended to direct the Israelites in proper conduct religiously and ethically for the good of the whole community. Adultery, for example, was considered such a serious crime because it disrupted the foundational unit of society, namely the family, the locus for the procreation of children. The Israelites viewed violations of marriage through adultery as damaging to the whole community and not just to the individuals involved. Today such punishments for adultery would be untenable. Also, many have pointed out that women were more penalized than men and held to a stricter standard of sexual exclusivity than were men. However, the point of the law was to guarantee sexual fidelity within marriage because the consequences of infidelity were and are so profound for so many people (parents, children, in-laws, and the entire community).[4]

The Israelites believed that God was as concerned with intimate personal issues that affected others as God was with overtly religious matters. Marriage and sexual integrity, then, were seen as extensions of the covenant between God and people as well as a place where that covenant should be lived out. When trying to understand any difficult law within the Bible, it

THE LAW AND GOD'S PROMISE

The law in Exodus, Leviticus, Numbers, and Deuteronomy covers a multitude of religious and social situations. The law itself represents the human response to God's promise, first established with Abraham. In order to get a sense of the range of concerns covered by the covenant at Mount Sinai, read Exodus 20–24. After reading these laws, answer the following questions:

- What types of laws do you find in these passages?
- Identify and describe those laws that relate to marriage, sexuality, and children. Do these laws seem appropriate or relevant for people today?
- What laws in these passages are problematic for you? Should they still be binding for people today who consider the Bible to be God's revelation? Why or why not?
- What is your overall sense of the covenant based on these laws? How would you describe its mandates both religiously and socially?
- How would you describe the relationship between covenant laws in general and marriage as a covenant specifically?

---

3. See Carvalho, "Reading the Law through a Contemporary Lens," in *Encountering Ancient Voices*, 89–97.

4. Ephraim Neufeld reviews Israelite marriage in *Ancient Hebrew Marriage Laws* (Toronto: Longmans, Green and Co., 1944).

is helpful to ask what the purpose of the law might have been at the time it originated and whether there is any insight or wisdom in that ancient purpose that still resonates today.

IN THE LAND

The history of the people in the land is not as idyllic as one might expect, given their special relationship with God. If the Exodus occurred sometime in the mid-thirteenth century, it took about two hundred years for the tribes of Israel to coalesce into a unified whole and to establish a kingdom. The Scriptures began to be written at the height of the golden age of the kingdom under King David in the eleventh century. However, corruption, politics, and old tribal rivalries survived, leading to the eventual division and destruction of the kingdom. Two kingdoms were formed (Israel in the north and Judah in the south), both of which were pressed upon and ultimately destroyed by competing world powers in subsequent centuries.

During the time of the divided kingdom, many prophets emerged in Israel who sought to challenge the kings and prominent citizens of the capital cities of Samaria and Jerusalem. The prophets returned to the notion of covenant in order to assess the problems and challenges their kingdoms faced. The prophets attributed these problems to the people's failure to live up to their end of the covenant. One such prophet was Hosea.

Hosea took as a wife a woman named Gomer, who was a prostitute. Hosea saw in his marriage to Gomer a parallel relationship to that of the Israelites and their God. By the mid-eighth

HOSEA AND GOMER

Hosea 1–3 describes the tumultuous marriage between Hosea and Gomer. By marrying Gomer, Hosea is fulfilling his prophetic calling by symbolically living out in his own life the struggles that stress the relationship between the Israelites and God. In order to reflect on the meaning of this prophetic work more fully, read Hosea 1–3 and answer the following questions:

- Describe the nature of the infidelity that Hosea experiences. What type of infidelity has God experienced?

- The prophet redeems his wife and restores her to good standing. How is this act related to God's action on behalf of Israel?

- How would you characterize Hosea's forgiveness of Gomer? Consider both his emotional state and his actions.

- Should Hosea's extraordinary compassion for Gomer be a model for marriages today? Why or why not?

century BCE, when Hosea prophesied, the kingdom of Israel had compromised its integrity by admitting foreign religious practices (which were deemed immoral). The ruling class had become corrupt and exploitative of those less affluent. Thus Israel had strayed and become unfaithful to the covenant. Similarly, Gomer strayed and was unfaithful to her husband. Under such circumstances, Hosea was permitted and indeed required by religious law to cast out his wife and even to stone her. But he refused to do so, instead recovering her from her debasement and welcoming her back into his home. Rather than repudiating her for her infidelity, Hosea redeemed Gomer and treated her as his queen. By treating her with such compassion and steadfast love, Hosea helped Gomer to transform into the person she was meant to be all along.

This is also how Hosea depicts God's action in Israel's history. Although Israel strayed miserably, God nevertheless remained faithful and compassionate. Even when the affectionate love between the people and God was stressed by Israel's faithlessness, God's actions revealed a deeper love that could withstand the greatest challenges. This metaphor of active and steadfast spousal love became the archetypal Old Testament image for God's covenant with the people of Israel. Moreover, since marriage could be seen as a metaphor for God's relationship with his people, the very perception of marriage was exalted. Marriage came to be seen as a place where service, forgiveness, and steadfastness not only could but *should* be present, because in marriage people have the opportunity to live out God's love personally.

IN THE WRITINGS

Although prophets such as Hosea worked to encourage the Israelites to return to their covenant obligations, the kingdoms of Israel and Judah were too compromised by political instability and corruption to withstand the forces of Assyria and Babylon for long. By the year 722 the northern kingdom had been destroyed by Assyria (2 Kings 17:1–41). By 586 the southern kingdom had been destroyed by Babylon (2 Kings 24:8–25:21). In the event known as the Babylonian exile, the citizens of Jerusalem were carried away in chains, having been overrun by the great general Nebuchadnezzar. This experience was devastating to Israelite identity, indeed the most ruinous event in Israel's history. Among the worst tragedies of the exile was the destruction of the Temple in Jerusalem, which was the centerpiece of Israelite religion. Torn from their homes, the Israelites faced the challenge of trying to understand why they had enjoyed freedom and prosperity in the promised land of Canaan, only to lose it.

In reflecting on this loss, the Israelites composed some of the finest literature in the Hebrew Bible. They compiled and edited their history and stories into a version of the Old Testament that we would recognize today so as to lovingly record all that had been. They also wrote beautiful poems and stories reflecting on the meaning of human life, suffering, hope, and the consolation of God's everlasting love. Much of the Writings comes from this period. Although this literature is not explicitly concerned with Israel's history vis-à-vis the covenant with God, it is fundamentally concerned with the meaning of covenanted life.

One of the most beautiful texts of the Writings, the Song of Solomon, is a poetic exploration of the theme of covenanted love. In its current form the Song of Solomon is probably derived from a poem that would have been read or acted out during ancient wedding ceremonies. On one level, it may certainly be read as a poem about the ecstatic pleasure of physical and sensual love. Many modern interpreters are inclined to read it precisely in this vein. However, for most of its history, Hebrew and Christian interpreters alike have seen in the poem, respectively, an allegory of God's love for the people of Israel or Christ's love for the church. It is fascinating to note that even after a period of cultural destruction, exile, and devastating loss, the Israelites were best able to express their sense of covenant relationship to God in terms of the fullness of human intimacy between spouses.

Reading this poem I am always struck by the tenderness and joy that the lovers express and find in one another. Consider these verses:

I delight to rest in his shadow, and his fruit is sweet to my mouth. (2:3)

His left hand is under my head and his right arm embraces me. (2:6)

How beautiful is your love, my sister, my bride, how much more delightful is your love than wine, and the fragrance of your ointments than all spices! (4:10)

Set me as a seal on your heart, as a seal on your arm; for stern as death is love, relentless as the nether world is devotion; its flames are a blazing fire. Deep waters cannot quench love, nor floods sweep it away. (8:6–7)

It is not surprising that readers see in this poem a sensuous description of physical love. The imagery of the poem invites such a reading. What is surprising, however, is that readers have often seen in these same images poetic descriptions of divine-human love. I find it stunning to think that people could be to God more delightful than wine and fragrance, more beautiful than any other, and loved with a relentless passion. What great comfort to imagine God holding people as a lover would, with one hand supporting the neck and the other embracing the body. It is a remarkable witness to divine love that the Israelites saw in this poem a statement about their relationship with God, even after all the suffering they experienced within their history. It is equally remarkable that only in the metaphor of physical love within marriage could they adequately express their experience of divine love.

SUMMARY

The exploration and exposition of the meaning of God's covenant relationship with the Israelites is the unifying theme of all Hebrew literature. Whether the Israelites were writing during the high point of the kingdom united under David or exiled by the waters of Babylon, they wrote about their covenant. Whether they were writing history, poetry, or legend, they wrote about their covenant. For the covenant defined them.

Moreover, the idea of the covenant shaped the Christian community, which came to understand the work of Jesus in the New Testament as establishing a new covenant with God.

In order to grasp fully the meaning of covenant between God and the people of Israel, one needs to read the Scriptures. The selections discussed here are meant to sensitize us to the depth of experience and contemplation that the Israelites invested in the notion of what it means to share a covenant with God. For in their experience, God was not an impersonal power beyond conception, nor was God a fickle deity to be lured and manipulated through deeds and rites. The all-powerful God of creation and history was, in the experience of Israel, as close as a lover and as involved in their lives as a spouse. The lived experience of marriage became a place and opportunity for the people to experience and practice covenanted life, which they believed to be instituted and ordered by God himself. Indeed, the Israelites believed that God's covenant promise was most concretely fulfilled in the context of marriage through the blessing of children. On the one hand, the Israelites used the incomparably close human relationship of marriage in order to express how God and the people interrelate. On the other hand, the steadfast and tireless fidelity of God to the people became the paradigm or ideal model for actual marriages.

APPLICATION TO FAMILY AND MARRIAGE TODAY

The Israelites self-consciously made the connection between human marriage and divine-human love. Although the family structures that characterized the biblical Israelites did not always live up to the covenant ideal, the concept of covenant remained as a rule and judge of conduct and character within marriage. If we reflect for a moment upon what this model reveals to us about human marriage, three points emerge. First, a theology of the family and marriage grounded in the biblical notion of covenant affirms that marriage is a sacred reality. In other words, although marriage and family life have obvious social, legal, and even political dimensions, the human experience of marriage and family life transcends mere sociological analysis. It is a reality that, when it points toward the ideal, becomes a condition for human beings to experience the divine.

In what way does this occur? Take again the example of Hosea's love for Gomer. His love is not a passive affection or sentimentality. It is, rather, a love expressed in terms of saving action. Hosea recovers and restores Gomer, not because she merits it by her past behaviors, but because she has an inalienable worth in his eyes. He transcends his baser inclinations to anger, jealousy, and retribution in order to achieve both her restitution and the salvation of their marriage. No mere legal or social explanation of marriage can account for love's desire to overcome weakness, loss, and the hurts people are all too capable of inflicting upon one another. In Hosea we see the human acting as the divine in order to reach beyond human feeling. True interpersonal love that seeks excellence and wholeness in one's beloved causes goodness to flourish in both lover and beloved. It is in this sense that marriage may be understood as a sacred reality.

This brings us to the second point, which is that covenant love is not passive feeling or sentimentality. It is rather compassionate action and fidelity. It is expressed in terms of what is done as opposed to what is felt. Although the emotional dimensions of love should not be diminished or disparaged, a mere affective sense of love is antithetical to the biblical notion of covenant love. Covenant love is love expressed in behaviors that are constant, redeeming, restorative, patient, and steadfast, even when the emotions would instruct us to behave otherwise.

A final point is that covenant love is indissoluble. Invoking the comparison between a contract and a covenant is useful here. A contract is a legal agreement that binds two parties to one another under a specific set of conditions and for a specific purpose for a specified time. Covenants, on the other hand, are unconditional, and while they may be legal, they cannot be broken or forfeited in the same fashion as a contract. For example, one does not establish a set of conditions upon which a friendship will depend and then write it on parchment to be signed by the friends. And when a friendship is challenged by a betrayal or failing, one does not merely cancel it and begin anew with someone else. Covenants involve the whole person and the measure of the person's character in a covenanted relationship is the sincerity and commitment one brings to upholding the relationship. As covenant relationships largely define human beings, they cannot be rejected without causing permanent damage to the persons rejecting them. In this sense covenants are indissoluble, for they involve the entire character and identity of the persons involved.

When we say that a biblical sense of covenant founds a Christian theology of marriage, we are saying that marriage is:

- A sacred reality
- Based on active love
- Indissoluble

These three points will frame the entire Christian outlook on family and marriage, and they find their origin in the long and meandering history of the biblical Israelites who came to know themselves by coming to know God. Their covenant is the beginning revelation of God's love, and indeed, of love itself.

Questions for Review and Discussion

1. What is "revelation"? What are some of the issues modern readers face when turning to the Bible for guidance and instruction?

2. How would you define God's covenant with the people of Israel?

3. Identify and summarize the biblical selections cited within this chapter that relate to marriage as a covenant. When viewed together, how would you summarize the Hebrew Bible's view of marriage?

4. Legal material in the Bible can be difficult to reconcile with modern attitudes and concepts of rights. How do you think we should regard biblical laws? How do these laws relate to the claim that the Bible is divine revelation?

5. Evaluate the marriage between Hosea and Gomer. Does Hosea do the right thing? How can or should marriage be a context for redemption?

6. God is typically depicted as the husband and the Israelites as the wife in the God-Israel marriage metaphor. Some have suggested that this endorses the idea that men ought to play a god-like role over their wives in human marriages, even having the authority to punish their wives as God punishes Israel. How do you evaluate this suggestion? Is it problematic for you?

7. What is the difference between a covenant and a contract? Should marriage legally be one or the other? How might you conceive of the differences between the two legally?

8. Do some brief research on the legal differences between marriage contracts and marriage covenants. What arguments would you make in favor of or against legal marriage covenants versus legal marriage contracts?

9. Does a covenant need to be a legal or civil reality in order to be binding?

Resources for Further Reading

Old Testament Resources

Lawrence Boadt, *Reading the Old Testament: An Introduction* (Mahwah, NJ: Paulist Press, 1984).

Corrine Carvalho, *Encountering Ancient Voices* (Saint Paul: Anselm Academic, 2006).

Covenant Marriage Resources

John Kippley, *Sex and the Marriage Covenant: A Basis for Morality* (San Francisco: Ignatius Press, 2005).

Craig Hill, *Marriage: Covenant or Contract* (Northglenn, CO: Harvest Books, 1992).

Bernard Cardinal Law, *Christian Marriage: A Covenant of Love and Life; A Pastoral Letter* (Boston: Roman Catholic Archbishop of Boston, 1998).

John Cardinal O'Connor, *Covenant of Love: Pastoral Reflections on Marriage* (Liguori, MO: Liguori Press, 1991).

John Tarwater, *Marriage as Covenant: Considering God's Design at Creation and the Contemporary Moral Consequences* (Lanham, MD: University Press of America, 2006).

John Witte, Jr., and Eliza Ellison, eds., *Covenant Marriage in Comparative Perspective* (Grand Rapids: Eerdmans, 2005).

3

JESUS' LOVE AND MARITAL CHARITY

Often we think of love as sentimentality, feelings of affection, attraction, and chemistry between people. Sometimes we refer to the experience of affection and attraction as "love at first sight" or "falling in love." This emotion-based understanding of love is popular for good reason. When people fall in love, they enjoy the feeling of attraction to each other, happiness in each other's presence, and longing for each other in times of absence. As important as attraction and affection are to the experience of love, sparks between people can wane as quickly and unexpectedly as they began. A Christian theology of marriage requires a concept of love that is more sustainable and enduring than a passive concept of love that simply "happens." Charity, the love modeled by Jesus in the New Testament, is precisely the kind of enduring and sustainable love that is the foundation of a Christian theology of marriage.

Love in the New Testament entails something more profound and lasting than feelings of affection and attraction. Affection and attraction are healthy and human attributes of love, but when viewed from a scriptural perspective, the capacity to give and receive love is rooted in the human relationship to God: "We love because [God] first loved us" (1 John 4:19).

The biblical Israelites came to understand the ideal of human love as modeled after God's steadfast love for them. The first Christians also interpreted love as modeled after the relationship between God and human beings. However, the Christian lens for interpreting this relationship differed from that of their Hebrew predecessors in that Christians came to experience and understand God's love in the person of Jesus. For Christians, Jesus is the revelation of God's love. Pope Benedict XVI's encyclical letter *God is Love* confirms this reality:

We have come to believe in God's love: in these words the Christian can express the fundamental decision of his life. Being Christian is not the result of an ethical choice or a lofty idea, but the encounter with an event, a person, which gives life a new horizon and a decisive direction. Saint John's Gospel describes that event in these words: "God so loved the world that he gave his only Son, that whoever believes in him should . . . have eternal life" (3:16). In acknowledging the centrality of love, Christian faith has retained the core of Israel's faith, while at the same time giving it new depth and breadth.[1]

The New Testament record of the life, words, and actions of Jesus offers a transformed picture of the human capacity to love and be loved. The renewed potential for love between humans and God is identified by the New Testament authors as a *new covenant* with God, which is both a preserving and deepening of the Old Testament notion of covenant. Christian theology, including the theology of marriage, emerges from this new covenantal notion founded in the potential for love, redemption, and peace that the life of Jesus represents as remembered in the biblical record.

TOOLS

Just as it was necessary to consider the Hebrew Scriptures, it is all the more necessary to consider the New Testament in a discussion of Christian marriage, because the New Testament contains the first and fullest documents we have about Jesus, his ministry, and the earliest Christian communities. Some basic knowledge of the New Testament will help us in our discussion of its concept of love. The New Testament, like the Old, is a compilation of documents that came to have special revelatory meaning for the followers of Jesus. There are twenty-seven books of the New Testament, which were authored between

roughly 51 CE and 130 CE. The books are divided into four literary genres: gospels, epistles, acts (history), and apocalyptic.[2]

The four Gospels are books about the life and ministry of Jesus. They are close to biographies in form, but they do not attend to details in the same way that we would expect a modern biography to record facts about a person's life. A better way to think of the Gospels is that they are theological interpretations of Jesus, written by people who were transformed by the meaning of his life. We do not know who the human authors of the texts were, although traditionally they have been attributed to Matthew, Mark, Luke, and John.

Most scholars argue that the Gospels were written between thirty and seventy years after Jesus' death and Resurrection, leading them to conclude that they were not written by people who actually knew Jesus during his lifetime. This helps to explain the occasional discrepancies in chronology or point of view that we encounter when we do a side-by-side comparison of the Gospels. Such discrepancies are understandable when we remember that the Gospels were written not simply to record data, but to spread the news about the meaning of Jesus' life, death, and Resurrection (*gospel* means "good news").

The Book of Acts is an early church history written by the same individual who wrote the Gospel of Luke. Acts tells the story of the first Christians and the spread of Christian faith throughout the world. Acts tells how Jesus' life brings salvation to the whole world, concluding with the arrival of the apostle Paul in Rome. This trajectory demonstrates that the Christian

---

1. *Deus Caritas Est*, §1.

2. There are many excellent resources for introductory study of the New Testament, which typically explain the context of the writings as well as provide specific and detailed analysis of each of its books. Some resources I find useful in teaching this material include: Stephen Harris, *The New Testament: A Student's Introduction* (Boston: McGraw Hill, 2002); Bart Ehrman, *The New Testament: A Historical Introduction to the Early Christian Writings* (New York: Oxford University Press, 2004); and Daniel Harrington, *Interpreting the New Testament: A Practical Guide* (Michael Glazier Books, 1990).

faith, which began in an eastern province of the Roman Empire, successfully spread to the very capital of the empire and to every sort of person within the empire.

The Epistles of the New Testament include the oldest writings of the Christian canon. The earliest were written by Paul to address specific issues confronting the first Christian churches. Paul, and missionaries like him, spread the message of Jesus by making trips to distant cities, taking up residence within the communities they visited, and working to establish churches with the locals. After they had helped a community get on its feet, they would move on to new territories. Missionaries wrote letters to keep in touch with the churches they established and address any problems they encountered. Many of the letters Paul wrote survived and were circulated broadly because of the wisdom and truth they conveyed about the way a Christian community should behave, how it should be organized, and what it should believe.

Other letters dating to a later period were written by a range of authors for a variety of reasons. Some expressed a particular theological point of view of importance to the author; others were written to safeguard believers against false or wrong interpretations of Jesus, church leadership, or morals. These letters were addressed to Christians generally, unlike the letters of Paul, which were mostly written to specific congregations. They are commonly called "Catholic Epistles," because they are universal (i.e., "catholic") in intent.

The Book of Revelation is apocalyptic in theme and content, focusing on events that will lead up to the end of this present world and usher in the world to come. The meaning and significance of this book garner particular debate because of the ambiguity of its apocalyptic imagery and messages. It draws heavily upon Daniel, Ezekiel, and other Old Testament books, and is intended to give hope to people who experience suffering and persecution in this life by the promise that they will be vindicated in the next.

As with the Old Testament, we do ourselves a disservice if we read the New Testament without employing the tools of modern Scripture scholarship available to us. This is particularly important in our study of marriage and family within the New Testament, because at times the New Testament reflects conflicting points of view on the value and meaning of intimate relationships. For example, in the Gospel of Luke, Jesus speaks to a gathering of people about what is required of them if they want to be disciples. Jesus says, "If anyone comes to me without hating his father and mother, wife and children, brothers and sisters, and even his own life, he cannot be my disciple" (14:26). In this same Gospel, however, Jesus shows profound compassion to a grieving father named Jairus, whose daughter has died, and brings the girl back to life (8:49–56). In the letter 1 Timothy, bishops and deacons are allowed to be married only once and must manage their households and children well (3:1–13). Why does Jesus respond to a father's grief in one passage while instructing people in another to forsake their human attachments if they want to be his followers? Why are leaders of the Christian churches permitted to marry and have children, if such attachments distract from being true followers of Christ?

These complicated questions can be negotiated more successfully when we are attentive to issues such as literary genre, original source material, authors of the texts, time frames and contexts during which the various books were written, and the purpose of the writing. Even a cursory look at Christian history between the years 30 and 130 CE will reveal that in every decade of that century Christians faced new challenges as communities of believers attempted to understand the significance of Jesus' life and to preserve his memory. They also faced challenges as they accommodated to the broader Roman

Empire in which Christianity ultimately spread and flourished as an institution. What was happening at any given time influenced what people wrote about and emphasized. While the books in the New Testament may differ in purpose, style, and authorship, we can confidently acknowledge that each of the books in its own way serves the goal of spreading the good news about Jesus and the transformative impact of his life.

WHO WAS JESUS AND WHY DOES HE MATTER FOR MARRIAGE?

The New Testament is our best source about Jesus. No other ancient documents detail his life, nor have any significant archeological remains from the first century been unearthed that mention him. The Gospels, the most detailed accounts of Jesus' life in the New Testament, date to several decades after Jesus lived and were written as testimonies about Jesus' meaning for believers. Thus it is sometimes difficult to be certain of specific historical facts about the life of Jesus, but the New Testament texts remain our best source of information about this man and the beliefs of his followers.

There have been many efforts at reconstructing the historical life of Jesus over the past centuries, and scholars disagree about the historical accuracy of some data.[3] Certain aspects of Jesus' life are almost universally agreed upon, while others (such as his birth to a virgin mother or his performance of miracles) are debated. Most scholars agree that Jesus was born around the year 4 BCE in the province of the Roman Empire called Judea. Although almost nothing is known about his early childhood, adolescence,

or young adulthood, the Gospels indicate that he was born to observant Jewish parents named Mary and Joseph. Jesus was baptized around his thirtieth birthday by a preacher in the Galilee region named John, after which time he began his ministry as an itinerant teacher. After only a few years of preaching, Jesus traveled to Jerusalem during the Passover feast in the fourth decade of his life. His teachings and actions aroused the suspicion of both the religious high court and the Roman governor. He subsequently was arrested, tried, and executed by Roman soldiers.

This thin sketch of Jesus' life in no way captures the richness of his story or the impact of his life on his followers. It is for this reason the Gospels were written: to tell the story of Jesus' life and work in its full meaning. To appreciate the impact of Jesus' life on his original followers, a bit of background information is necessary. At the time of Jesus' life, Judea had been a province of the Roman Empire for several decades. Prior to the Roman conquest, Israel had been independent for only about one hundred years, having been occupied by various foreign powers from the eighth through the second centuries BCE. The impact of foreign colonization on the Israelites and their culture had been devastating. Samuel Oyin Abogunrin, in his commentary on the Gospel of Luke, describes how this history particularly impacted women and children:

> The presence of foreign troops created havoc since the local populace had to provide for the various needs of [a moving army]. Women and children were captured. Such women were vulnerable to rape. This created a special problem for Jewish women because even if a Jewish woman had only been in danger of being raped a pious

---

3. Some useful resources for investigating historical questions about the life of Jesus include Gerd Theissen and Annette Merz, *Historical Jesus: A Comprehensive Guide* (Minneapolis: Augsburg Fortress Publishers, 1998); Luke Timothy Johnson, *The Real Jesus: The Misguided Quest for the Historical Jesus and the Truth of the Traditional Gospels* (San Francisco: HarperSanFrancisco, 1997); and Daniel Harrington, *Jesus: A Historical Portrait* (Cincinnati: Saint Anthony Messenger Press, 2007).

Jew could not sleep with her because she might have been defiled.[4]

Long centuries of occupation had worn down the people of Israel, but out of their historical suffering hope emerged for deliverance and redemption. This hope was reinforced by prophets who foretold Israel's salvation throughout the ages.[5] Jesus emerged as one among a tradition of Hebrew prophets who spoke of the hope for a new kingdom. What was distinctive about Jesus' message, however, was that it was contrary to what people generally expected when they think of power and kingship. Jesus' ministry most empowered those who were socially marginalized. This included the sick, lame, bleeding, poor, and mentally ill, as well as those whose professions made them outcasts, such as tax collectors and prostitutes.[6]

Time and again, Jesus seemed to violate the religious law.[7] He frequently did so through his ministry to people who were considered impure. This ministry took many forms. Sometimes he laid his hands on them, sometimes he dined with them, sometimes he merely addressed them in parables or proverbial sayings, sometimes he performed deeds that his followers interpreted as miracles. In all of these cases, his actions and words worked together to portray a vision of the kingdom of God as one in which the most holy and noble citizens would be the very people who in the present world are weakest and most

THINK ABOUT IT

What would life be like for us today if we were deported from our homes and families, forced to speak a foreign language, to eat foreign foods, to tolerate foreign gods and statues in our places of worship, all the while being denied the freedom to practice our own forms of worship, work, and culture? These were the conditions that had plagued the Israelites for centuries prior to Jesus' birth. Can you think of any comparable modern-day situations? How might marriage and family life be affected by foreign occupations and wars?

demeaned. Children, women, the poor, the sick, those in prison, the suffering, the grieving, the persecuted—Jesus said these would be the first in the kingdom of God.

It should be noted that women and children in particular were vulnerable in Jesus' day, because they had relatively few freedoms and low legal status.[8] Consider family structures for a moment. When we think of family in the present era, we are likely to think of a small nuclear family comprised of a mother, a father, and their children. In the time of Jesus, both pagan and Hebrew families were structured quite differently. For starters, there were usually more people living together than is common now. Grandparents, extended kin, household servants and slaves (and their families), adopted children, and others often shared the same household.

---

4. Samuel Oyin Abogunrin, "Luke," in *The International Bible Commentary: A Catholic and Ecumenical Commentary for the Twenty-First Century*, ed. William R. Farmer (Collegeville, MN: Liturgical Press, 1998), 1369.

5. For example, Isa 49–52; Jer 31–33; Ezek 37.

6. Rosemary Radford Ruether discusses Jesus and his work with the marginalized in her text *Women and Redemption: A Theological History* (Minneapolis: Fortress Press, 1998), especially in chapter 1, "In Christ No More Male and Female: The Question of Gender and Redemption in the New Testament," 13–43.

7. For example, Matt 12:1–14; Luke 6:6–11.

8. See, for instance, Gillian Clark's *Women in the Ancient World* (Oxford and New York: Oxford University Press, 1989).

A household was governed hierarchically by a primary male.[9] The male held supreme authority over the activities and lives of the people in his household and made such determinations as how property could be used and distributed, who could marry, to whom children would be married, and how the goods produced by the family members would be sold and traded. Wives, children, and servants were not empowered to make such arrangements for themselves as they were legally the property of the male head of house. Sexual exclusivity was required for females, but a fair amount of sexual license was permitted to men in the form of prostitutes, plural wives (in some cultures), and concubines. In the Hebrew family, males alone had the prerogative to divorce. In Greek and Roman families, children were very vulnerable. They could be abandoned as infants and even sold into slavery.

Large family networks of the New Testament era acted as small corporations, and the welfare of individual family members depended upon the welfare of the whole. In this regard, families played a crucial role in the stability of the broader social structure. Families met many of the economic and physical needs of their members, but not without some obvious costs and risks to the individual members, especially women and children. Carolyn Osiek speaks to these dangers in the following passage:

> The lives of children in the New Testament world were precarious. Infant and childhood mortality were high, and the poor sanitation, nutrition, and health practices of the urban populace meant that many were malnourished and deprived. Methods of contraception and abortion were dangerous, arbitrary, but nonetheless practiced. The most usual method of family limitation, however, was the abandonment of unwanted babies, especially daughters, who were a liability to poor families not in a position to gain in wealth and influence through marriage. There is no way of knowing how many children died of exposure. But many of them were picked up and raised, usually as slaves. So common was this practice that there was Roman legislation about it specifying, for instance, that if an adult brought up in this manner could later prove free birth, he or she was to go free. Most legal systems allowed for the sale of children as slaves by parents, sometimes for a limited time, sometimes indefinitely.[10]

Moreover, Osiek notes:

> Daughters carried the potential danger of shaming the family through their misconduct or violation, and thus were a constant worry, lest they not remain virgins until marriage, lest they not please their husbands, lest a good marriage not be found for them.[11]

Although it would be unfair to assume that all marriages or families in this time were negatively characterized by abandonment, slavery, and so on, it would also be naïve to assume that all members of the family flourished under such conditions. By contrast, the values that Jesus preached and behaviors he modeled contradicted worldly expectations about many things, including the status of women and children. In the Gospel of Luke, for example, Jesus visits the home of a woman named Martha. Martha here

---

9. See Christine Gudorf, "Western Religion and the Patriarchal Family," in *Religion and Sexual Health*, ed. Ronald M. Green (Dordrecht, Netherlands: Kluwer, 1992), 99–117.

10. Carolyn Osiek, "The New Testament and the Family," in *The Family*, ed. Lisa Sowle Cahill and Dietmar Mieth (Maryknoll, NY: SCM Press and Orbis, 1995), 3–4.

11. Ibid., 5.

SERMON ON THE MOUNT

Jesus' Sermon on the Mount — or Sermon on the Plain, as it is called in Luke — is one place where his teachings run profoundly contrary to general conceptions of power and strength. Read Matthew 5:1–12 and Luke 6:20–26. Afterward, answer the following questions:

- Who will be blessed in the kingdom of God and what will their rewards be?
- How does the passage in Matthew differ from that in Luke?
- How do the final verses in Luke, in particular, counter common opinion about success and power?
- How do success, power, and wealth relate to marriage and family life? How might the reversal of expectations about these things alter your views about what a successful, affluent, or upwardly mobile family should be?

is busy entertaining her guest, serving food and so on, while her sister Mary sits at Jesus' feet listening to him speak. When Martha complains to Jesus that her sister is unhelpful, Jesus replies, "Martha, Martha, you are anxious and worried about many things. There is need of only one thing. Mary has chosen the better part and it will not be taken from her" (10:41–42). Here Jesus affirms Mary's choice to set aside her customary responsibilities as a woman in order to hear his teachings.

One can imagine that such teachings were provocative but also inspiring to many underdogs, because Jesus offered an alternative for self-understanding and conduct. As a result, Jesus was also a threat to those who held positions of religious and civil authority because those in power had much to lose if people started to view and value themselves differently. Jesus was ultimately arrested and

executed because of the threat he seemed to pose. And under the governor of Caesarea, Pontius Pilate, whose main concern was maintaining order in the volatile province of Judea, arrests and executions that demonstrated a total disregard for real justice were common.

Had Jesus merely died on the cross, his followers would have no doubt been saddened and disillusioned by their loss. They would have seen him as a valiant and noble preacher who met with the end that all true prophets risk: public humiliation and death. But something dramatic happened to Jesus' disciples that changed not only what they thought but how they behaved. They experienced Jesus as resurrected, and they proclaimed him risen among them. Now it is true that no eyewitness of the Resurrection recorded his or her thoughts in the New Testament. It is also true that the Resurrection as a historically verifiable event cannot be proven. Here it is helpful to remember the purposes of the Gospels. They were not written to prove the Resurrection; rather, they were written to tell people about what the disciples experienced. And what they experienced was Jesus alive and walking among them three days after his death!

This experience was so powerful that Jesus' followers reconvened and began to proclaim the miracle of the Resurrection, even at great personal risk. Jesus' Resurrection showed them several things. For one, Jesus' teaching about the kingdom of God was now understood in a different light. It would not be a kingdom of the present world but a kingdom of another kind. The spiritual kingdom of God erased distinctions of gender and class and race.[12] People could interact on a whole new level, as equals in light of their baptism. The frailties and injustices of human life now appeared tragic but not final because there emerged a hope for life beyond this world in which justice and righteousness would prevail. The future of all humankind could be anticipated in the Resurrection of Jesus, God's revelation of the destiny to which all people are called.

Followers of Jesus began to see themselves in a special community, so intimately interrelated as to constitute one body, the body of Christ. Their special relationship to one another as individual parts of this body promised fellowship and friendship in ways previously thought impossible, among each other and with God. Although their lives were still fraught with challenges, their participation in the family of Christian believers, the body of Christ, seemed to them a foretaste of a perfect life beyond this one, when the kingdom of God would be fully realized, a kingdom that reflected the values that Jesus had preached and for which he ultimately died. Moreover, this newfound sense of meaning in human life had significant consequences for how Christians would understand marriage and the meaning and value of family life.

THE MEDITERRANEAN FAMILY VERSUS THE BODY OF CHRIST

If we carefully read the many references to family and marital life in the New Testament, something surprising emerges. The passages do not present a unified and ideal picture of family and marital love. Despite the New Testament's predominant endorsement of love, there is no uncomplicated way to read the New Testament passages on family and marriage.

The large, multigenerational families characteristic of the era that were described above had a great deal at stake in keeping the loyalty of all of their members. If individuals converted to Christianity, it could result in economic and interpersonal hardships for the other members who did not convert. To make matters more complicated, Christians believed that in their baptism they entered into a new kind of family comprised of other baptized Christians. Jesus himself validates this transference of biological family for family of faith in a dramatic way. The Gospel of Matthew[13] records the following incident:

> While [Jesus] was still speaking to the crowds, his mother and his brothers appeared outside, wishing to speak with him. Someone told him, "Your mother and your brothers are standing outside, asking to speak with you." But he said in reply to the one who told him, "Who is my mother? Who are my brothers?" And stretching out his hand toward his disciples, he said, "Here are my mother and my brothers. For whoever does the will of my heavenly Father is my brother, and sister, and mother." (Matt 12:46–50)

It was not one's family of origin but the members of the body of Christ who enjoyed unity and mutual status, regardless of race, class, age, or gender. This thinking was simply unprecedented in its day and age. The Christians did not immediately strive to change all social conditions that perpetuated inequalities and oppression, but they nevertheless believed that before God all people were genuinely equal and created with an inalienable dignity. Such thinking was disruptive to patriarchal family structures that

---

12. This is the sentiment conveyed in the early baptismal formula found in Gal 3:27–28, which reads: "For all of you who were baptized into Christ have clothed yourselves with Christ. There is neither Jew nor Greek, there is neither slave nor free person, there is not male and female; for you are all one in Christ Jesus."

13. See also Luke 8:19–21.

QUESTIONS REGARDING JESUS' FAMILY

Did Jesus have brothers and sisters? Did he have a wife and children? How did Jesus experience his own sexuality? The New Testament does not answer these questions, and no extra-biblical testimony provides historically reliable answers either. While the Bible is silent, there is no reason to assume that as a human being Jesus did not experience sexual desires, just as there is no reason to assume that he acted on those desires or married and had children. Similarly, while the birth narratives in Matthew and Luke support Mary's virginity at the time Jesus was born, the New Testament remains silent on the question of her virginity after that. The New Testament does speak of Jesus' "brothers" and "sisters," but these terms could also be used more broadly of cousins or other relatives. There is no uncontested evidence that either supports or contradicts the possibility of Jesus' siblings.

Christians hold a variety of opinions about these matters, most of which pertain to doctrines such as Jesus' divinity. The Roman Catholic Church remains relatively silent on the issue of Jesus' sexuality, while it teaches that Mary remained a perpetual virgin before, during, and after Jesus' birth. What do you think?

operated on the assumption that people were in fact not equal but ordered according to gender, age, race, and class.

Lisa Sowle Cahill explores these ideas at length in her work *Family: A Christian Social Perspective*.[14] Here Cahill argues that many New Testament passages seem to recognize that families, as such, were not always conducive to an individual's spiritual growth in relationship with God or participation in the body of Christ. Some New Testament passages call for a repudiation of one's family of origin and a celebration of one's family in Christ. For example, in the Gospel of Matthew a potential disciple of Jesus requests that before accompanying Jesus he be permitted to bury his father. Jesus replies, "Follow me, and let the dead bury the dead" (8:22). On the question of discipleship, Jesus states, "If anyone comes to me without hating his father and mother, wife and children, brothers and sisters, and even his own life, he cannot be my disciple" (Luke 14:26).

Difficult passages such as these make more sense when interpreted as part of a broader critical commentary on family structures that interfered with personal freedom and faith formation. The wisdom of the New Testament is that all human beings are part of one's family. Biological kin relationships, then as now, can interfere with faith commitments. This was a big risk when a family's corporate identity relied on the individual's commitment, as it did in the world of the New Testament. Moreover, biological kin relationships can also mask a failure to love. Then as now, it is often easy to be loving and neighborly to those to whom we feel a biological obligation. It is seldom as easy to extend ourselves in the same way to those we see as strangers or to whom we feel no obligation. Families, as such, can actually mask our obligation to extend ourselves to others who need our active love, support, and care.

While some passages seem to renounce family life, others endorse the family as an

---

14. Lisa Sowle Cahill, *Family: A Christian Social Perspective* (Minneapolis: Augsburg Fortress Publishers, 2000).

important place for people to experience love and to live out their human responsibilities to one another. In both Matthew (19:3–9) and Mark (10:2–12), Jesus provides lengthy teachings on marriage and divorce, in which Jesus cites the creation accounts in Genesis as the foundation for marriage. Jesus acknowledges that men were in the past permitted by Moses to leave their wives, but he insists that this was only because of the hardness of their hearts. Under Jesus' new teaching, divorce is illicit (unless the marriage was unlawful in the first place) and remarriage to another is a form of adultery. Matthew includes in his account (19:10–12) a comment that those who are unmarried and can accept their situation ought to remain unmarried for the sake of the kingdom of God. Like Mark, however, Matthew follows Jesus' teaching on marriage and divorce with an affirmation of the goodness and blessing of children (Matt 19:13–15 and Mark 10:13–6). Two other short proscriptions against divorce may be found in Matthew 5:31–32 and Luke 16:18. The marriage teaching in Mark 10 reads as follows:

> He set out from there and went into the district of Judea [and] across the Jordan. Again crowds gathered around him and, as was his custom, he again taught them. The Pharisees approached and asked, "Is it lawful for a husband to divorce his wife?" They were testing him. He said to them in reply, "What did Moses command you?" They replied, "Moses permitted him to write a bill of divorce and dismiss her." But Jesus told them, "Because of the hardness of your hearts he wrote you this commandment. But from the beginning of creation, 'God made them male and female. For this reason a man shall leave his father and mother [and be joined to his wife], and the two shall become one flesh.' So they are no longer two but one flesh. Therefore what God has joined together, no human being must separate." In the house the disciples again

questioned him about this. He said to them, "Whoever divorces his wife and marries another commits adultery against her; and if she divorces her husband and marries another, she commits adultery." And people were bringing children to him that he might touch them, but the disciples rebuked them. When Jesus saw this he became indignant and said to them, "Let the children come to me; do not prevent them, for the kingdom of God belongs to such as these." "Amen, I say to you, whoever does not accept the kingdom of God like a child will not enter it." Then he embraced them and blessed them, placing his hands on them. (Mark 10:1–16)

The teachings on marriage and divorce in these passages do not deal with the range of situations that might lead a couple to divorce, which we will take up in chapter 11. They do, however, emphasize that the reason divorce was permitted under Mosaic Law was to accommodate the hardness of men's hearts. Women were not permitted to initiate divorce under Mosaic Law, but they were vulnerable to abandonment under the law. Jesus' teachings here seem to speak primarily toward the protection of women from callous or unjustifiable divorces. Likewise, Jesus' commentary on the value of children that immediately follows the teaching on marriage is a powerful endorsement of this outcome of marriage. The kingdom of God belongs to children and those who are child-like. In such passages we see not a repudiation of marriage and family life but a validation of it.

Indeed, marital love is so respected in the New Testament that over time it came to be compared to the union between Jesus and the church. This sentiment is expressed in the Letter to the Ephesians, a later text of the New Testament. One of the main themes of this letter is that Christians, by virtue of their baptism, share in one mystical body, headed by Christ. All parts of the body need to work together in order for the body to function as a whole. In Ephesians 5:21–33, love between husband and wife is discussed:

> Be subordinate to one another out of reverence for Christ. Wives should be subordinate to their husbands as to the Lord. For the husband is head of his wife just as Christ is head of the church, he himself the savior of the body. As the church is subordinate to Christ, so wives should be subordinate to their husbands in everything. Husbands, love your wives, even as Christ loved the church and handed himself over for her to sanctify her, cleansing her by the bath of water with the word, that he might present to himself the church in splendor, without spot or wrinkle or any such thing, that she might be holy and without blemish. So [also] husbands should love their wives as their own bodies. He who loves his wife loves himself. For no one hates his own flesh but rather nourishes and cherishes it, even as Christ does the church, because we are members of his body. "For this reason a man shall leave [his] father and [his] mother and be joined to his wife, and the two shall become one flesh." This is a great mystery, but I speak in reference to Christ and the church. In any case, each one of you should love his wife as himself, and the wife should respect her husband. (5:21–33)

As contemporary readers, many of us will find this passage troubling because it is hierarchical, with the male partner given a position of authority over his wife. No amount of scriptural gymnastics can erase this basic inequity. If we recognize that the ancient family structures of Christians at that time reflected a patriarchal or male-headed structure, then it becomes quite obvious why the author would have assumed this structure to be normative for husbands and wives. Ephesians 6:1–9 also assumes that children and slaves will be subordinate and obedient to the heads of their households.

The original audience would not have reacted to marital hierarchy negatively, but might well have been scandalized by Ephesians for other reasons: the letter insists that husbands and wives should serve one another mutually. Even more, husbands are to care for their wives as they would for their own bodies. This is a remarkable challenge in an age in which women were not afforded high status and certainly were seen as inferior to male heads of house. The human couple is instructed to model in their life together the same kind of loving service, fidelity,

CHRIST AND THE CHURCH AND RELATIONSHIP OF SPOUSES

The comparison of the relationship between spouses to the relationship between Christ and the church, made by the New Testament authors, is a lofty one with many possible implications. What might some of these implications be, especially for Christian spouses? In your discussion you might consider the following questions:

- In what ways does the comparison hold? In what ways does it not?

- Does the association of Christ with the husband and the church with the wife hold implications for differing gender roles in marriage? If so, is this problematic?

- What if we were to reverse the comparison, comparing the relationship between Christ and the church with the relationship between spouses? In formulating your answer, consider the challenges, blessings, victories, and even failures of human marriage.

and obedience that Jesus modeled to all people in his human life.

That loving service of Jesus to human beings is carried on in the church. So intimate is the relationship between Christ and the church that they are seen as one body, just as the human couple is identified as one body in the creation story in Genesis. Marital love, modeled after Christ and the church, becomes an opportunity to find one's truest self in the mutual and steadfast commitment to one another's ultimate well-being.

CHRISTIAN CHARITY AS A FOUNDATION FOR MARRIAGE

Although there are ambiguities in the New Testament regarding family life, there is no ambiguity regarding Jesus' principle commandment to love one another. When pressed by the Pharisees to answer which of the religious laws is greatest of all, Jesus replies, "You shall love the Lord, your God, with all your heart, with all your soul, and with all your mind. This is the greatest and the first commandment. The second is like it: You shall love your neighbor as yourself. The whole law and the prophets depend on these two commandments" (Matt 22:37–40). To love one another and God is the focal point of Jesus' message and ministry.

What type of love is this? The love that Jesus models is not a passive or merely emotional kind of love. It is rather a love that seeks active service and justice, and includes acts of physical and material care for one another. It always aims at seeking the preservation of the other and the realization of justice and equity among people, particularly with respect to physical needs. The word for love that is used predominantly in the New Testament, *agape*, refers to self-giving love,

as opposed to *eros* (the love of desire) and *philia* (the love of mutual friends). Agapic love is self-giving and sacrificial. In agapic love, people find personal fulfillment in the flourishing of one another; their own good is found foremost in the good of another.

The love of neighbor that Jesus commands and demonstrates through his own example does not merely mean experiencing feelings of goodwill toward people whom one knows only in passing. Jesus' parable of the Good Samaritan is an elaboration not on charitable acts but on neighborliness.[15] It is no coincidence or mere detail that it is a Samaritan who helps the injured man on the road, a man whom religious elites passed by. Samaritans had long been territorial enemies with the Judeans, and the enmity between the two peoples was great. By telling a story in which a Samaritan helped a Judean man, Jesus reveals that concrete acts of love—such as caring for another's physical well-being or financing medical care—are what is required of Christians for all people, even supposed enemies. The love people are to show one another is to be as great as the love and care they have for themselves.

The First Letter of John commands this remarkable kind of love of all Christians. This letter boldly asserts that God is love: "God *is* love, and whoever remains in love remains in God and God in him" (1 John 4:16). The experience of love is an experience of the very *being* of God. Moreover, the love of God is not a feeling of passive affection or even holiness. It is not found in private spiritual piety. Rather, loving God is loving one's neighbor, and loving one's neighbor is loving God. First John 3:17–18 affirms this when it says, "If someone who has worldly means sees a brother in need and refuses him compassion, how can the love of God remain in him?

---

15. Luke 10:29–37.

Children, let us not love in word or speech but in deed and truth." In 1 John 4:20–21 we read, "If anyone says 'I love God,' but hates his brother, he is a liar; for whoever does not love a brother whom he has seen cannot love God whom he has not seen. This is the commandment we have from him: whoever loves God must also love his brother."

Loving those before one's eyes is not, according to the New Testament, a feeling of kindheartedness toward people but loving service that meets fundamental human needs. That is why 1 John insists that the true Christian is one who sees his brother in need and gives in order to meet that need. The early Christian communities felt so passionate about this that they strove to live communally, giving according to ability and taking according to need. The second chapter of the Book of Acts tells how the early Christians lived and worked in common so that the needs of all would be met. In this common lifestyle they exalt, rejoice, and enjoy the favor of God, and add new members to their community.[16] To love, as expressed in Scripture, is to act in concrete ways that are moral and strive for justice.

One of the most beautiful passages in the New Testament on the nature of love is expressed in the First Letter to the Corinthians. Here Paul situates his discussion of love in a broader discussion of spiritual gifts that human beings experience and share with their community of believers. No gifts, he argues, are useful apart from the spiritual virtues of faith, hope, and love. What is more, even faith and hope fall away if a person does not experience love. Paul goes on to explore the characteristics of love:

> Love is patient, love is kind. It is not jealous, [love] is not pompous, it is not inflated, it is not rude, it does not seek its own interests, it is not quick-tempered, it does not brood over injury, it does not rejoice over wrongdoing but rejoices with the truth. It bears all things, believes all things, hopes all things, endures all things. Love never fails. If there are prophesies, they will be brought to nothing; if tongues, they will cease; if knowledge, it will be brought to nothing. . . . So faith, hope, and love remain, these three; but the greatest of these is love. (1 Cor 13:4–8, 13)

Paul's exposition reveals something beautiful about love that differs from our contemporary, common usage. It expresses a long-term disposition to be totally for another person in such a way that helps to build up and sustain the other while not indulging one's own pettiness.

APPLICATION TO FAMILY AND MARRIAGE TODAY

Because of the different types of passages in the New Testament on marriage and family, it is clear that a rule or guide for responsible interpretation is necessary. The principle of active and just love may be precisely the interpretive tool we need. This is especially the case when we seek to apply teachings in the New Testament to marriage and family life today. For instance, we considered several passages prohibiting divorce. It makes sense that such prohibitions would be in the New Testament in an era in which women could be the unwitting victims of abandonment or an unjust divorce. A prohibition against divorce in this context is consistent with the rule of love because it functions as a protection of women. However, the prohibition against divorce cannot be taken as a blanket rule to be applied as a norm in all situations. For example, a situation of domestic violence that threatens a woman's life cannot be

---

16. Acts 2:42–47.

considered a marriage that models the love of Christ for the church. The divorce does not put the woman in jeopardy as much as the marriage. In such a situation, the rule of love would argue in favor of the woman's safety.

Thus one must interpret and apply the New Testament teachings on family and marriage in ways consistent with the overarching themes of the New Testament, principle among them being that God is love. This message that Jesus reveals to his followers creates the possibility of a new covenant with God and new potential for love among human beings. Like the covenant between God and the people of Israel, Christianity proclaims a covenant of divine-human love. This covenant is indeed proclaimed by Christians to be all the more perfect because it was perfectly realized in the life and deeds of Jesus.

The Christian concept of love challenged families in the New Testament to find a more perfect expression of mutual service and love. Families and marriages are not inherently perfect; they are rather opportunities for us to grow deliberately into God's love through a commitment to active service to one another. Moreover, families have the obligation to extend themselves beyond their immediate kinships to the whole family of Christ—and indeed to all human beings. In summary, the New Testament encourages human beings in marriage and family life to:

- Model their love after Christ's love for the church
- Love their spouses as themselves, as their own bodies
- Love actively in concrete deeds
- Love God through the love of one another
- Manifest love in mutual service, obedience, and loyalty

Questions for Review and Discussion

1. Explain the difference between a "biological family" and the "family of faith." According to the example of Jesus in the Gospels, which type of family should have priority?

2. Cite examples of New Testament passages that seem to diminish the value of family and marriage. Cite other examples that seem to uphold the value of family and marriage. How do you reconcile such passages?

3. How does love of neighbor relate to love of intimates in the New Testament? Who might be defined as a neighbor? Is it realistic to think that people can or should love neighbors as their own families?

4. How are justice and love related?

5. Describe charitable love in the New Testament. Of what does it consist? How does this kind of love differ from affection-based love? Do the two kinds of love oppose or reinforce one another?

6. Cite several examples of pop-culture depictions of love, marriage, and family life, from movies, celebrity news, television programs, or the like. How would you describe the values and qualities of love and marriage in these depictions? How would you compare these qualities with love in the New Testament?

7. What gender issues surfaced for you in reading through this material?

8. Can human marital love truly imitate the relationship between Christ and the church, as described by Paul in Ephesians 5?

Resources for Further Reading

New Testament Resources

Bart Ehrman, *The New Testament: A Historical Introduction to the Early Christian Writings* (New York: Oxford University Press, 2004).

Daniel Harrington, *Interpreting the New Testament: A Practical Guide* (Collegeville, MN: Liturgical Press, 1990).

Stephen Harris, *The New Testament: A Student's Introduction* (Boston: McGraw Hill, 2002).

Resources for Christian Love and Family in the New Testament

Benedict XVI, *God is Love: Deus Caritas Est* (San Francisco: Ignatius Press, 2006).

Bernard Brady, *Christian Love* (Washington: Georgetown University Press, 2003).

Ken Campbell, ed., *Marriage and Family in the Biblical World* (Downer's Grove, IL: InterVarsity Press, 2003).

Lisa Sowle Cahill and Dietmar Mieth, *The Family* (Maryknoll, NY: SCM Press and Orbis, 1995).

Lisa Sowle Cahill, *Family: A Christian Social Perspective* (Minneapolis: Augsburg Fortress Press, 2000).

Livio Melina and Carl Anderson, *The Way of Love: Reflections on Pope Benedict XVI's Encyclical Deus Caritas Est* (San Francisco: Ignatius Press, 2006).

4

HISTORICAL DEVELOPMENT AND MARRIAGE

You may have noticed in recent years attempts to define marriage as a union between one man and one woman via state constitutional amendments, a proposed Federal Marriage Amendment, and legislative actions (some of which have made it to the ballot). These acts would preclude not only same-sex marriages but also polygamous marriages. Such initiatives raise questions. On what grounds can or should the government define who can be married? Was marriage always a matter to be legislated by the government? Has marriage always been between one man and one woman? What if one's religion allows for plural spouses? Are marital practices matters of freedom of religion?

Marriage practices, laws, and norms do in fact change over time. Such a revelation may run contrary to popular thinking. Especially in our era, when attitudes toward marriage seem to be undergoing a transition, there is a temptation to think of marriage as a fixed reality that has never changed until now. If we like the fixed reality, we want to preserve "family values" or get back to the "good old days," when marriage was simple and the roles of husband and wife were clearly defined. If we do not like the fixed reality, we say marriage is passé and confining—and thus increasingly subject to divorce. Both attitudes miss a fundamental truth about marriage, however: marriage is always undergoing change and always related to social issues outside itself.

The institution of marriage experiences historical development across cultures and over time. Changes within Christian marriage are related to historical developments within Christianity in general. This chapter will explore the theme of the historical development of marriage within the Christian tradition. Our goal will be to situate the discussion of the development of marriage within the wider discussion of the historical development of the Christian church and faith.[1] The aim of this discussion is twofold.

---

1. People's understanding and articulation of Christian faith and practice have varied from the beginning of the Christian era. Today there are hundreds of different Christian worshipping communities, some very ancient, some recent. Major divisions

First, it is important to understand that marriage structures and customs are alterable. Second, and more importantly, when we move beyond thinking of marriage as an institution, we are free to think of marriage as a dynamic journey between spouses, with open possibilities for creative and loving choices.

The historical-developmental point of view enables us to see dynamism, vitality, and potentiality in every dimension of Christian faith. In contrast, an institutional point of view sees Christian faith as an unchanging structure, fully formed from the beginning, and moving through time without regard to current realities. A historical-developmental view shows that while the basic teachings about the centrality of Jesus' life and its saving effect on human beings remain unchanged, Christians in every era face the task of appropriating and refining the Christian message in new contexts.

The church may be thought of as a dynamic community of people, both lay (non-clergy) and ordained (clergy), who both inherit and pass down the traditions, Scriptures, theologies, and material properties of their foremothers and forefathers. Members of that community inhabit the traditions they have received and contribute by bringing to them their own perspectives, shaped by contemporary experiences. An analogy might be inheriting a family recipe. The recipe comes with a certain list of things to do and include in the meal preparation. Over time, as a person uses the

TECHNOLOGY, LIFESTYLE, AND MARRIAGE

Consider for a moment the impact of technology and lifestyle on the ways people experience faith, moral debates, and means of worship. To watch Mass on television or listen to a homily over the internet would have been an impossibility just decades ago. The first Christian communities could not have imagined ethical questions surrounding reproductive technologies, such as in vitro fertilization. Even reading the Bible or documents produced by church leaders, something we take for granted because of our easy access to print materials, would have been very difficult or impossible for many in the ages before the printing press. As an exercise, list and discuss ten ways that you think contemporary experience affects the theology of family and marriage.

recipe for himself, he may add a spice or change an accompanying dish, thus preserving even while transforming the recipe as he makes it his own.

Because people's faith does not exist in a vacuum removed from other aspects of social life, the church—understood as a composite of the faithful—must regularly resituate itself to its context. In order for the faith to be meaningful to people in any age, it must be pliable enough to address present questions, concerns, and issues. The pliability of Christian faith is expressed well by the Roman Catholic Church in the documents of the Second Vatican Council, which describe the whole Christian church by the term "pilgrim."[2] This term opposes the notion of church as a rigid building or institution in favor

include the Eastern Orthodox, Roman Catholic, and Protestant communions. This textbook will discuss some of the corresponding variances with regard to marriage; our intent here is to provide a framework that, while derived from a Roman Catholic perspective, would also be appropriate for any Christian theology of marriage. In this chapter, the use of the terms *church* and *faith* are intended to speak broadly of the history of Western Christian worshipping communities, insofar as the history here being discussed predates the Protestant Reformation.

2. See especially *Lumen Gentium*, §48–51, "The Pilgrim Church." Used by permission.

of the notion of the church as a living, journeying community of people.

The changes within the church from one era to the next are best understood not as contradictions but as developments and refinements. As the church gains greater insight into a particular area or aspect of life, Christians accommodate that insight into their theologies and teachings. This developmental process can be seen in all aspects of theology, and the theology of family and marriage is no exception. Teaching and practice have progressed over the eras into what we today consider normative. What is more, today's lived experience will shape how people think about marriage from a Christian theological perspective into the future.

TOOLS

In order to understand developments within the Christian church historically, one must ask what was happening in the world at any given time. The study of the church and its history is called *ecclesiology*.[3] Some aspects of ecclesiology include:

- The nature and purpose of the church
- The presence of the Holy Spirit in the church
- Structure and major divisions of leadership
- History of clergy and papacy
- Relationship to and development of religious orders
- Physical location in the world

- Church relationships to politics and political leaders
- Financial and economic concerns
- Social context surrounding major doctrinal developments
- Relationship of the church to theological and scriptural scholarship
- Official church teachings
- Relationship to major technological or scientific developments
- Relationship to philosophical movements and non-religious institutions of higher learning
- Impact of and involvement in major world events, such as wars and natural disasters
- Role and history of women and groups with limited leadership opportunities or representation in the church
- Role of lay people, lay ministries, and popular movements within the church
- Relationship among different Christian worshipping communities
- Relationship between Christian and non-Christian worshipping communities

This list is partial and could be expanded or refined in any number of ways. All of these features and more comprise the historical context of the church. These features are related, and when we come to a better understanding of any one of these aspects, we gain greater insight into why the Christian worldview was as it was at any given point in history. Of course, this would be the work of many books.[4]

---

3. For recent and well-regarded treatments of ecclesiology, consider Roger Haight, *Christian Community in History: Ecclesial Existence* (New York: Continuum, 2008) and Bernard Prusak, *The Church Unfinished: Ecclesiology Through the Centuries* (Mahwah, NJ: Paulist Press, 2004).

4. Two approachable introductions to church history that I have found helpful for beginners are Bruce Shelley, *Church History in Plain Language*, 3rd ed. (Nashville: Nelson, 2008) and Timothy Paul Jones, *Christian History Made Easy: 13 Weeks to a Better Understanding of Church History* (Torance, CA: Rose, 1999).

We will address major historical developments in the church between the origin of Christianity in the first century and the scholastic period ending in the mid-fifteenth century, because the theology of family and marriage developed dramatically over this period. We will reserve a discussion of subsequent eras until chapter 6, when we take up the discussion of the history of marriage in the contemporary period.

A HISTORY OF THE CHURCH AND MARRIAGE

Beginning of the Church: 30–200

The church's life begins with the foundation and formation of the Christian religion. This period is marked by the teaching and ministry of Jesus, Jesus' disciples and the first converts, and by the formation of the first domestic churches. In this era there were as yet no grand cathedrals. There was no New Testament either, because the books of the New Testament were still being written and were beginning to be circulated. In addition, church structures, practices, and leadership roles were just being discovered. The early church was at the very beginning of its historical journey, much like a young child learning to walk and talk.

The church grew in two significant ways at this time. First, the Christian community transitioned from a Jewish sect into a community largely influenced by a Gentile population. Initially, missionaries such as the apostle Paul traveled to synagogues throughout the Roman Empire to spread the good news of Jesus. They encountered many Jews, but they also held an appealing message for Gentile or pagan converts. A big question facing the early Christians was whether Gentile converts to Christianity needed to observe the Jewish Law.[5] We see this question raised throughout the letters of the New Testament. Eventually Christianity grew away from its Jewish origins, and Christian observance of Jewish rituals and laws faded away.[6]

The second way in which the church grew during this period was in its manner of leadership and organization. The first Christians believed that Jesus would be returning to them immediately, and so they were not highly structured in either leadership or organization. People responded freely when they felt that the Spirit called them to do something for the church,[7] and there was no need to plan for a long-term future because the future was soon to be interrupted. When Jesus did not return as expected, however, they had to reorient to accommodate the delay.[8] This reorientation toward a delayed second coming of Jesus marked a significant development in

---

5. Paul elaborates on this theme at length in Rom 3:21–4:25 and Gal 3:6–18.

6. The distancing of Christians from the synagogue, largely based on their claim that Jesus was the Messiah of Jewish ancestral hope, can be seen especially in the Johannine literature (The Gospel of John, the Letters of John, and the Book of Revelation).

7. The spiritual leadership of the church and rules for proper assembly are the subject of 1 Cor 11:2–14:40. The model of leadership described by Paul contrasts starkly with 1 and 2 Timothy and Titus, where the model of church organization is much more structured and hierarchical. Scholars argue that 1 and 2 Timothy and Titus are pseudonymous, written by someone other than Paul at a much later date. Presumably the charismatic style of leadership found in 1 Corinthians became insufficient in later decades, especially as controversies over doctrine began to emerge.

8. Concerns about believers who had died before the anticipated return of Christ and the timeframe of that return are addressed in 1 Thess 4:13–5:11, followed by commentary on mutual support and church conduct in 5:12–22. Apparently some were afraid that those who had died would miss the resurrection. There were also questions about how the community should conduct itself while waiting for Christ's return. These issues show that the delayed return caused both doctrinal and organizational development in the fledgling church.

beliefs and necessitated new forms of structured organization among early Christians.

Family and household structures played an important role in the life of the church in this era, even while their relationship to the church as families would not be clearly defined for several hundred years. In the infancy period of the church, family and marriage reflected the broader Mediterranean culture and practices, discussed in the previous chapter.[9] Both Jewish and Mediterranean families were large kin groups, dominated by a male head of house. The household provided protection for individual family members, even while it was often limiting and oppressive.[10] At the beginning of the Christian era, only citizens of the Roman Empire could be legally married. "Christian marriage" per se was a matter of the faith of believers. In other words, the only thing that differentiated a Christian marriage from other kinds of marriages was the decision on the part of the couple to live out their faith together.

Before there was a church hierarchy or church buildings, of course, there could be little official church involvement in marriages. That is, marriages could not be overseen by a priest nor could they take place within church walls. It was the Roman custom to contract marriages by the consent of the fathers of the bride and groom.[11] Often this occurred when children were very young. A bride price and dowry would be agreed upon by the fathers of the bride and groom. The bride price was the compensation the groom's family would give to the bride's father for the loss of his daughter; the dowry was the portion of the bride's inheritance that would accompany her into her marriage. When the agreed time arrived, a festive meal or meals would be shared, along with other accompanying rituals, and the bride would leave her father's home to go to her new husband's house. No more official paperwork or oversight was required to contract a marriage (or to end one).

We may be startled at the small role love seems to play in this arrangement, but love as "affection" was not the primary reason that people married at the time. People married primarily to produce offspring and to make good alliances between families for purposes of inheritance and property transmission from one generation to the next. Individuals surely loved one another, but they did so by living out the basic duties and responsibilities required by their roles. A husband's responsibilities included providing material support for his wife. A wife's basic responsibility was sexual exclusivity to her husband for the purpose of providing legitimate (male) heirs.

Although men of higher classes had the option of sex with their female slaves or concubines, adultery (sex with another man's wife) was treated with the most severe punishment: death. The severity of the penalty demonstrates how seriously marriage was taken. The fabric of society rested upon the proper transmission of property and lineage. Christians took the marriage obligation so seriously that divorce was considered a deep violation and hence impermissible,[12] even though Roman custom allowed for regular divorce and remarriage.

---

9. A comprehensive treatment of this family structure, including discussions of childcare, child labor, divorce, and class structure, may be found in Keith Bradley, *Discovering the Roman Family* (Oxford and NY: Oxford University Press, 1991).

10. See also Charles Reid, Jr., "The History of the Family," in *The Family*, ed. Lisa Sowle Cahill and Dietmar Mieth (Maryknoll, NY: SCM Press and Orbis Books, 1995), 10–17.

11. Joseph Martos discusses the father's role in early Jewish, Roman, and Christian marriage in his essay "Marriage: A Historical Survey," in *Perspectives on Marriage: A Reader*, 3rd ed., ed. Kieran Scott and Michael Warren (Oxford and NY: Oxford University Press, 2007), 29–68.

12. See especially Jesus' Gospel prohibitions against divorce, as discussed in chapter 3.

ROLE OF WOMEN IN THE CHURCH

What role did women play in the early Christian movement? This question is much debated, but recent scholarship in women's studies and the New Testament has revealed that women played an important, if not leading, part in the Jesus movement of the first century. In the Gospels, Jesus spends time with women and even learns from them (for example Mark 7:24–30; Luke 8:1–3). In the letters of Paul, women are addressed as leaders of household churches as well as fellow-workers, deaconesses, and even apostles (Rom 16:1–16; 1 Cor 16:19; Phil 4:2–3; and Philem 2). The discovery of Gnostic Christian literature in the past two centuries, moreover, has shed new light on the leadership of prominent women, such as Mary Magdalene. Once considered a woman of ill-repute, Mary Magdalene is portrayed as a favorite disciple and church leader in the Gnostic texts.

The question of women's roles in the church as portrayed in the New Testament has significance today because the Bible is often seen as establishing precedence for contemporary practice. When there is debate about the meaning of New Testament passages or when passages conflict, modern interpreters have to make judgments about how (or whether) to apply biblical teaching today.

As an exercise, compare the passages cited above with the instruction for the conduct of women in 1 Timothy 2:8–15. What differences do you find in the attitude toward women in these passages? How might you account for the differences, and how do you think Christians today might deal with the conflicting attitudes toward women's leadership roles in the church evident in these passages?

The major ways in which families interacted with the infant church were by providing material support (including physical space for gathering, worship, and meals) and a natural organizational structure. The material support and structure of households led to the natural emergence of domestic or household churches. The structure of the male-headed domicile, however, also led to an emergent patriarchal (male-headed) leadership within the domestic churches. To be sure, male dominance in both domestic and public spheres was normative in its day, but the New Testament indicates an impulse toward egalitarianism on the part of the first Christians.[13] Over time, as the developing church became distanced from the immediacy of Jesus' life and the first Christians who felt themselves to be directly led by the Holy Spirit, the order of the household began to give shape to the order of church governance. The pattern of emergent patriarchal headship in the church is documented in 1 Timothy especially, which mandates appropriate conduct of male leaders, women, and slaves.[14]

---

13. This egalitarian impulse is supported primarily by Jesus' positive relationships with women, especially as recorded in the Gospel of Luke and by the early baptismal formula in Gal 3:28.

14. Elisabeth Schussler Fiorenza explores the ways in which the potential of an egalitarian Christian community gives way to a patriarchal structure within the New Testament in her highly regarded work *Bread Not Stone: The Challenge of Feminist Biblical Interpretation* (Boston: Beacon Press, 1984 and 1995).

Growth of the Church in the Greco-Roman World: 200 – 400

During this period, the church was melding with the broader Greco-Roman culture. Greek philosophy influenced the way Christians thought about their faith. Great debates arose about the nature of God and Christ, preserved in the writings of leaders of the church, often referred to as the "fathers."[15] Conflicts over what Christians should believe prompted meetings of bishops (synods and councils) to sort out and define true Christian faith versus false interpretations of it. In these meetings, *orthodoxy* (correct doctrine) began to be formulated.[16]

During this time Christians also experienced persecution by Roman authorities, for their faith prevented them from paying divine honor to the Roman Emperor, which the Romans insisted was their duty as citizens of the empire. As a result, Christians were often seen as socially subversive and were easily made scapegoats in times of social duress. Persecutions plagued Christians throughout the third century, giving rise to the heroic tales of Christian martyrs. The persecutions ended dramatically in the fourth century when Emperor Constantine converted to Christianity and ended persecutions of Christians.

After his conversion Constantine pursued policies that essentially Christianized the Roman Empire. This began the period of institutional Christianity, with all the advantages and temptations of a state religion. Constantine built churches, included Christian holidays in the calendar, used Christian insignia on public and military images, and gave special privileges to bishops. The effort to canonize or select the writings to be included within the New Testament occurred during this time. Also the doctrine of apostolic succession was formed. This meant that legitimate leadership of the church had to be passed down from one bishop to the next in proper order as it had been since the time of the apostles (who were the original bishops). Desert monasteries were formed where intensely spiritual people could pursue a contemplative life. Finally, because the state was now predominantly Christian, it became increasingly important to settle theological debates and to standardize Christian documents, worship practices, and beliefs. As a result, this period also witnessed the first ecumenical (universal) councils at Nicaea, Ephesus, Chalcedon, and Constantinople, which were convened to settle disputes about major Christian doctrines.

The same challenges that the Greek philosophical tradition posed to theological development in general began to influence the thinking on the theology of the family. Even in the earliest days of Christianity, there was some debate about whether it was good for people to marry. As we recall, Christians at that time anticipated the immediate return of Jesus. Preparing for future generations of this world was not their concern: it seemed better to them to prepare themselves spiritually as individuals. To marry and have a family could possibly interfere with spiritual preparation, so there was some ambivalence toward the good of marriage among early Christians.[17]

This initial ambivalence toward family and marriage was heightened in the Greco-Roman

---

15. Hence this is termed the *patristic* period, from the Latin *pater* (father).

16. Alister McGrath, in *Historical Theology: An Introduction to the History of Christian Thought* (Oxford and Malden, MA: Blackwell Publishers, 1998), provides an outstanding and student-friendly introduction to Christian historical eras. He touches on both theological issues and the contexts that gave rise to them. His discussion of patristic theology is particularly useful here.

17. Rosemary Radford Ruether speaks specifically to this tension within the New Testament community in her discussion of family and anti-family traditions in the New Testament in her work *Christianity* and the *Making of the Modern Family: Ruling Ideologies, Diverse Realities* (Boston: Beacon Press, 2000), 25 – 35.

period of Christian development because Greek philosophy harbored a negative attitude toward women and the physical body.[18] In the Greek system, characterized by Plato, the highest good was thought to be disembodied spiritual existence. Individual human souls were believed to originate in and belong most fully to the spiritual realm, where they were believed to be free from change, decay, and death. Since bodies obviously are not free from change, decay, and death, *corporeality* (embodiment) itself was blamed for human spiritual disorders such as greed, gluttony, lust, and perversion.

If it were not for our bodies, we would not experience temptations and distractions, so they reasoned. Greek philosophers argued that if we could bring our bodies under control through disciplining bodily cravings or appetites, we would attain spiritual and intellectual excellence that would more quickly return us to our proper home in the spiritual realm after bodily death. The more spiritual one was, the more likely one was to escape the physical realm and return to purely spiritual existence.

Women were considered physically and spiritually inferior because of their reproductive monthly cycles, which seemed to reveal a closer relationship between the female soul and the body. The processes of menstruation, gestation, and lactation were seen as necessary evils for reproducing heirs. Women were also largely denied education, civil rights, and access to participation and leadership opportunities within the public sphere. Complicating matters even more, there was often an age disparity between teenage brides and their older grooms. The result was a culture in which men and women occupied little common ground. The philosophical bias against femaleness and the indoctrinated sociological differences between men and women resulted in a widespread attitude of negativity toward women and ambivalence toward the spiritual good of marriage and family life.

To be sure, the growing Christian community was never wholly negative in its attitude toward women, bodies, and marriage. Drawing on the Hebraic stories in the biblical book of Genesis that proclaimed God's creation as good, and indeed marriage as good, Christians logically had to uphold marriage and family life as a noble lifestyle designed by the goodness of God. And yet, the philosophical denigration of the physical in favor of the spiritual made an indelible imprint on the Christian mindset.[19]

One might say that two classes of Christians emerged as a result of this influence: those who married and those who remained celibate. The latter became the monks and nuns, giving rise to the monastic traditions in which individuals often subjected their bodies to rigorous ascetic practices and lived in isolation or in spiritual communities separated from the mainstream culture. Celibate males were not typical of the early clergy, and the original bishops and priests were not required to remain celibate. Nevertheless, the celibate lifestyle was celebrated as spiritually higher than the married lifestyle, and it would centuries later become normative for the ordained clergy.[20]

---

18. Nancy Tuana discusses the role of women in Greek philosophy, particularly Aristotle and Plato, in *Women and the History of Philosophy* (St. Paul: Paragon House, 1992), 13–33.

19. Rosemary Radford Ruether discusses the ambivalence of Christianity regarding embodiment in her consideration of the synthesis of Hellenistic and Hebraic creation stories in *Gaia & God: An Ecofeminist Theology of Earth Healing* (New York: HarperCollins Publishers, 1992), 15–31.

20. This remains true of Roman Catholic clergy even today, although since the time of the Reformation, Protestant ministers typically marry.

The Fall of the Empire: 410–600

The growth that Christianity experienced in the fourth century did not continue unaltered into the next century. By the early 400s the Roman Empire was invaded by warring tribes who came down from Northern Europe. By 410 Rome itself was sacked. By the end of the fifth century, the whole Empire lacked political stability. Conquering Germanic peoples migrated throughout the Empire, bringing with them a militaristic and feudal culture. Church buildings, properties, and offices at this time often fell under the control of feudal lords rather than bishops. This resulted in conflict over who had the authority to name *ecclesiastical* (church) leaders. Consequently, the bishops and priests of the church often fell under obligation to feudal lords as well.

Much of the stability of the church at this time resulted from the presence of monastic communities, which continued to flourish. These communities were largely responsible for preserving theological traditions, charitable works, faith, and worship life during a time of widespread socio-political transition. Especially because monastic scribes preserved written material, these communities were instrumental in maintaining and growing the treasury of Christian literature and learning.

Although there was by this time still no ecclesial or church formula for marriage, the meaning of marriage was an important topic as Roman customs and laws gave way to Germanic practices. We see in this period a great deal of reflection on Christian lifestyles. Among the most significant contributions to the reflections on marriage from this period are the writings of

Augustine (354–430), the giant of theological orthodoxy from the patristic age. Augustine's thoughts on marriage are very important, both because of his status and also because they reveal the ongoing tension mentioned earlier within Christianity over the quality and purpose of married life.

Augustine experienced this tension deep within himself, as he records in his monumental work of Christian spirituality *The Confessions*. There he relates the struggle he experienced over his intellectual and spiritual conversion to Christianity. His internal conflicts over his sexual urges were a large part of his conversion process, and he only considered himself completely converted when he could finally decide to forego sexual activity altogether. This tension is reflected in his writings on marriage and family.

In his principle work on family and marriage, *On the Good of Marriage*, Augustine holds that marriage is a good and holy institution that manifests the good of children, proper direction of sexual urges, and companionship of spouses. Long before it was customary to do so, Augustine argued that marriage is a *sacramentum* (a sacred mystery), in that it reflects the sacred bond between Christ and church. Despite this exceptionally high regard for marriage, Augustine argued that sexuality is inherently stained by the sin of lust, of which no act of conjugal intercourse can be free. As a result, no sexual activity, even within marriage, is free from the stain of sin in Augustine's eyes.[21]

The conflicted thinking on marriage and the potential evil of sexual desire led many churchmen of Augustine's day to reject the notion of marriage as *sacramentum*. Others, such as

---

21. *On the Good of Marriage*, §6 reads, "Further, in the very case of the more immoderate requirement of the due of the flesh, which the Apostle [Paul] enjoins not on them by way of command, but allows to them by way of leave, that they have intercourse also beside the cause of begetting children; although evil habits impel them to such intercourse, yet marriage guards them from adultery or fornication." From *Nicene and Post-Nicene Fathers: First Series*, edited by Philip Schaff (Peabody, MA: Hendrickson Publishers, 2004), 3:401.

Augustine's mentor Ambrose (340–397), argued alongside Augustine[22] that marriage was *indissoluble*, meaning that it could not be separated by divorce. The thinking that marriage was indissoluble, coupled with the notion that remarriage resulted in adultery while the divorced spouse was still living, began to be reinforced officially by church councils in the 500s and 600s.[23] This development reflects a need on the part of the church to reinforce its ideal of Christian marriage at a point in history when marriage was still a family matter yet cultural norms regarding families were undergoing dramatic change.

Cultural changes stemming from the different marital practices of Romans and Germanic tribes ultimately forced the church to become more actively involved in marriages.[24] In the Roman custom, people were considered married at the time that the fathers of the bride and groom gave consent for their children. Once betrothed, the two individuals could not be engaged to another person. The marriage was considered binding and valid at the time of the consent. In the Germanic custom, people were considered married at the time of the first sexual intercourse between the couple. To have sexual congress was what bound two people in matrimony rather than a contract negotiated between the fathers of the bride and bridegroom.

The simultaneous practice of these very different notions of marriage created an enormous amount of confusion, frustration, and injustice. Those operating under the Roman custom would have believed a marriage to be valid at the time of the consent of the parents; but betrothed children often disregarded their parents' contracts, giving their consent to another and sealing that union through intercourse. Through sharing sexual intercourse, people often entered into private and clandestine marriages in order to avoid marriages that had been arranged for them. Divorce and polygamy were also serious problems with the landholding nobility. Marriages were contracted and abandoned excessively for the purposes of gaining land, producing heirs, and acquiring political and military alliances. There were no laws per se that bound couples in marriage, so people often turned to members of the clergy to help them sort out their conflicts. There was as yet no formula for marriage regulated by the church; such a form would come in the centuries that followed.

The Medieval Period: 600–1200

In the seventh and eighth centuries, Europe was still plagued with political instability. Popes and kings vied for power over one another even as they worked together from time to time in order to stave off foreign threats. In an effort to demonstrate that the church had ultimate authority over kings, Pope Leo III crowned Charlemagne (742–814) "Holy Roman Emperor" on Christmas day in the year 800. This act indicated that popes had the power to determine who would be recognized as the legitimate political authority. Although in subsequent generations old feuds between the political and ecclesial (church)

---

22. *On the Good of Marriage*, §32 reads, "Therefore the good of marriage throughout all nations and all men stands in the occasion of begetting, and faith of chastity: but, so far as pertains unto the People of God, also in the sanctity of the Sacrament, by reason of which it is unlawful for one who leaves her husband, even when she has been put away, to be married to another, so long as her husband lives. . . . The marriage bond is [not] loosed save by the death of the husband or wife." From *Nicene and Post-Nicene Fathers: First Series*, ed. Philip Schaff (Peabody, MA: Hendrickson Publishers, 2004), 3:412.

23. Martos, *Perspectives on Marriage*, 45.

24. For a detailed discussion of the differences in Roman and Germanic practices, consult Phillip Lyndon Reynolds, *Marriage in the Western Church: The Christianization of Marriage During the Patristic and Medieval Periods* (Leiden: Brill Press, 1994).

authority would resurface regularly, the time of Charlemagne marked a return to the overtly Christian character of Europe.

In addition to the resurgence of church authority over political leaders, by the eleventh century monasteries had become the primary centers for education and scholarship in Europe. Many monks focused on the spiritual reform of church leaders as well as the whole Christian world. This reform movement led to the widespread implementation of a new form of church law called *canon law*, which had both civil and ecclesial authority over people's lives. By the mid-thirteenth century, the hierarchical church organization, with supreme power vested in the bishop of Rome (the pope), was again a visible, political power.

This period also marked the age of the Crusades (1095–1204), which were intended to free conquered regions in Palestine and Eastern Europe from Islamic rule, and the development of scholastic theology. The Crusades had reawakened theological debate among Christians, Jews, and Muslims, and they had also reintroduced into the West the work of the Greek philosopher Aristotle. In order to demonstrate how Christianity was inherently reasonable in the face of competing truth claims, scholastic philosophers such as Peter Lombard (1100–1160), Thomas Aquinas (1225–1274), and Bonaventure (1221–1274) developed comprehensive systematic treatments of the faith that relied heavily on reason and logic-based argumentation. Their work became some of the most important theology in Christian history, and even today it carries great authority for believers.

With the resurgence of church authority in the form of canon law and the emergence of scholastic theology came new practices and theologies regarding family and marriage. On account of increased church involvement, marriages began to take place in public, leaving behind the older concept of marriage as a family matter. Couples began to announce their intent to marry before the wedding, giving an opportunity for anyone who had a previous claim to marriage to come forward. The public place of choice for marriage celebrations became the steps of the church, where the exchange of vows and gifts would take place to be followed by entrance into the church for blessing by the priest. Eventually the priest became involved in the actual blessing of the gifts and the couple on the church steps. Finally, the wedding ceremonies moved inside the walls of the church itself.[25]

Marriage was incorporated into canon law, largely to correct the abuses of marriage that stemmed from differing customs, frequent divorce, and polygamous unions. In order to determine what constituted a valid and legal marriage and what kinds of marriages could be dissolved, a canon lawyer named Francis Gratian (twelfth century) offered a workable solution. Drawing from both the Germanic and Roman customs, Gratian argued that a valid marriage required the consent of the people marrying, but it also required consummation by sexual intercourse. Thus the Latin formula of *ratum et consummatum* (consent and consummation) became accepted. Marriages that were contracted but never consummated were valid but separable in a divorce overseen by a proper ecclesial authority. Marriages that were consummated were de facto considered inseparable. Marriages that occurred in private were considered valid but illegal, while marriages that occurred in public were legal unions recognized in the eyes of the church. With this new formula, the notion of a church marriage was born.[26]

---

25. Martos, *Perspectives on Marriage*, 48–49.

26. Ibid., 50.

WHAT CONSTITUTES A MARRIAGE?

Can people marry one another privately, or does some witness or external authority need to be present? What if people are denied the right to marry by an external authority, such as by an owner in the case of a slave? When does a marriage occur—at the time of the wedding, or during the engagement, or even during courtship? What conditions make a marriage valid or invalid? These kinds of questions challenged Christians in the first millennium, and even today they continue to be revisited. What do you think constitutes a marriage? Are there differences between valid and legal marriages, and what conditions can (or should) govern each?

APPLICATION TO FAMILY AND MARRIAGE TODAY

By the height of the Middle Ages, marriages within the church tradition had undergone tremendous development. Where once marriages were a family matter, they now were overseen by the church and recognized as an indelible part of the faith life of believers. Divorce was more limited and polygamy was largely under control.

Over the time that marriage had grown into an ecclesial reality, much debate had occurred before scholastic theology finally recognized marriage as a sacrament. The precise nature of a sacrament will be considered in the following chapter, but it is helpful here to recognize a core understanding: a sacrament is an activity presided over by the church that is believed to communicate God's grace in a special and transformative way. Many were still suspicious of marriage because it was believed to be an inferior state to that of ordained, celibate life. Nevertheless, marriage had become incorporated into the main practices of the church.

The great benefit of studying the development of marriage and family life is that we can see that even within the Christian tradition, marriage has not been a static reality. It has changed in theory as well as in practice. The form of marriage has developed over the ages. At first it was a family matter, while later it became a matter of the church's involvement. Once marriages were arranged between the fathers of brides and grooms, while later marriages were contracted by the couple themselves.

There have also been different rules for different classes of Christians over the ages. In some eras, it was considered normative and acceptable for members of the nobility to have more than one wife. Through the eleventh century, it was considered acceptable for Catholic clergy to marry. There have also been different reasons given for marriage. Marriage was first considered to be for the explicit purpose of having children while more contemporary ages see marriage as for the purpose of fellowship and mutual love between the spouses. Marriage has been considered a grace-filled expression of Christian life for centuries, but how Christians understand the grace of marriage is an ongoing topic of theological reflection.

When we realize that marriage is not a static institution that people walk into, as if they are walking into a military compound, we become liberated to recognize that marriages, like the institution of marriage itself, are dynamic and developmental. This is particularly the case in the contemporary era, when old understandings of marriage are undergoing transition and new attitudes toward marriage are being formed. The faith tradition that speaks to marriage is vibrant so long as it is alive and dynamic; it is dead when it binds us in ways that bear no connection to our contemporary contexts and experiences. In chapter 6 we will discuss further developments in Roman Catholic thought regarding marriage that occurred from the thirteenth century through the present, but before we can turn to that discussion a careful consideration of the notion of the sacramental or graced dimension of marriage is necessary. To that we now turn.

Questions for Review and Discussion

1. Name several reasons why at first Christian thought was conflicted over the good of marriage.

2. Describe how marriage changed from the beginning of the Christian era until the Middle Ages.

3. In what ways has marriage been part of the broader reality of the Christian church historically?

4. Why did Augustine reason that marriage was indissoluble? Do you agree or disagree with his thinking?

5. Describe some of the gender issues within family dynamics in the eras here considered. Are these or related issues present today?

6. Why did people marry in the past? Why do you think people marry today?

7. Is there value to arranged marriages? What role, if any, do parents (or extended family members) play today in the choice of spouses for children?

8. Marriage was not always a matter of the state or the church. What are some reasons that justify state involvement in marriages? Church involvement?

Resources for Further Reading

Resources for the Historical Development of the Church and Theology

Thomas Bokenkotter, *A Concise History of the Catholic Church* (New York: Doubleday, 2005).

Alister McGrath, *Historical Theology: An Introduction to the History of Christian Thought* (Oxford: Blackwell Publishers, 2000).

Bruce Shelley, *Church History in Plain Language* (Nashville: Thomas Nelson Publishing, 2008).

Resources for the Historical Development of Marriage

Stephanie Coontz, *Marriage: A History; From Obedience to Intimacy, or How Love Conquered Marriage* (New York: Viking, 2005).

Mary Hartman, *The Household and the Making of History: A Subversive View of the Western Past* (Cambridge and New York: Cambridge University Press, 2004).

Glenn Olsen, *Christian Marriage: A Historical Study* (New York: Crossroad Publishing Co., 2001).

Kieran Scott and Michael Warren, *Perspectives on Marriage: A Reader* (New York and Oxford: Oxford University Press, 2007).

Marilyn Yalom, *A History of the Wife* (New York: HarperCollins Publishers, 2001).

5

MARRIAGE AS SACRAMENT

In the previous chapter, we discussed the development of marriage throughout the first Christian millennium. That discussion ended with the Catholic Church recognizing marriage as a sacrament.[1] This chapter will explore that affirmation. It is important to emphasize that when we talk about the historical development of marriage, we are talking not only about developments in how marriages were arranged, how they were celebrated, and how they were managed by men and women over the ages, but also and perhaps more importantly, about how the meaning of marriage has been understood by married people and by those with a particular investment in marriage.

While marriage is one of the earliest and most widespread of ritually observed practices, the meaning of marriage has varied among cultures. Some cultures have perceived marriage merely as a stabilizing social arrangement that cooperates with the natural mating habits of humans, while others have ascribed to marriage great cultural or religious significance. Even within Christianity, not all people recognize marriage in the same way, either historically or today. The Roman Catholic understanding of the meaning of marriage is distinguished by the claim that marriage is a sacrament. This means that Roman Catholicism recognizes marriage as bearing the highest spiritual significance. Catholicism also holds that married couples have a special meaning and relationship to the Catholic Church.

TOOLS

The sacramental theology of marriage is rooted foremost in how Catholicism understands God's being, God's relationship to creation, God's Incarnation in Jesus, and God's ongoing presence in the life of the Catholic Church and indeed in the whole Christian people. The discussion here

---

1. Note that "church" is capitalized when referring to a specific worshipping community; thus "Roman Catholic Church." When referring to the universal Christian church, the lower case is used.

attempts to establish how Catholicism articulates this theology, especially for the benefit of readers who may be unfamiliar with it. Students who are already immersed in the principles of Catholic sacramental theology may wish to jump directly to the discussion of the sacrament of marriage.

REFLECTION ON GOD

In order to understand the concept of marriage as a sacrament, we first need to consider the underlying concept of sacramentality. We must begin with the notion of the universe as God's creation, because sacramentality is grounded in the belief that elements of the natural world communicate God's grace. Christians believe that God created the universe, which is another way of saying that everything has its being and origin in God. Nothing exists in and of itself and for its own sake except for God.

The Christian faith rooted in the Hebraic understanding of God holds that there is only one God from whom all else comes. The authors of the creation stories in Genesis believed that the one God was the origin of all things, and they attempted to offer a hymn of praise to this glorious foundation of all creation in their writing.[2] The notion of God alone as having an independent being unique from anything else may sound somewhat lofty and theoretical, but if we think in practical terms it quickly becomes clearer. Consider for a moment all of the ways in which elements of the natural world, including human beings, relate to and rely upon one another in an intricate chain of interdependence.[3]

Even though as human beings we experience ourselves as unique individuals, we are very much a part of a continuum of being that stretches backward and forward across time. We rely on one another as a human community, and we rely on the natural world, in which we live and breathe, from which we eat and drink, and within which we work, play, laugh, grieve, transmit new life, and pass away. All things of the natural world, ourselves included, relate to and depend upon on one another in similar fashion. Neither amoeba nor star system exists independently. Human beings are no different, being at last neither our own source of being nor in control of our own ultimate destiny.[4] In short, all creation is dependent on something else for its existence and sustenance.

In order for there to be anything at all, everything must come from something. All the things we have mentioned have a traceable cause and origin, but eventually something uncaused and primary must precede everything else that is caused.[5] That something from which all else primarily originates is what Christianity calls "God."

Now, one might argue that God is not independent from the rest of creation. Indeed, many have held that the natural world is divinity itself. This point of view is called *pantheism* (meaning "god is everything"). The problem with this point of view from the Christian perspective is

---

2. We need not read the creation stories in Genesis literally in order to find them theologically meaningful. Indeed, we can surmise that the authors never intended for their work to be read as a literal and historical account of creation, because they included two stories side-by-side with different accounts and orders of creation, even employing different names for God.

3. Sallie McFague's now classic text *The Body of God: An Ecological Theology* (Minneapolis: Fortress Press, 1993), 207–12, provides an outstanding resource for reflecting on the networks of interdependence and interrelationship of elements of the natural world.

4. Indeed, the eighteenth-century Protestant theologian Friedrich Schleiermacher described this level of self-awareness that leads to religious awareness as a "feeling of absolute dependence."

5. This is essentially an aspect of Thomas Aquinas's cosmological argument for the existence of God, located in the *Summa Theologiae* Ia, q. 2, a. 3. A good introduction to this argument may be found in Peter Kreeft's edited and annotated summary of Aquinas, *Summa of the Summa* (San Francisco: Ignatius Press, 1990), 60–70.

that it reduces God to a mechanistic function of biochemical processes. God has no free will and no personhood in pantheism, as God is not individuated from the universe per se. A cornerstone of Christian faith, by contrast, is the belief that God relates to human beings freely and personally. It is precisely free personhood that characterizes how God was understood by the authors of the Bible as well as how Christians continue to interpret their own historical experience of God.

Christianity thus teaches that God is a free and personal being who chooses to create the world. A Christian view of the world does not perceive it as merely random natural processes carrying out mindless operations. Rather Christians perceive purpose, beauty, and meaning that transcend the natural world and point to something beyond nature itself. That something is the source of purpose, beauty, meaning, freedom, hope, love, and everything else that gives life direction. In short, Christianity understands God as this source or ground of being.[6]

THE SACRAMENTAL PRINCIPLE

The sacramental principle holds that all of creation is imbued with God's grace. To say it another way, the physical world is a medium for the divine. The Catholic Church teaches that the presence of God's grace throughout creation is specially and fully present in Jesus. In order to teach this concept, I sometimes use the analogy of a painting in a museum. If we study the painting, we learn something about the artist. However, if we actually speak to the artist, we learn something more about the artist than was communicated through the painting alone. According to Catholic Church teaching, we might say that the encounter with Christ is akin to having a conversation with the artist rather than just encountering the artwork.

This teaching invites several questions that are helpful for discussion. In what substantive ways do you think a Catholic might differentiate between God's grace in nature and God's grace in the Church? Do you think grace is present in nature, and if so, does it require special revelation in order to be fully accessible to human beings? If grace permeates all of nature, how do you think the Catholic Church might understand the ways in which other animal and plant life not only reveals but also experiences God's presence?

GOD'S RELATIONSHIP TO CREATION AS THE GROUND OF SACRAMENTALITY

Having established this basic understanding of God's relationship to creation, we can begin to understand what Catholicism means when it declares that the world is sacramental. "Sacrament" implies "sacred," so to say the world is sacramental is to say it is sacred. Catholicism teaches that the world is sacred because it is the loving expression of God who creates it. As physical creatures who are a part of the world, human beings cannot step outside the world to encounter God directly. It is only through physical realities of creation, such as our bodies and

---

6. David Tracy speaks to this in *Blessed Rage for Order* (Chicago and London: University of Chicago Press, 1996), 187: "The question of God's reality, the divine necessity or impossibility, is not a question of interest only to those with a taste for arcane subjects. In fact, the question of properly conceiving God's reality—precisely as the objective ground of our most basic faith in the meaningfulness of our lives—is of crucial existential import for all concerned with the need to articulate an objective ground for faith."

brains, that people can know anything about the world in general as well as anything about God in particular. In other words, physical or material realities are the only media through which people can know God. Because Catholicism teaches that the world communicates God to people, it says that the world is graced. Anything in the world can be a medium of grace, such as a rainbow, a friend, a song, because all of these things can be reflections of the beauty and goodness of God.

In short, this is how Catholicism understands sacramentality in the world. If we believe that the universe is created by the loving intent of a Creator, then the creation itself becomes a means of knowing and understanding the Creator. The world thus becomes a holy place of encounter with God.

JESUS AND THE SACRAMENTS

Catholicism holds that the grace of creation in the natural world is present to all peoples of all faiths and creeds in all eras of human existence. It further holds that any religion that recognizes God's presence in the universe is responding to this same phenomenon, whether it is referred to as an experience of grace or identified by some other name.[7] What makes the Catholic notion of God's grace unique is the belief that God has not

only *generally* disclosed Godself in all of nature, but that God has *particularly and fully* disclosed Godself in the person of Jesus.[8]

In the unique event of the life of Jesus of Nazareth, Catholicism sees a total and perfect revelation of God. Catholic belief is that Jesus is the *Incarnation* of God[9] and that his divinity is revealed through his actions and teachings, his life and death, and his Resurrection. Completely open to God's grace, Jesus (who is both fully human and fully divine) understands what God wills and responds in total loving obedience to God's free gift of self. All the beauty, purpose, and meaning of life that is indirectly revealed in nature becomes explicitly articulated in Jesus, who teaches in word and deed how human beings can know and love God in true and lasting friendship.

This is what is meant by the theological term *incarnation*, which means "enfleshment." The very being of God becomes *incarnated* or enfleshed in the person of Jesus. What was transcendent and indescribable became immanent and accessible in Jesus. The grace that was everywhere undefined became uniquely definitive in Jesus. As the physical, bodily medium, Jesus became the human person in whom the sacrament of creation is totally realized and the encounter with God is totally possible. Thus, for the Catholic faith, while God's grace in creation remains present everywhere in the natural world,

---

7. Consult Vatican Council II's document *Nostra Aetate*, §1–2.

8. That Jesus is the primordial sacrament, whose sacramental presence is carried on in the life of the Church and lived out specifically in the seven great sacraments of the Roman Catholic Church, is the subject of Edward Schillebeeckx, *Christ the Sacrament of the Encounter with God* (New York: Sheed and Ward, 1963).

9. The Catholic understanding of God is Trinitarian. This means that God is three-in-one. The three aspects of God are called *persons*, which are distinguished by their relationships to one another as Father, Son, and Holy Spirit. Some contemporary Christians are more comfortable with other names for the persons of the Trinity, such as Creator, Redeemer, and Sustainer. The persons of the Trinity are believed to be inherently relational, such that even if God were entirely alone God would still experience relationship. It is the second person of the Trinity that Catholicism teaches became incarnate or embodied in the person Jesus. Based on this Trinitarian understanding of God, it is appropriate to speak of Jesus as God and also to speak of Jesus as having a relationship to God. Many early Christian councils of the fourth through the sixth centuries finally resulted in the formulae for expressing beliefs in Jesus' Incarnation and the Trinity. The standard text on these councils is J. N. D. Kelly, *Early Christian Creeds*, 3rd ed. (New York: Continuum, 2006).

it is perfectly revealed in the unique life of Jesus.

The life of Jesus ended in his death by crucifixion, but Christian faith holds that Jesus was resurrected three days after his death. This claim does not refer to a physical resuscitation; it refers to a transformed state of being in which Jesus enjoys ongoing life in the presence of God. The Gospel accounts of Jesus describe a period of time during which the risen Jesus was able to speak with and even dine with his friends, but that period ended with his ascension into heaven. Without his immediate leadership, the disciples floundered until they experienced the outpouring of the Holy Spirit upon their community during the feast of Pentecost. This outpouring of the Spirit is recounted in the second chapter of the Book of Acts in the New Testament and marks the beginning of the worldwide church.

This event in the Scriptures signifies not only the beginning of the Jesus movement, but the ongoing presence of God incarnate or enfleshed. Although the grace of God could no longer be experienced through the human being Jesus in his mortal form, it could now be experienced through other human beings by virtue of their participation in the church. The church became the place where Christians continued to experience the direct revelation and transmission of the grace of God in concrete and tangible forms.

MORE ABOUT SACRAMENTS

The Catholic Church did not always recognize seven sacraments. Indeed, it took centuries for the sacrament of marriage to be recognized officially in Church teaching. That the number of sacraments has varied historically suggests that sacramentality itself is open to interpretation. Since the Catholic Church teaches that sacraments, instituted by Christ and celebrated by the Church, communicate grace in special ways, what aspects of human life do you think could plausibly be considered sacraments? Can you argue that there are any missing from the seven sacraments? Likewise, can you argue that any of the seven sacraments should be eliminated?

Christians even called themselves the body of Christ, because they believed that through their baptism they became the ongoing presence of Jesus in the world. Although Jesus could no longer use his own hands to heal believers, his followers, after his guidance and inspired by his Spirit, could use their hands on Jesus' behalf. In this faith, then, the church became the place where God's grace could be especially experienced in a direct and tangible way. Specifically, the Catholic Church came to recognize over time seven distinct moments in the worship life of believers during which grace is particularly felt and in which the healing effects of God's grace are mediated through the Catholic Church. These moments are: baptism, Eucharist, confirmation, reconciliation, anointing of the sick, holy orders, and marriage.[10]

---

10. The seven sacraments of the Catholic Church relate to and reinforce one another in poignant ways. It is worthwhile to consider each sacrament individually and then to ask how the sacraments complement the meaning of the others. However, such a study is outside the scope of our present discussion, the focus of which is the sacrament of marriage. Where appropriate, I will comment on the relationship of marriage to the other sacraments, but for a fuller introduction to sacramental theology, see David Power, *Sacrament: The Language of God's Giving* (New York: Herder & Herder, 1999) and Michael Lawler, *Symbol and Sacrament: A Contemporary Sacramental Theology* (New York: Paulist Press, 1987).

THE SACRAMENT OF MARRIAGE: GOD'S GRACE AMONG SPOUSES

To say that marriage is a sacrament is to invoke all of the discussions thus far in this book. Marriage as a sacrament first emerges from the principle of *sacramentality*. Based on God's creation, all of nature is graced. The natural bond of love between a man and a woman is itself by nature a holy and sacred reality. To love and to be loved and to rear children out of a loving union communicate a fundamental grace in the couple. What is this grace? It is the blessings of joy, happiness, laughter, wisdom, companionship, and stability that come from human partnership.

However, the Christian notion of the meaning of marriage does not stop with the appreciation of the natural goodness that comes out of becoming a couple. For surely such joining together is not always joyous, nor is it immediately obvious in nature that one man and one woman should live exclusively in one marriage and should stay in a marriage throughout life. Many variations on marriage are naturally possible. Historically both men and women sometimes chose to have more than one spouse (polygyny/polyandry). Some people mate or partner with someone for a brief period of time and then move on to a new partner (serial monogamy). Some marriages are arranged or serve only financial or political interests; the spouses may have little in common. With all of the various ways in which human beings could partner, the natural grace of marriage becomes murky and undefined.

Largely due to this murkiness, in the Catholic faith the sacramental quality of the marriage has over time been given a specific definition and specific significance. This definition has its origins in the sacred literature of the biblical Hebrews. The Israelites perceived the union and love between spouses as a covenant akin to the covenant between God and the people of Israel.[11] Like the love Hosea demonstrates for Gomer, covenant love is steadfast and forgiving. It has the ability to heal and correct error and sin over the meandering course of a relationship, safe in the knowledge that no matter how many times one might fail eventually righteousness will prevail. Because covenant love is foremost rooted in the reality of God's love for the Israelites, the covenant marriage becomes the locus for experiencing God's grace between the human spouses.

This same notion of covenant underlies the Christian notion of charity in the New Testament.[12] Charity is not mere affection or eroticism. It is rather active love that seeks justice and goodness on behalf of the beloved. When one experiences charity for another, he or she loves the other because the other is God's creation. One wants to see in the other total human flourishing and will work to see that flourishing realized. One is less invested in personal gain and outcomes than in the welfare of the other, and it is in the goodness of the other that the self finds its own happiness. This is a selfless sort of love, and it was modeled perfectly in the sacramental life of Jesus. Moreover, the Catholic Church has historically seen in the opening miracle of the Gospel of John, in which Jesus turns water into wine at the wedding feast of Cana, an affirmation of the sanctity of marriage.[13]

Throughout the subsequent centuries, explored in the previous chapter, Christian charity and covenantal love increasingly came to be recognized as a warrant for understanding

---

11. See the discussion of covenant in chapter 2.

12. Likewise, reference the discussion of charity in chapter 3.

13. John 2:1–11.

marriage not only as a human good but also as an expression of God's grace that intricately relates to the life of the church. Herbert Vorgrimler's *Sacramental Theology*[14] documents the historical decisions relayed in theological writings and church statements of the Middle Ages and Reformation era that increasingly defined marriage as a sacrament.[15] For instance, Vorgrimler cites the following examples:

- Pope Alexander III (d. 1181) promoted the idea that marriage is valid when the couple offers their free consent, and it becomes indissoluble once the marriage is consummated.
- Peter Damian (d. 1072) and Peter Lombard (d. 1160) both include marriage in their list of sacraments.
- The Second Lateran Council of 1139 and the Council of Verona of 1184 argue in defense of church marriages, with the latter actually naming marriage a sacrament for the first time in a doctrinal statement by the Roman Catholic Church.
- The Council of Florence in 1439 affirms marriage as a sacrament that signifies the union of Christ and the Roman Catholic Church.
- The Council of Trent in 1547 numbers matrimony as one of the seven sacraments of the Roman Catholic Church.[16]

Today the Roman Catholic Church's Code of Canon Law (1055–1165) discusses specific components of the sacrament of marriage. It begins, "The matrimonial covenant, by which a man and a woman establish between themselves a partnership of the whole of life and which is ordered by its nature to the good of the spouses and the procreation and education of offspring, and which, between the baptized, has been raised by Christ the Lord to the dignity of a sacrament. For this reason, a valid matrimonial contract cannot exist between the baptized without it being by that fact a sacrament."[17] This teaching, affirmed regularly in the official teachings and practices of the Church,[18] confirms marriage as a sacred or graced way of life that is intimately related to the whole sacramental life of the Roman Catholic Church.

HOW IS MARRIAGE A SACRAMENT?

It is helpful to consider aspects of marriage in order to illustrate not only *that* it is a sacrament but also *how* it is a sacrament.[19]

Marriage Models Jesus' Love for the Church

The relationship between Jesus and the church is understood as itself an archetypical kind of love that, in ordinary human relationships, can

---

14. Herbert Vorgrimler, *Sacramental Theology* (Collegeville, MN: Liturgical Press, 1992).

15. For a useful complement, see Richard McBrien's discussion of the history of matrimony in *Catholicism*, new ed. (New York: HarperCollins Publishers, 1994), 852–55.

16. Vorgrimler, *Sacramental Theology*, 294–97.

17. Can. 1055, §1–2.

18. Odile M. Liebard edited a useful volume of teachings on sexuality and marriage, dating from the nineteenth through the latter quarter of the twentieth century in *Official Catholic Teachings: Love and Sexuality* (Wilmington, NC: McGrath, 1978).

19. Several books help illuminate these aspects of marriage, including William Roberts, *Marriage: Sacrament of Hope and Challenge* (Cincinnati: St. Anthony Messenger Press, 1988); Michael Lawler and William Roberts, *Christian Marriage and Family: Contemporary Theological and Pastoral Perspectives* (Collegeville, MN: Liturgical Press, 1996); and Michael Lawler, *Marriage and Sacrament: A Theology of Christian Marriage* (Collegeville, MN: Liturgical Press, 1993).

best be experienced in marriage. In other words, marriages are the proper context in which human beings can manifest total self-gift to one another in a way that mirrors and reflects the love of Christ for the church. How Christ lived, loved, and sacrificed for his followers should be reflected in how spouses love one another and their family. As a sacrament, marriage is recognized as a physical, material reality in which God's grace, revealed specifically through Jesus, can be experienced in concrete and practical terms. Marriage and family life provide enormous opportunities for compassion, forgiveness, service, and sacrifice.

A Model of Covenant and Charity

In marriage there must be room for individuals to be themselves, but there is no room for selfishness. Marriages do not get far on the basis of kindly feelings alone. Love for one's spouse and one's children is lived out actively in day-to-day choices. Moreover, the family is a locus for charity expressed beyond itself through acts of social service, participation, and alms. As covenants, marriages are not easily undone. The birth of children, furthermore, irrevocably changes the lives of parents and even extended family members. Both the responsibilities and opportunities of marriages provide occasions for spouses to grow as authentic, spiritual, steadfast, and whole persons, reflecting God's covenantal love for human beings.

Relationship to Sacraments of Initiation

As mentioned above, the Catholic Church recognizes seven sacraments. These seven sacraments are organized into three categories. The Sacraments of Initiation include baptism, confirmation, and Eucharist. They are called Sacraments of Initiation because they represent an individual's entrance and journey as an integrated member of the Roman Catholic Church. Through

baptism and confirmation, a person becomes a full member of the Church. Through reception of the Eucharist (sometimes called Communion), a person is strengthened and nourished in one's Christian journey. The sacrament of marriage is related to baptism, confirmation, and Eucharist in that it is an expression of the lifestyle and journey within the Church to which members of the community of believers are called. Spouses experience this journey and make decisions about their lifestyle *as spouses*, and as such they live out their baptismal promises together.

Relationship to the Sacraments of Healing

The Sacraments of Healing include reconciliation and anointing of the sick. Reconciliation represents the spiritual, psychological, and moral healing that must occur from time to time in any relationship—in this case between the individual and the Church. Anointing of the sick represents the need for physical blessing and psycho-spiritual healing of persons enduring sickness and facing the end of life—both of which can also distance a person from the life of the worshipping community. Marriage is related to the Sacraments of Healing because it calls upon spouses to manage and respond in loving compassion to the spiritual and physical needs and shortcomings that characterize all human lives. Forgiveness and healing grace, mediated by the sacramental life of the Church, are fundamentally the reason for the Church's very existence. Marriage and family life provide an essential location for these realities to be experienced in daily life.

Marriage as a Sacrament of Vocation and Commitment

The Sacraments of Vocation and Commitment include holy orders and matrimony. These sacraments represent the ways in which a person physically brings grace to others through personal presence and service. In the sacrament of holy orders, an individual is ordained and thus dedicates his life to serving others, with whom one generally does not have intimate attachments, according to the needs of the Church. In the sacrament of matrimony, spouses live out a spiritual vocation or calling to live in fidelity and service within the context of family responsibility.

Marriage is a spiritual vocation in which the husband and wife function as the priests who confer the sacrament of matrimony upon one another. Spouses become spiritual ladders for one another to climb, as each one supports and shepherds the growth of the other toward a full and mature faith in God. This dimension is also present in the manner in which parents shepherd and support their children toward spiritual holiness. Marriage is in this sense truly a religious vocation because it draws upon and seeks to address the deepest spiritual needs of spouses and their children.

Indeed, one could argue that marriage is the greatest sacrament because in this context alone new covenants of love, born of the bloodshed of mothers in birth, come into being. Of course, children can be born outside of Christian marriage and indeed outside of marriage altogether, but the sacrament of marriage recognizes and celebrates the grace that comes to a child who is born to parents in a wedded covenant of true charity. As a sacrament, marriage becomes not only a civil reality authorized by a marriage license that is provided by the state. It becomes an ecclesial reality, recognized as elemental to the very being of the Church.

THE RITE OF MARRIAGE

In the Catholic Church, liturgical practices are often referred to as "rites." Rites have established components and an order that the Church deems as standard. The celebration of the Rite of Marriage has several necessary components. First, there is an introductory dialogue between the celebrant and the couple getting married. This is followed by the consent of the couple, during which the individuals clearly state their free consent to marry one another. Subsequent to the consent is the blessing and exchange of rings. After the blessing, general intercessions or prayers are offered, followed by the nuptial blessing over the newly married couple. The concluding rite, which consists of the Lord's Prayer, the sign of peace, and the final blessing, ends the celebration. Couples may also wish to have their wedding rite within the context of a Communion Rite or a Mass. In these cases, couples would also include in their weddings readings from Scripture (called the Liturgy of the Word) and either the Communion Rite (in which case the attendees receive communion) or the Liturgy of the Eucharist (in which case the bread and wine of communion are consecrated before being received).

Sacramentals of Marriage

In a marriage ceremony, physical elements called *sacramentals* symbolize the grace that spouses intend to confer upon one another. These may include the lighting of a large candle from the flames of two smaller candles, representing the oneness in body that two people bring about through their union. Similarly, it could be the veiling together or tying of a cord around one another, which also represents unity. It usually involves the exchange of rings, which in their circular shape express an eternal reality—without beginning and ending. The couple exchanges a kiss to signify their physical union. These ritual elements signify the graces of unity and love that will be experienced by the couple and their family over their life together.

An Ecclesial Reality of the Roman Catholic Church

In the Catholic Church, marriage is an aspect of the Church itself. This may sound odd, but it is important to remember that the Church is not a building or set of documents. It is, rather, a community of living human beings. To the extent that married human beings are part of that community, their marriage becomes a place where the Church itself exists. Catholic marriages and families are not only a place where the Catholic Church may be found, they are a place where the values and beliefs of the Catholic Church (and indeed the Christian community as a whole) are expressed to the broader human community. This sentiment is summed up well in the Second Vatican Council document, *The Church in the Modern World*:

> Families will generously share their spiritual treasures with other families. The Christian family springs from marriage, which is an image and a sharing in the partnership of love between Christ and the church; it will show to all people Christ's living presence in the world and the authentic nature of the church by the love and generous fruitfulness of the spouses, by their unity and fidelity, and by the loving way in which all members of the family cooperate with each other.[20]

SPECIAL CONSIDERATIONS

Because the Catholic Church understands marriage to be a sacrament, certain related considerations follow. These are helpfully recounted in Richard McBrien's discussion of marriage in his comprehensive treatment of Catholic faith entitled *Catholicism*.[21] We will discuss many of these considerations elsewhere in this text, but they are worth noting here.

The first consideration is that a sacramental marriage is indissoluble, meaning it is incapable of being dissolved or separated by divorce, based on Jesus' teachings in the New Testament as well as on the theology of marriage as representing the bond between Christ and the church. From the time of Augustine onward, Christian theologians argued that marriage between two baptized Christians was indissoluble. Just as Jesus cannot be divorced from the church, baptized spouses cannot be separated from one another. Once a marriage is contracted through the free consent of the couple, followed by sexual consummation, it is considered indissoluble. This teaching is affirmed in the Code of Canon Law 1056 and 1141.

Distinctions to the claim of indissolubility of marriage, however, were being made as early as New Testament times. In 1 Corinthians 7:10–16, Paul argues that a convert to Christianity is not bound to stay with a non-converted spouse. Today, this principle still holds. The Roman Catholic Church will allow a Catholic convert to remarry under its auspices, following the divorce of a non-baptized person, on the grounds of this so-called "Pauline Privilege." Similarly, under what is known as the "Petrine Privilege," deriving its name from the convention of identifying the pope with Christ's disciple Peter, the pope may dissolve a marriage between a Catholic and a non-Christian for a serious reason (such as the desire of a Catholic party to marry another baptized person upon the divorce of a non-Christian). Of course, it should be noted that what the Catholic Church allows or not is an internal matter. Whether the Catholic Church will recognize a marriage or a divorce has little bearing on the civil legality of a marriage or a divorce. It does, however, bear on the relationship of a Catholic to his or her Catholic Church community.

---

20. *Gaudium et Spes*, §48. Used by permission.
21. McBrien, *Catholicism*, 859–61.

This last point raises the issue of Catholic divorces, which of course do occur. The specific issue of divorce will be raised in chapter 11 of this book. For now, it is useful to note that because marriage is considered indissoluble, the Catholic Church believes a marriage to be binding, even in the event of a civil divorce, unless the Catholic Church itself issues a declaration of nullity. A declaration of nullity may be sought from a marriage tribunal, which is a Church court, on the grounds that the marriage was somehow deficient at the time of its inception. If some defect in free consent or consummation can be demonstrated, the marriage tribunal will grant an annulment. This means that while a wedding took place, a sacramental marriage never actually occurred. Care for divorced persons in the Catholic Church, as a result, requires thoughtful consideration and ministering.

APPLICATION TO FAMILY AND MARRIAGE TODAY

To return to the opening paragraphs of this chapter, marriage can have many different meanings for many different people in many different contexts. It has not always been considered a sacrament, even by Christians. Even when it has been considered a sacrament, it did not and does not always carry with it the same implications for interpersonal happiness and mutual friendship that it does today. In subsequent chapters we will consider some of the historical failures that were manifest in marriage, just as we will consider what happens when marriages fail. It is helpful to remember that when we are talking about the contemporary Catholic notion of marriage as a sacrament, we are talking about an ideal to which baptized believers are called. This ideal is obviously not always realized, and it

is never realized automatically or effortlessly just because two people marry.

Marriage, according to the Catholic Church, is a sacrament inherently because of what it signifies and what is potentially present within it. This correlates with the notion that a sacrament is not dependent upon the quality of the minister to be effective. If the priest that baptizes me is inebriated at the time of my baptism, my baptism is no less valid. If sacraments required perfection on the part of their ministers in order to be effective, no sacrament would ever be able to confer grace. So in this sense, marriage is a sacrament by virtue of the grace that it signifies, apart from the spouses in the marriage.

On the other hand, the grace of sacraments cannot be effective in the lives of recipients unless they are open to and present to its transformative quality. Marriage is not a sacrament by accident or by magic. It is a sacrament because married persons choose to live it as such. The grace of marriage is achieved imperfectly, because spouses are imperfect. This imperfection in human beings creates a gulf between what human beings experience in actuality and what we seek in our deepest aspirations. The ideal itself is a form of grace in that it gives spouses a vision and goal to move toward.

While other Christian communions may not use the term *sacrament* to describe the sacredness of marriage, for Christians, any marriage rooted in the love of Christ (or God for the Israelites) is an expression of grace. Christian marriage is distinguished from other types of marriage because of the biblically derived goal to which spouses should strive, not because of the guarantee that the goal will be achieved. The core meaning of marriage as a sacrament is that it is a lifestyle that invites spouses to grow in the love of Christ in a permanent and indissoluble union with one another. The challenges of living this sacrament are issues for further consideration.

Questions for Review and Discussion

1. How does God's relationship to creation underlie the Catholic principle of sacramentality?

2. Why does Catholicism see the church, and specifically the Catholic Church, as the ongoing presence of Christ in the world today?

3. Name and describe the Catholic Church's seven sacraments.

4. Describe how marriage models the love between Jesus and the church.

5. Describe how marriage relates to the other sacraments of the Catholic Church.

6. What does it mean to say that marriage is an ecclesial reality of the Catholic Church?

7. What are some of the special considerations that arise out of the Catholic Church's understanding of marriage as a sacrament, especially pertaining to divorce and separation?

8. Do you think only Catholic marriages are or can be sacraments? Does any church need to pronounce marriage a sacrament in order for the marriage to confer grace?

9. How would you describe the graces of marriage?

10. Compare the ideal of marriage as sacrament with your perception of actual marriages. Where might you actually find the sacramental quality of marriage being lived out between spouses and among their families?

Resources for Further Reading

Resources for Sacramental Theology

Michael Lawler, *Symbol and Sacrament: A Contemporary Sacramental Theology* (New York and Mahwah, NJ: Paulist Press, 1987).

David Power, *Sacrament: The Language of God's Giving* (New York: Crossroad, 1999).

Herbert Vorgrimler, *Sacramental Theology* (Collegeville, MN: Liturgical Press, 1992).

Resources for the Sacrament of Marriage

Todd Salzman, Thomas Kelly, and John O'Keefe, eds., *Marriage in the Catholic Tradition: Scripture, Tradition, and Experience* (New York: Crossroad, 2004).

Michael Lawler, *Marriage and the Catholic Church: Disputed Questions* (Collegeville, MN: Liturgical Press, 2002).

Michael Lawler, *Marriage and Sacrament: A Theology of Christian Marriage* (Collegeville, MN: Liturgical Press, 1993).

Pontifical Council for the Family, *Preparation for the Sacrament of Marriage* (Boston: Pauline Books and Media, 1996).

William Roberts, *Marriage: Sacrament of Hope and Challenge* (Cincinnati: St. Anthony Messenger Press, 1983).

6

MODERN MARRIAGE
AND HOW WE GOT HERE

In the previous two chapters, we looked at the historical development of marriage, resulting in a Catholic theology of marriage as a sacrament. We will now consider the history of marriage from the Middle Ages until the present. Marriage has changed from previous eras, and understanding the history underlying modern marriage is essential to grasping those changes and the challenges, benefits, and expectations that modern couples experience.

The meaning of marriage is in transition. Old models of marriage have been called into question, and new models are still being discovered. People want marriage to be fulfilling personally, but how to achieve that remains unclear. Women's social roles and opportunities have changed, granting women more economic freedom than in the past. As a result, women and men may enter into marriage on a more equal footing, but vestiges of old roles still color what husbands and wives expect from each other in marriage.[1] Some people simply opt not to marry, while others seek marriage as a right that has been denied them.[2]

To understand how and why certain changes in marriage occurred, we will explore some major cultural and intellectual developments from the Middle Ages to the present and their impact on marriage. Then we will consider modern marriage, focusing on how expectations of marriage have changed dramatically in recent decades and the challenges in living out marriage as an expression of covenant, charity, and sacrament in the modern world.

---

1. Peter Marin's article "A Revolution's Broken Promises," in *Perspectives on Marriage: A Reader*, eds. Kieran Scott and Michael Warren (Oxford and New York: Oxford University Press, 2007), 167–75, is an excellent resource for considering the gulf between what people today want and expect from their marriages and what they are willing to do for it. This article also quite helpfully explores transformed attitudes toward sexuality and the expectations from marriage.

2. While many heterosexual couples opt to delay marriage or to forsake it altogether, many same-sex couples lobby for the right to marry for both political and spiritual reasons. As an example, Stephen Pope's article "Same-Sex Marriage: Threat or Aspiration?" in *Perspectives on Marriage: A Reader*, eds. Kieran Scott and Michael Warren (New York and Oxford: Oxford University Press, 2007), 141–46, explores reasons both for and against same-sex marriage.

TOOLS

A brief sketch of the historical periods that helped to shape the context of Christianity in Europe and North America from the Middle Ages to today is helpful in understanding the development of marriage. Marriage has never existed in a vacuum, and just like all else in human life, it has in part been formed by its broader context. As with our first look at historical periods, discussion here is limited to thumbnail sketches. It should be noted that historical overviews are notoriously difficult because they can only discuss generalities, and in the process many distinctions and nuances are lost. Moreover, the discussion here focuses not on marriage in a global context but rather on developments within western Christendom from the Middle Ages to the present. Even within this limited geographic focus, detailed treatments are necessary for more focused study of marriage and family life in any of these eras.[3] The periods we will consider now are the Renaissance, the Reformation, the Enlightenment, and the eighteenth to twentieth centuries.

Renaissance: Fourteenth to Sixteenth Centuries

Renaissance means "rebirth" and refers to a cultural movement in Europe that witnessed a great recovery and revival of classical sources from ancient Greece and Rome.[4] Originating in the Tuscany region of Italy, the movement spread throughout Europe for two centuries, affecting art, literature, architecture, and education. A number of factors contributed to this movement. Among them was Florence's uniquely wealthy, politically powerful, and artistically influential Medici family. Another factor was the aftermath of the Black Death, also known as the bubonic plague, a pandemic bacterial disease that killed millions throughout Europe, the Middle East, and Africa in the fourteenth century. In its wake Europe's devastated population found new social mobility as labor and industry, especially for men outside the land-owning nobility, began to expand outside the home and into the public realm of the guild.[5] Moreover, the spread of Islam into Europe in previous centuries reintroduced into the West lost or neglected classical literature that had been preserved in Islamic libraries; the most influential of these works were those of Aristotle.[6] These and other factors led particularly the wealthy classes to a widespread fascination with ancient Latin and Greek sources, broader popular literacy, and patronage of highly ambitious art and architectural projects.

The great educational movement of this era is called *humanism*.[7] As the name suggests,

---

3. Several excellent resources for study of marriage from the Middle Ages forward include: David Herlihy, *Medieval Households* (Cambridge and London: Harvard University Press, 1985); Frances and Joseph Gies, *Marriage and the Family in the Middle Ages* (New York: Harper & Row, 1987); Steven Ozment, *When Fathers Ruled: Family Life in Reformation Europe* (Cambridge and London: Harvard University Press, 1983); and Beatrice Gottlieb, *The Family in the Western World from the Black Death to the Industrial Age* (New York and Oxford: Oxford University Press, 1993).

4. See Thomas Bokenkotter's discussion in "The Unmaking of Christendom 1300–1650," in *A Concise History of the Catholic Church* (New York: Doubleday, 2004), 173–258, for a detailed yet accessible treatment of the state of the Church from the Renaissance through the Reformation. Bokenkotter here details the political and economic tensions of the era, the corruption of the Renaissance papacy, the internal reforms, and ultimately the Protestant break from authority to the pope. For a general introduction to the Renaissance period, consult Paul Johnson, *The Renaissance: A Short History* (New York: The Modern Library, 2000).

5. Rosemary Radford Ruether, *Christianity and the Making of the Modern Family: Ruling Ideologies, Diverse Realities* (Boston: Beacon Press, 2000), 61.

6. Bokenkotter, "Unmaking of Christendom," 158–72.

7. Alister McGrath's discussion of different schools of Renaissance humanism, including key philosopher-theologians and their impact on the church, is quite useful here. See *Historical Theology: An Introduction to the History of Christian Thought* (Oxford: Blackwell Publishers, 1998), 108–18.

humanism placed great confidence in the human being. In the previous era, scholastic thinkers would argue fine logical points in highly systematic ways, basing their truth claims on what biblical or theological authorities, such as Saint Paul or Augustine, had argued before them. The scholastic method was reserved for the learned elite, and it admitted little room for the speculation and reflection of the average person. Humanism reversed this trend by arguing that literacy and education were widely desirable; that truth should be related to observation; and that the human mind should be a tool for judging knowledge. Although there were many different emphases among humanist philosophers and authors, Christian humanists undoubtedly laid the intellectual foundation for the Reformation that followed.

Cultural developments stemming from the Renaissance and humanism affected how people experienced marriage and family life. By this time, Christian marriage had become widely accepted as a sacrament, and the governance of marriage had fallen under the auspices of the church. Previously marriage had been a family matter and only people of the nobility had public ceremonies to indicate that a legally binding union had occurred. However, once marriage was recognized as a sacrament, it became normative to have a priest preside over the ceremony, for the ceremony to take place within a church building, and for the church as an institution to oversee lawful and moral order in marital unions.

Outcomes of the shift to ecclesial marriage included restrictions on who could marry whom,

MARRIAGE BANNS

There is evidence in Christian writings from as early as the second century that some form of publicizing an impending marriage before one's bishop was considered desirable. The practice, which went out of vogue in the fifth century, was replaced in some places in Europe in the twelfth century by the publication of an impending marriage in the resident parish of the couple. The Council of Trent reinforced this practice as a matter of Church law.

Today, the Catholic Church still requires the names of people intending to marry to be published or announced three times prior to the wedding in the residential parish(es) of the couple. Failure to publish the banns may warrant ecclesial penalties on the couple and the parish priest, although a dispensation of the banns may be granted for serious reasons. Today, while the practice still serves as an opportunity for witnesses to bring forth any known impediments to the marriage, it also serves the happier purpose of announcing the forthcoming wedding.

public notification of marriages, and severe restrictions on the dissolution of marriages. If a marriage was to be a sacrament, it would have to exist between people appropriate to one another. People already bound to another by marriage, people related to one another through a blood relationship (called *consanguinity*), and people who had a spiritual relationship to one another (such as a godmother to a godson), were not permitted to marry. So that people could make known these kinds of impediments to marriage in a public forum, the Church began to publicize marriages before they occurred in what is called the *banns* of marriage.[8]

Divorce historically had been a viable, legal option to end a marriage. The Church now argued that, as a sacrament, marriage can never

---

8. See Ozment's discussion of Church regulation of marriage in *When Fathers Ruled*, 25–28.

be "undone" through human power. However, since the Church had the authority to determine barriers to divorce from the outset, it also assumed authority to determine after the fact whether some barrier to authentic marriage had been present from the beginning. The Church consequently had the power to determine not only who could marry, but also who could leave a spouse on the grounds the marriage contracted was invalid and a sacramental marriage in fact had never existed.

By the twelfth century, people were no longer married by the consent of their parents; they had to consent freely in order for a marriage to be binding. This marked an improvement in the conditions of marriage for individuals, because they could no longer legally be forced to marry against their will. However, one should be careful not to romanticize the state of marriage on this account. Marriage still was undertaken as a matter of social responsibility for the procreation of children. Moreover, the changing economic climate of the period, combined with the humanist movement, directly affected the way people understood and experienced marriage and family life.

In its revival of Greco-Roman sources, the humanist movement also spurred a renewed interest in classical understandings of womanhood. This led to debates about whether female nature was defective, whether and how the female could or should be educated, and how the alleged vices of the female might best be controlled. These debates have theological and historical significance in their own right, but we note them here for their impact on women in convents, in families, and in the polis at large.

Rosemary Radford Ruether chronicles these impacts in several scholarly works, including

Women and Redemption: A Theological History,[9] in which she notes that women's political citizenship and economic opportunities were dramatically curtailed in this age. Ruether observes that Renaissance Europe recovered and enforced ancient Roman law codes, which had regarded women as incapable of being legally responsible for themselves. As in the Roman Empire, women were required to have a male guardian for public interaction. Accordingly, as city states and kingdoms throughout Europe defined citizenship, property ownership, and political access, women in Renaissance Europe became increasingly excluded from public access and assigned to subordinate roles under a husband's headship.[10]

At the same time, women were increasingly separated from paid work. In the early Middle Ages, men and women worked together commonly in the economic activities of a household. As such, husbands and wives shared equally in skilled labor. During the Renaissance, men began to bring their labor into the public realm through membership in guilds. Guilds favored men and typically admitted women only if they were wives to guildsmen and served in auxiliary roles such as weaving wool for tailors to use, where the finished garment alone (produced by a male) would be saleable. Ruether describes the result of this separation of men's skilled, paid labor from women's unpaid, unskilled labor as follows:

The early modern period saw an accelerating process by which paid work was increasingly separated from domestic work as women were forbidden to engage in the paid economy. Baking, brewing, pharmacy, printing, even many areas of textile work, were separated into male-only workshops differentiated from the domestic roles of women, children, and servants in the household.

---

9. Rosemary Radford Ruether, *Women and Redemption: A Theological History* (Minneapolis: Fortress Press, 1998).

10. Ibid., 114.

Licenses and educational requirements, forbidden to women, heightened the exclusion of women from many kinds of work in which they had been previously engaged beyond the family on the basis of family-taught skills.

This differentiation of female housework and male paid work was the sharpest in the emerging middle class. It meant that the widow of a middle-class artisan or businessman no longer shared in the skills by which he had made a living and had little possibility of continuing such work in his absence. Low paid drudge work was always available for the woman without male support, but it became increasingly impossible for a woman to support herself by skilled work.[11]

The outcomes for marriage and family life were twofold: women's place in the emergent middle class society was increasingly restricted to the home, and the home was changing from a place of cottage industry to a private sector separated from the commerce of men's labor. The home was, furthermore, redefined by the superior status of the husband, who became responsible for the legal guardianship of his wife and children as they lacked access to broader social roles. The alternative to this lifestyle for women remained vowed religious life in a convent, which option would be challenged by the Protestant Reformation soon to follow.

Reformation: Sixteenth to Seventeenth Centuries

The Protestant Reformation refers to a series of reform movements that took place within the Church during the sixteenth and seventeenth centuries.[12] As with the Renaissance, a number of cultural factors combined to produce the Reformation. These factors include the greater education of the populace and more widespread literacy that grew out of the humanist movement; the mass production of affordable print materials through the development of the printing press; theological and ecclesial reform efforts on the part of scholars and churchmen during the fifteenth century; frustration on the part of European kings, who owed both taxes and political allegiance to the bishop of Rome; and high-level corruption in the Church itself stemming from the excessive lifestyles of the Renaissance popes and bishops. The climate was ripe for reform, and when it occurred it tore through Europe and the Church with vigor and violence.

The movement did not begin as an orderly plan to create new Christian churches with new rites, creeds, liturgies, and theologies. Rather, the Reformation began with waves of protests (hence, the term *Protestant*) and was only formalized through the development of new creeds and church structures in the generations after the first breaks from allegiance to Rome had occurred. Moreover, the Protestants frequently disagreed among themselves about matters of doctrine, worship, and church structure. As a result, the movement was not uniform and many varieties of Protestant churches emerged. Many within the Catholic Church itself sought reforms and enacted a Catholic Reformation (sometimes called the *Counter-Reformation*), resulting in a variety of moral reforms, the birth of new religious orders, and the clarification of Catholic teachings at the Council of Trent (1547–1563).

The outcomes of the Reformation, both for Catholics and Protestants, were mixed. On the negative side, Europe witnessed a series

---

11. Ibid., 115.

12. For a recent introduction to the Reformation, see Alister McGrath, *Reformation Thought: An Introduction* (Oxford: Blackwell Publishers, 2001). For a classical collection of primary source Reformation readings, see Hans Hillerbrand, ed., *The Protestant Reformation* (New York: Harper Torchbooks, 1968).

of religiously inspired wars. Political rivals used divided loyalties to the Protestant or Catholic churches strategically to galvanize popular sentiment.

On the positive side, when these wars ended, a sense of necessary tolerance for religious freedom and diversity emerged. Driven mostly by an awareness that a consensus would not be reached, a newfound sense of denominationalism and peaceful co-existence among Christians emerged. The class differences between the peasantry and the nobility were called into question, since nobles and monarchs were seen by the masses as historically collaborating with the old order of the Catholic Church. Although the revolutions that would overthrow these monarchies would be violent, modern Western notions of democracy have their roots in these revolts. Humanist efforts at strengthening and educating the masses were taking hold. People no longer uncritically accepted beliefs about the final value and merit of their lives. They were reading and thinking for themselves, both Catholics and Protestants. A religiously aware and critically minded populace sowed the seeds for greater accountability by the organizational and institutional churches. Finally, the Roman Catholic Church underwent a much-needed internal reform, resulting in a better-educated clergy, a greater commitment to holiness, a rejection of the abuses of ecclesial offices, and the birth of social justice-oriented religious orders.

Both Catholics and Protestants witnessed the emergence of a new emphasis on the human person as a spiritual being, whose relationship with God was personally defining. The role of the Church for Catholics was still central to a person's faith life, but for all persons in the wake of the Reformation, a greater awareness of the individual was being realized. What had begun

in the humanist movement was developed in the Reformation and would be carried to its height in the Enlightenment period to follow. This trend was reinforced in the Protestant churches, even when they achieved highly developed structures for leadership, confessions, and bodies of theology, because these churches never played the sacramental role of mediating grace to their flocks in the same way that the Roman Catholic Church did to its flock.[13]

Among the many areas of life that Protestant Reformers sought to liberate from ecclesial control was marriage. Key Reformers rejected the theology of marriage as a sacrament, along with the other Roman Catholic sacraments, except baptism and Eucharist. Marriage, according to Protestant thought, was not the church's responsibility to order or control. The Reformers, furthermore, rejected the Catholic Church's insistence that the celibate lifestyles of priests and nuns constituted a higher order of life than that of marriage. They emphasized that it was both right and natural for men and women to marry, according to the biblical teachings in Genesis, and they sought to enforce this belief in both their teachings and actions (including seizing and forcibly "liberating" women from convents and cloisters).

Steven Ozment's critical investigation of family structures in the Reformation era, entitled *When Fathers Ruled: Family Life in Reformation Europe*, explores the contradictions and hypocrisies of the medieval Catholic Church teachings on marriage and sexuality as well as the patriarchal family ideal that Reformers championed as God's design. Ozment notes that while the Catholic Church upheld marriage as a sacrament, it also harbored a grave mistrust of sexuality. The old Augustinian fear that, even within the context of marriage, sex is tainted by lust continued

---

13. Protestants tend to emphasize the role of the Bible in the formation of personal faith, while Catholics tend to attach personal faith to the sacramental mediation of the Catholic Church.

to inform how clergymen understood sex. As a result, excessive emphasis on sexual sins and guilt forced an unnatural and unhealthy attitude toward the body and sexuality. Moreover, some corrupt clergymen openly kept concubines and visited brothels, which suggested to many that a celibate life was impossible even for those who aspired to it.[14]

Leading Protestant Reformers, concerned about such problems, embraced marriage as the normative state for men and women.[15] Moreover, the Reformers denied that their churches should be empowered to regulate marriage through their codes of impediments, because they saw church involvement as often corrupted by mercenary, ulterior motives. With the rejection of the concept of marriage as a sacrament came the consequent rejection of the notion that marriage was indissoluble. As a result, Protestant churches had no need for an annulment procedure. For valid reasons, marriages could end in divorce, permitting the former spouses to remarry.

Ruether notes an ambivalence in Reformation theology regarding the status of women and marriage. On the one hand, women and girls in Protestant territories were no longer encouraged or forced to enter convents. For those who did not want a celibate lifestyle, this marked an improvement and some liberation from oppressive attitudes toward sexuality and childbearing. At the same time, women were not seen as equivalent to men, either in creation or in their lived experience in the world.[16] The only proper alternative to the celibate lifestyle, Ruether relates, was an intensely patriarchal household, in which the ideal of the male head of house was reinforced by women's reduced participation in political and economic spheres. Ozment summarizes the transformation of marriage that occurred in Protestant regions of Europe as follows:

> In Protestant territories monasteries and nunneries were dissolved and their physical structures and endowments given over in most instances to public charitable and educational uses. Marriage laws became simpler, clearer, and more enforceable and were applied less arbitrarily. . . . Reversing the practices of centuries, the Reformation made it more difficult for the immature and unestablished to enter a valid marriage; at the same time those with a just and proper cause could, for the first time, divorce and remarry with the church's blessing.
>
> Most significantly, a home and family were no longer objects of widespread ridicule, a situation that lasted until modern times. The first generation of Protestant reformers died believing they had released women into the world by establishing them firmly at the center of the home and family life, no longer to suffer the withdrawn, culturally circumscribed, sexually repressed, male-regulated life of a cloister. And they believed children would never again be consigned at an early age to involuntary celibacy but would henceforth remain in the home, objects of constant parental love and wrath, until they were all properly married.[17]

In sum, although one may see the Protestant rejection of marriage as a sacrament as demoting the status of marriage, Protestants on the whole argued that marriage was a proper and natural state. Conversely, the Roman Catholic Church continued to uphold and elaborate upon

---

14. Ozment, *When Fathers Ruled*, 9–12.

15. This is particularly the case of Martin Luther, who was perhaps the strongest supporter of marriage and the greatest critic of a celibate clergy.

16. Ruether, *Women and Redemption*, 117–26 and *Christianity and the Making of the Modern Family*, pp. 73–79.

17. Ozment, *When Fathers Ruled*, 49.

the theology of marriage as a sacrament, and in refutation of the Reformers it devoted the twenty-fourth session of the Council of Trent (1563) to considering and endorsing the sacrament of marriage. The fact that the Catholic Church continued to view marriage as a sacrament did not, however, elevate married persons to the spiritual status of celibates in the Church's eyes. The Catholic Church would not recognize the spiritual equality of married and celibate lifestyles for roughly four hundred years.

Enlightenment: Seventeenth to Eighteenth Centuries

The Enlightenment refers to a movement within Western philosophy that explored the possibilities and limits of human reason.[18] It is sometimes even referred to as the "Age of Reason," because philosophers of this movement trusted in the competence of human reason to know and understand everything necessary about the world. The shift toward the human person and human reason that was begun centuries earlier was now in full flower. Especially as the authority of the Catholic Church had been successfully challenged by the Reformers, people had a new confidence and freedom to question and investigate matters of faith and science.

Situated in secular universities, philosophers scrutinized matters of faith that had long gone unchallenged. Even the deepest convictions of Christian faith were brought under critical and scholarly investigation, including the belief in miracles and Jesus' Resurrection. Christian philosopher-theologians argued for alternative ways of understanding Jesus' life, focusing on the moral example he set rather than his divine nature. As such, many aspects of the Christian

story were considered unnecessary, while all elements deemed necessary were required to be inherently compatible with reason.[19]

Although philosophers and theologians in subsequent eras have found fault with the Enlightenment's arguably arrogant assumptions regarding human reason, the Enlightenment as a movement even today profoundly influences contemporary beliefs about the capacity of the human mind, the potential for human good, and the basis of human social equality. Among its legacies is the ideal (certainly not realized by Enlightenment thinkers themselves) that through the application of reason-based inquiry, we can engage one another mutually, dialogically, and without prejudice, because the rational faculty is what fundamentally connects us as human beings.

In the world of the Enlightenment, the Christian churches lost their prior authority. Roman Catholics found the authority of the Church shaken in the sense that there were plausible alternatives. Protestant churches rarely enjoyed the authority that the Roman Catholic Church had wielded at the peak of its political and secular power.

The Enlightenment ideals that led to new methods of philosophical, political, and scientific inquiry had also helped to reshape popular aspirations for democratic representation in government and broader social freedoms. These ideological shifts resulted in democratic revolutionary movements that attempted to cast off the yoke of both church and monarchy. In place of these old power structures, people sought to create representative governments in which males, at least, could have a voice. The civil government emerged, and with it, civil marriage. The state became the entity that recognized and conferred

---

18. For a brief documentary history, see Margaret Jacob, *The Enlightenment: A Brief History with Documents* (Boston: Bedford/St. Martin's Press, 2000).

19. For example, Immanuel Kant's *Religion Within the Limits of Reason Alone* (1792).

the legality of marriage. In some countries, religious marriage was outlawed and civil marriage became compulsory. In other instances, a religious ceremony followed the legal ceremony, but a legal ceremony before a state representative was what established the legal marriage. In still other instances, a religious ceremony established the marriage, so long as the celebrant was licensed by the state to celebrate marriages (thus, acting de facto as an agent of the state). In any of these forms, the normative model of marriage in Western culture since the eighteenth century has placed the legal dimension of marriage and divorce within the domain of the state.

The meaning of marriage also underwent dramatic change as a result of the new ideals of reason and personhood that the Enlightenment espoused. Stephanie Coontz details many of these changes in her discussion "From Yoke Mates to Soul Mates."[20] Coontz notes that during this era people increasingly entered into marriages for the sake of love as opposed to political reasons or a sense of social obligation. Moreover, while households still remained patriarchal, the division of labor took on new meaning under the model of a love-based marriage. Men were to support their families economically by working outside of the home, while women were to provide emotional support for their families within the home. Although Enlightenment thinkers still maintained that there were basic anthropological differences between men and women (with women being essentially inferior),[21] Enlightenment-era people increasingly assented

to the notion that marriages should be founded on reason and justice.[22] Coontz helpfully summarizes these developments as follows:

> During the eighteenth century the spread of the market economy and the advent of the Enlightenment wrought profound changes in record time. By the end of the 1700s personal choice of partners had replaced arranged marriage as a social ideal, and individuals were encouraged to marry for love. For the first time in five thousand years, marriage came to be seen as a private relationship between two individuals rather than one link in a larger system of political and economic alliances. The measure of a successful marriage was no longer how big a financial settlement was involved, how many useful in-laws were acquired, or how many children were produced, but how well a family met the emotional needs of its individual members. Where once a marriage had been seen as the fundamental unity of work and politics, it was now viewed as a place of refuge from work, politics, and community obligations.[23]

From the Eighteenth through the Twentieth Century

In the aftermath of the Reformation, the intellectual shifts of the Enlightenment, and the social changes wrought by industrialization, a series of new ideas began to take root, particularly among the lower economic strata of society. Church and political establishments alike were transformed by these ideas.[24] A newfound sense

---

20. Stephanie Coontz, "From Yoke Mates to Soul Mates," in *Marriage: A History; From Obedience to Intimacy, or How Love Conquered Marriage* (New York: Viking Press, 2005), 145–60. Used by permission of S J Coontz Company.

21. Consult Nancy Tuana's discussions of Kant, Rousseau, and Locke in *Woman and the History of Philosophy* (St. Paul: Paragon House, 1992).

22. Coontz, *Marriage*, 146.

23. Ibid.

24. A well-regarded, scholarly treatment of the religio-political history of this period is Hugh McLeod, *Religion and the People of Western Europe 1789–1970* (Oxford and New York: Oxford University Press, 1981).

of national identity bound together people of common language and culture. Moreover, a sense of the right to democratic *enfranchisement* or the right to vote emerged. The ancient monarchies and land-holding nobility, long supported by the institutional churches, possessed wealth and power that were utterly lacking among the poorer classes. Yet these classes had recently come into a sense of their own dignity and potential power as a unified body politic, resulting in a series of democratic revolutions throughout Europe and America.

Exemplifying these revolutions were the American and French Revolutions, in which the poor and middle class in both colonial America and in France had grown weary of the financial and political burdens of supporting an oppressive monarchy. Armed with a democratic sense of government and classic liberal ideals (derived from the Enlightenment),

popular movements overthrew monarchical regimes. By the mid-nineteenth century, the popular sentiments in America and France were echoed in revolutions throughout Europe. Peasants rose up and sought to destroy church and monarchy alike, as both represented entrenched political and social hierarchies that had historically resulted in mass economic oppression and marginalization.

The success of European and American revolutions varied from the establishment of parliamentary governments and a free press to a mere change of rulers without any significant accompanying social reforms. The poor and middle classes, however, were poised for political and economic advancements that would continue to develop in the following decades. The democratic ideals and intellectual developments of these eras set the stage for modern Western culture.

HOW THINGS HAVE CHANGED

Think of all the ways our lives are different today from previous centuries. For example, we travel relatively easily, safely, and cheaply in ways that once would have been inconceivable. Computers and the internet allow for instantaneous communication with people all over the world. Modern physics has reshaped how people think about the origins, purpose, and destiny of human life and the cosmos itself. Consider the following list of discoveries and developments since the mid-nineteenth century that have changed human experience. Describe how life might have been prior to these developments and how it is today. In particular, how have these developments changed people's experience of marriage and family life?

- Pasteur's discoveries in microbiology in 1859 and the consequent ability to diagnose and treat bacterial infection

- Invention of moving pictures in 1878

- Development of radio in 1895

- Development of the mass-produced automobile in 1902 (Oldsmobile) and 1914 (Ford)

- Women's Suffrage: 1920 (USA), 1928 (UK), 1944 (France)

- First FDA-approved oral contraceptive in 1957

- Development of the microprocessor and first PCs in the 1970s

The diversity and scope of social, cultural, technological, ideological, and political developments emerging out of these political and intellectual revolutions have been truly novel in the human experience. No single word or phrase can capture the breadth of the modern situation; almost all aspects of the Western world underwent a process of modernization. The broadening of political and economic opportunity for the poor and middle classes, coupled with a reduction in the authority that religious bodies exercised over such areas as research, education, and industry, resulted in considerable developments in human experience and understanding.

For example, modern science has dramatically affected how people understand human personhood. In 1859 Charles Darwin published his work *Origin of Species*, which postulated the theory of evolutionary biology. The ramifications of this theory were far-reaching, especially in the way it undermined the uniqueness of the human being among animal species. To the extent that the nature of the human species was called into question, both Protestant and Catholic Christians reacted with concern. Many Protestant Christians responded by proposing a fundamental set of Christian beliefs, among them belief in the literal inerrancy of the Bible. The Catholic Church responded with the publication in 1907 of Pius X's *Lamentabili Sane* (Syllabus of Errors), which condemned the errors of modernist thought and theory. Neither Protestants nor Catholics, however, were able to control or silence modern thought, including evolutionary theory. Dialogue and debate over evolutionary theory has, for the most part, replaced authoritarian control over how

people, including Christians, are to understand the human person. This more open model of inquiry and investigation characterizes the contemporary and more democratic approach to life among modern Western people.

Women's Liberation

There have been many outcomes of this more democratic, popular attitude. In particular, the women's movements of the nineteenth and twentieth centuries have seriously influenced marriage and family life.[25] These movements opened and continue to open doors for women's political liberation and economic independence, both of which have had an enormous impact on marriage and family life.

Among the greatest successes of these movements has been the increased awareness of the need for women's freedom and opportunity for economic independence. It should be noted that women have always played a part in the workforce, with the exception of upper-class females who could afford to have domestic tasks done by paid or unpaid female servants. However, since the advent of modern industry, domestic life has been in flux due to women's broadly increased presence in the public labor sector. When women and families moved into urban settings to pursue employment, the family unit was forced to accommodate women's greater access to the public arena.

Working conditions within and outside the home have not always been favorable to women, especially in the area of pay. Even today, much female labor goes unpaid, while women who are paid have historically received a fraction of

---

25. There are a number of fine introductions to the study of feminist theory and its culturally transformative developments since the nineteenth century. One useful and lucid text for students is *Andrea Nye, Feminist Theory and the Philosophies of Man* (New York and London: Routledge Press, 1988). Anne Clifford accomplishes a similar task for feminist theology in her work *Introducing Feminist Theology* (Maryknoll, NY: Orbis, 2006), in which she offers a broad introduction to the themes and issues of Christian feminism in global perspective.

the income realized by their male counterparts.[26] In the early industrial period, women's labor conditions were nothing less than abysmal, as remains all too often the case for women and children factory workers in developing countries.[27] But in first-world contexts, women's lot has markedly improved in matters of social access and employment, largely due to legislative actions brought about through feminist reform efforts of the past hundred and fifty years.

The feminist reform movements of the nineteenth century focused on securing for women the right to vote. These reformers argued that until women were recognized legally as autonomous, self-governing adults, even within the context of marriage, women were vulnerable to a plethora of personal and social injustices.[28] Political enfranchisement, which occurred for women in Europe and America in the early to mid-twentieth century, was only a portion of the battle for social equality. The women's movements of the 1960s and 1970s strove to realize entirely the social participation that women had sought a century earlier.

FEMINIST THEOLOGIES

Feminist theologies have a serious stake in women's roles in the Christian churches as well as in family life. However, feminists do not all agree with one another about the way to best achieve their goals, just as they do not all agree on the actual goals. The range of feminisms extends from the politically and ideologically conservative to the radical social reformist. Some feminists define women's concerns in terms of patriarchy, while others see women's concerns as more entrenched in racial and class concerns. As feminists have become increasingly aware that no single voice or perspective can adequately address all women's concerns, feminist discourse has taken on a "roundtable" model of dialogue and discussion. Sallie McFague has argued that an even more adequate metaphor for feminist discourse is that of the quilt, in which all persons are able to contribute a piece in order to craft the whole.

As new theories about gender, sexuality, and personhood began to circulate widely, women began to question the age-old assumptions that they were naturally caregivers, gentle of demeanor, suited for light labor, and ultimately satisfied by marriage and motherhood.[29] Women have since been seriously studying disciplines and pursuing careers that had previously been denied

---

26. Ruether's discussion of American families in the year 2000 in *Christianity and the Making of the Modern Family*, 194, includes detailed U.S. government statistics comparing wage earnings by race and gender according to educational status. In every bracket, from high school education to graduate and professional degrees, men earned significantly more than women and whites significantly more than blacks. White women's earnings were frequently comparable to those of black men of the same educational status, while black women consistently earned less than either white women or black men with the same level of education. White men were the highest paid in every category.

27. While discussion of marriage or women's conditions in a global context reaches beyond the scope of this chapter, a number of useful resources may be consulted for in-depth consideration of these dimensions of women's modern experience. Two such resources include Rosemary Radford Ruether, *Women Healing Earth: Third World Women on Ecology, Feminism, and Religion* (Maryknoll, NY: Orbis, 1996) and Uma Narayan, *Dislocating Cultures: Identities, Cultures, and Third World Feminism* (New York and London: Routledge Press, 1997).

28. Indeed, it was largely women's vulnerability within marriage that drove the women's suffrage movement. Key to women's political liberties, women suffragists recognized the need to debunk the Christian household codes whereby men were seen as having divine sanction to govern women both within and outside of the household. This sentiment is boldly expressed in Elizabeth Cady Stanton's introduction to The Woman's Bible, first published in 1895 and 1898.

29. This is the great insight of French feminist Simone de Beauvoir's *The Second Sex* (1949).

to them. Furthermore, with the advent of oral contraceptives, women gained an enhanced ability to moderate when and how many children they bore. Western women now have the option to regulate reproduction, to live independently of male guardians, to retain their own names in marriage, to pursue meaningful work, and to hold leadership positions in most strata and spheres of society.

Today, feminisms exist across a wide continuum of positions, commitments, and agendas. Concerns about racial equality, gender and sexuality, class differences, and even ecology help to shape the feminist dialogue. Women striving for liberation in past decades faced different struggles from those of women today. It is easy to forget how much has changed in the course of only several decades. While women's challenges differ today, especially in regard to demographic and geographic contexts, they are by no means unrelated to the tasks of earlier women's reform efforts. To the extent that women continue to work for genuine mutuality and equality in all matters—pay, government participation, child and domestic support while working outside of the home, equal participation in church and worship communities, laws protecting women against violence and sexual abuse, sexual freedom, reproductive choice—the women's movement constitutes a continuing push toward a more just and inclusive society.

APPLICATION TO MARRIAGE AND FAMILY LIFE TODAY

We should not be surprised that modern marriage has been undergoing tremendous changes. The impulse for popular literacy in the humanist movement of the Renaissance resulted centuries later in a more broadly educated citizenry than ever before. The turn to the individual person as the source and authority for religious experience—the legacy of the Reformation—leaves all Christians today with a profound sense of the personal nature of faith and the right to religious freedom. The Enlightenment's championing of reason continues to shape confidence in scientific and scholarly inquiry, even while we recognize the limitations of reason. The women's movements have transformed how women (and consequently their families) think about and experience work, family, and selfhood. These developments have culminated in possibilities for how women and men regard everything from personal identity to citizenship to sexuality.

Women's roles have historically been severely circumscribed to domestic duties and support roles within a predominantly male labor force. Within the Christian theological tradition, women have been subordinated in both doctrine and practice to male headship. Accordingly, men in all spheres were historically burdened with bearing the public, economic, and spiritual responsibilities of their families. These realities for both men and women distorted not only their self-knowledge but also their ability to relate to one another on genuinely mutual and just terms. However, the combined outcomes of the historical developments we have here considered have opened heretofore unprecedented options for men and women.

Modern Western people are suspicious of traditions that smack of bygone values from bygone eras. Marriage, being one such tradition, has been called into question. Particularly as marriage has historically favored the male sex and functioned as one of the mechanisms that severely limited women's social access, progressive thinkers, both men and women, mistrust it. People continue to marry, but expectations of marriage have been undergoing major transitions for decades. Marriage today is undertaken not only for the goal of procreation of children but also for companionship and love. In addition, people choose partners today for a wide variety and combination of reasons, some traditional, others quite novel. Consider, for example, the following possibilities why people today marry:

- Financial partnership
- Romantic attraction
- To obtain legal benefits, such as citizenship, tax breaks, or health insurance
- Money and social class standing
- Religious reasons
- Reproduction
- Friendship
- Companionship in old age
- Other—what other possibilities can you think of?

In previous eras, the goal of marriage was clearer as were the expectations about the roles and responsibilities of husbands and wives. Today, people want more from marriage than ever before, even while resisting the classic emphases on duty and responsibility that historically made many, especially women, feel trapped. In the face of the great unsettledness of modern persons, one might wonder what business people have marrying at all.

If today's men and women are uncertain about themselves and their expectations of one another, it seems unlikely that they will be successful at marriage. Responsibility and commitment to living out marriage intentionally, then, are critical in this day and age, even more so because so many alternatives are possible. Moreover, modern challenges to marriage are plentiful, including:

- A revised understanding of the meaning and purpose of human sexuality
- A newfound emphasis on gender-based difficulties in communication
- The challenge of ending domestic and sexual violence
- Prevalence of divorce
- Proper rearing of children within new family structures and models

The following chapters will take a close look at these issues, with a special emphasis on how each of these might be successfully negotiated.

Questions for Review and Discussion

1. Describe the European Renaissance. What impact did this movement have on marriage and family?

2. What is humanism? Was this movement pro-female, anti-female, or both?

3. What is the Protestant Reformation? What impact did it have on the understanding of marriage?

4. Describe the conflict between the Catholic Church's theology of marriage as a sacrament and its understanding of sexuality in the Middle Ages.

5. What is the Enlightenment? How did this movement help to redefine the meaning and purpose of marriage?

6. Describe your understanding of the relationship between labor and family life. How do changes in the workforce contribute to the way people understand the purpose and structure of family life?

7. Describe the goals of feminism. How has this movement contributed to the modern understanding of family and marriage?

8. What are three major issues you see as influencing marriage and family life in the twenty-first century?

Resources for Further Reading

Resources for the Making of the Modern Family

Frances and Joseph Gies, *Marriage and Family in the Middle Ages* (New York: Harper & Row, 1987).

Beatrice Gottlieb, *The Family in the Western World from the Black Death to the Industrial Age* (New York and Oxford: Oxford University Press, 1993).

Anne Kingston, *The Meaning of Wife* (New York: Farrar, Straus and Giroux, 2004).

Michael Lawler and William Roberts, eds., *Christian Marriage and Family: Contemporary Theological and Pastoral Perspectives* (Collegeville, MN: Liturgical Press, 1996).

Steven Ozment, *When Fathers Ruled: Family Life in Reformation Europe* (Cambridge, MA, and London: Harvard University Press, 1983).

Stephen Post, *More Lasting Unions: Christianity, the Family, and Society* (Grand Rapids and Cambridge, England: Eerdmans, 2000).

Rosemary Radford Ruether, *Christianity and the Making of Modern Family: Ruling Ideologies, Diverse Realities* (Boston: Beacon Press, 2000).

Also see resources from chapter 4.

CHAPTER 7

DIGNITY AND HUMAN SEXUALITY WITHIN MARRIAGE

Previously we established that the Roman Catholic tradition regards marriage most highly by naming it a sacrament. This affirms that marriage confers grace on a couple in a unique way. From financial stability to the joy of rearing offspring, the companionship and support in times of change or strife, the laughter late at night shared with a partner you have known intimately for decades; all of these elements comprise the state of grace that the married couple experiences. While Protestant communities may not call marriage a sacrament, they also regard marriage as a unique context for the experience of love and faith.

As previously noted, people do not automatically regard their marriages as sacramental or experience grace in marriage simply because they are married. Indeed, many work to destroy their marriages, even if unintentionally, through damaging words and deeds. The Catholic Church holds that it is the duty of the married couple to live out their marriages as sacraments in order to realize their highest potentialities. Simply put, married persons have to choose what they want their marriages to be and to mean.

The notion that people must make a choice about how they are to live as married couples opens ethical questions in the theology of family and marriage. What behaviors contribute to a good marriage? What personal characteristics best foster successful marriages? What decisions best reflect marriages as covenant, charity, and sacrament?

The ethical dimension of theology is called moral theology. Moral theology examines the ultimate good toward which human life is oriented, whether it is possible to know this good, and how best to respond to it.

Catholic moral theology takes direction from a number of authorities,[1] chief among them

---

1. Two useful introductions to Catholic moral theology include Charles Curran, *Catholic Moral Theology in the United States: A History* (Washington: Georgetown University Press, 2008) and Romanus Cessario, *Introduction to Moral Theology* (Washington: Catholic University of America Press, 2001).

the Bible, the official teachings of the Catholic Church, the classical sources of the theological tradition (such as works by Augustine or Thomas Aquinas), and lived human experience. Catholic teaching affirms that these sources confirm and shed light on truths revealed by God in Christian history and on truths that human reason discerns in nature. Based on the combined insights of these sources, the Catholic Church concludes that the foundation of all moral thinking about human life is the *dignity of the human person*. In this chapter we will consider how the Catholic Church arrives at the conclusion that dignity is the foundation of ethics. We will further consider the concept of human dignity as a foundation for marriage, and in particular, for sexuality within marriage.[2]

TOOLS

To understand the concept of dignity more fully, we will first look at morality as it is derived from natural law. This so-called teleological model of ethics argues that all things are good when they manifest their desired or intended ends.[3] (*Telos* is Greek for "end.") A teleological argument, for example, might be offered for why students should prepare for an exam. If a student prepares for an exam, she is more likely to score well on the test. She hopes to score well on the test because it means she will get a good grade in the class. If she gets high grades, she will graduate with honors and subsequently be more likely to find good employment. With good employment,

she will be more likely to enjoy a high quality of life, one where she not only has a job but is able to live out her unique personal talents and gifts, thereby fulfilling her purpose in life. From a teleological perspective, her test preparation benefits her whole life.

Many Catholic moral theologians argue that things in nature have natural processes and ends that can be observed and studied. The argument begins with the belief that the universe is created and ordered by God, and therefore the laws of nature and the processes by which things manifest their natural ends are designed by God.[4] In other words, the natural law is God's law, revealed generally in nature and specifically in Christian history.

Natural law has important consequences for Catholic moral theology because God's will is believed to be observable in nature. If that is so, human beings can look at the natural world, understand its processes, and align their behaviors to cooperate with the natural order and thereby with the will of God. The obvious example of such alignment with the divine will is biological reproduction. Everywhere in nature organisms reproduce themselves. Since animals are designed to reproduce, they are fulfilling their biological purpose or end when they do so. If God has created these organisms, then the "end" or purpose of their reproductive capacity, namely reproduction, is likewise intended by God. It follows that the reproduction of organisms according to their species also reflects the will of God for creation. When applied to human beings, the moral implication is that sexual fecundity is designed by God

---

2. As with the discussion of the sacrament of marriage, this chapter will focus on a Catholic understanding of human dignity as a foundation for thinking about sexuality within marriage. The author encourages students, however, to consider the wider applications of this line of thought to other Christian and non-Christian concepts of sexuality.

3. This classical line of reasoning is derived from a central dimension of Aristotle's thought. Monte Ransome Johnson, *Aristotle on Teleology* (New York and Oxford: Oxford University Press, 2008) provides a thorough study of this concept in Aristotle.

4. Thomas Aquinas gives classical expression to this theory, revisited recently in Stephen Pope, ed., *The Ethics of Aquinas* (Washington: Georgetown University Press, 2002). In particular, consult in this volume Clifford Kossel, SJ, "Natural Law and Human Law," 169–93.

for reproduction, and moral uses of sexuality will be directed toward the proper end of procreation.

This line of thinking raises a question. If we are part of nature, then is anything we *can* do natural and therefore moral? In nature one witnesses not only order but also aggression, virulence, and cancerous overgrowth, to name but a few imbalances. The Catholic answer here is that human beings do not manifest God's intent for nature perfectly because human free will has caused in nature a distortion through sin. This results in a gulf between what human beings actually do and what they ought to do. Both corporately and individually, human beings struggle to do consistently what is right and best. This situation is described by Christian theologians as human fallenness or sinfulness, which stems from the principle urge to do what feels best for ourselves rather than to live according to the ultimate *telos* or purpose of glorifying God and cooperating with God's will.[5]

The belief in human fallenness raises another question. If human beings are prone to sin, then how can they know what is right? What is more, how can they do what is right? Catholic theology holds that while human nature is corrupted by sin, human beings can overcome corruption because of Jesus' example and saving grace. Not only was Jesus a good teacher and friend (as many good prophets or leaders might be), but he was also the true Savior in that he made it possible for human beings to be freed from sin. Christians believe that Jesus' death *atoned* (made up) for human sins.[6] This means that his death

THE THEOLOGY OF SALVATION

What does it mean to say that Jesus saves people through grace? This question constitutes the part of Christian theology called *soteriology*. While Jesus' Incarnation, death, and Resurrection are the central foci of Christian faith, there has nevertheless been great debate throughout the ages over how Jesus' life is salvific. Theologians have proposed varying explanations, including theories of ransom, substitution, satisfaction, and moral example. Delores Williams notes, "As the history of classical Christian doctrine reveals, theologians since the time of Irenaeus and Origen have been trying to make the Christian idea of atonement believable by shaping theories about it in language and thought that people of a particular time understood and in which they were grounded."[7]

From age to age, Christians have had varying understandings of sin and salvation, but a consistent theme is that sin affects all areas of human existence. For this reason, Christians have argued that just as sin can damage marriage and family life, Christ's saving grace is needed to strengthen them.

---

5. Discussions of sin and how human beings are saved from sin permeate Christian theology. Systematic treatments of theology are useful in placing sin within the wider Christian theological framework. A helpful exploration of the topic may be found in Roger Haight, "Sin and Grace," in Francis Schussler Fiorenza and John Galvin, eds., *Systematic Theology: Roman Catholic Perspectives* (Minneapolis: Augsburg Fortress Press, 1991), 75–142.

6. One of the most fundamental questions of Christian theology is how Jesus' death saves humanity and overcomes sin, a topic known as *soteriology*. The range of thought in Christian theology is expressed in the selection of readings in John Sheets, *The Theology of Atonement: Readings in Soteriology* (Englewood Cliffs, NJ: Prentice Hall, 1967).

7. Delores Williams, *Sisters in the Wilderness* (Maryknoll, NY: Orbis Books, 1993), 162.

overcame the alienation human beings experience that separates them from God and from their intended purpose as creatures covenanted to God. Christianity teaches that through Jesus' gift of grace human beings are equipped to face the challenge of discerning God's will and striving to follow it despite the human inclination to sinfulness. The Catholic Church teaches that this grace is accessed in a unique (although not exclusive) way through communion with the Church and its sacraments. Protestant churches teach that this grace is accessed primarily through personal faith. In either case, Christianity holds that although people act imperfectly, they are nevertheless strengthened through grace to work toward the ideal in human behavior.

HUMAN DIGNITY: INDIVIDUAL AND SOCIAL

The two guiding principles that establish the primary road map for determining the right course of action in the Catholic tradition are the concepts of *social welfare* and the *intrinsic value of the human person*. These two ideas are equally important and mutually reliant for a just and balanced society. On the one hand, social welfare must be ensured. This means that the welfare of society, that is, genuine human social flourishing (not the greater good for the greater number of people) is necessary for true moral order. If individual goods were consistently placed before the goods of the whole, grave injustices that derive from unbalanced distribution of resources, wealth, and opportunities would run rampant. The individualism that typifies modern Western culture reflects some of these imbalances.

On the other hand, the intrinsic value of individual persons must be preserved in equal measure to the consideration of the whole. For example, imagine that a majority of people might benefit economically if a percentage of persons dependent upon public funds were eliminated. A society that would do such a thing would be entirely wicked in its lack of respect for individuals deemed socially undesirable.

The principle of human dignity keeps social welfare and the good of individual persons in balance.[8] Catholic theology teaches that human beings have their origin in the one God, the Creator. The story of God's creation in the book of Genesis conveys several ideas about why God creates, notably because creation is good and because God seeks a companionable relationship with God's creation. In a special way, human beings enjoy a freedom of self-determination and creativity that is akin to God's creative action.

In this way it is possible to say that human beings are created in the image or likeness of God.[9] This claim should not be understood in a literal or physical way, so that, by way of reversing the analogy, we imagine that God is roughly 6' 2", 220 pounds, red-headed, and athletic. We should also not assume that a claim of human likeness to God implies that ostriches, black widows, cherry trees, and supernovas bear no likeness to God. Christianity teaches that all of God's creation

---

8. The United States Conference of Catholic Bishops summarizes the Catholic social teaching on the life and dignity of the human person as follows: "The Catholic Church proclaims that human life is sacred and that the dignity of the human person is the foundation of a moral vision for society. This belief is the foundation of all the principles of our social teaching. In our society, human life is under direct attack from abortion and euthanasia. The value of human life is being threatened by cloning, embryonic stem cell research, and the use of the death penalty. Catholic teaching also calls on us to work to avoid war. Nations must protect the right to life by finding increasingly effective ways to prevent conflicts and resolve them by peaceful means. We believe that every person is precious, that people are more important than things, and that the measure of every institution is whether it threatens or enhances the life and dignity of the human person." Website of the United States Conference of Catholic Bishops, *http://www.usccb.org/sdwp/projects/socialteaching/excerpt.shtml* (accessed 4/22/09).

9. Genesis 1:27 reads, "God created man in his image; in the divine image he created him; male and female he created them."

in some manner reflects the divine being from whom it comes. This claim infuses all the world with enormous value and makes it imperative that people respect the unique, creative potential of every other human being because each person, however unlikely it may seem, carries the image of God within himself or herself.

A belief in the image of God within each person is corollary to the belief that an inalienable and inherent dignity defines the value of every human life. Belief in the core dignity of the person ties social welfare to the good of the individual. Society must be ordered in such a way that individuals can coexist freely, organize cooperatively, and flourish together. These conditions are the right of every human being solely on the basis that all are creatures of God. There is no claim that each person merits by his or her actions a certain level of respect. We would quickly struggle to respect the dignity of anyone if all of our unworthy qualities and behaviors became public knowledge. Rather, respect for human persons and the conditions that allow each individual to thrive is an a priori principle—that is, it precedes experience and guides the interpretation of experience. Belief in the goodness and value of human life means that a priori persons ought to uphold the dignity of every human being, from the weakest and the worst to the greatest and the best, not because people have earned it but because God has willed it.

Dignity of the human person is the guiding principle in Catholic social teaching. It will be the criterion called upon to determine right action in all manner of moral questions, from medical, to political, to lifestyle, to intimate questions of personal sexual behavior. The notion of human dignity is tied to the notion of the human person as a being created by God within a human society intended by God. Moreover, from a teleological point of view, God's creation is understood to be moving purposefully toward an end or a goal. The notion of an end or goal in nature is, once again, a matter of interpretation of data. Presented with the same information, physicists, cosmologists, and theologians might interpret the data before them differently. Catholic theology sees creation as moving through time toward a total redemption and restoration. This communal, cosmological process involves all of its constituent parts. Persons move toward their personal ends while the cosmos moves toward its cosmological end; again, the model is teleological.

By *ends*, we should not think exclusively of termination, death, or conclusion, although these ideas are included. Rather, we should think primarily of *meaning*, *purpose*, and *ultimacy*. In this light, human dignity is attached to the fulfillment—or at least the conditions where fulfillment might be possible—of human meaning, purpose, and ultimate value. This is the perspective from which the human person should be interpreted. The Catholic theological tradition sees human beings, like the sacrament

THE CONCEPT OF HUMAN DIGNITY

Evaluate the Catholic concept of human dignity from your own perspective. First, attempt to describe or restate your understanding of this principle of Catholic theology. Then describe your own point of view. What in your own experience or faith tradition supports or confirms this teaching? What counters it? Do you agree with this teaching? If so, why? If not, what do you consider to ground the value of human life? From your perspective, how should this value translate into intimate relationships?

of marriage, as bearers of the highest value. A foremost moral priority for Catholics is the establishment of conditions for flourishing so that people can achieve their creative potential, as bearers of the image of God. All aspects of human life, at the individual level and at all levels of human society, are to be seen within this framework. The dignity of the human person becomes a standard and judge of the adequacy of human behavior. What supports and uplifts human dignity leads people toward their proper ends; what degrades or denies that dignity stands counter to the created purpose of humanity.

PERSONAL DIGNITY AND MARRIAGE

In marriage, individuals are called upon to see their own dignity as well as that of their spouse in a special way. In married couples and their families the needs of the individual and the needs of the communal are interdependent. The welfare of one spouse cannot be separated from that of the other. If one is suffering, both are suffering. If the marriage is to survive over the long haul, the needs of husband and wife as individuals cannot be suppressed or ignored. Neither spouse can grow authentically if the personal growth of either spouse runs contrary to growth of the marriage collectively. The interpersonal communion of spouses lays a foundation for this type of mutuality, which is extended in turn to children, grandparents, cousins, and so on. The marital-family unit, then, may be thought of as a microcosm of society in general, in which the needs of individuals and the needs of the whole are inseparably interdependent. The sentiment is

expressed particularly well in Pope John Paul II's exhortation *On the Family*:

> Inspired and sustained by the new commandment of love, the Christian family welcomes, respects and serves every human being, considering each one in his or her dignity as a person and as a child of God.
>
> It should be so especially between husband and wife and within the family, through a daily effort to promote a truly personal community, initiated and fostered by an inner communion of love. This way of life should then be extended to the wider circle of the ecclesial community of which the Christian family is a part. Thanks to love within the family, the Church can and ought to take on a more homelike or family dimension, developing a more human and fraternal style of relationships.
>
> Love, too, goes beyond our brothers and sisters of the same faith since "everybody is my brother or sister." In each individual, especially in the poor, the weak, and those who suffer or are unjustly treated, love knows how to discover the face of Christ, and discover a fellow human being to be loved and served.[10]

To balance the needs and goods of individuals in a marriage, each partner must recognize and value the inalienable worth and dignity of the other. In such recognition, each individual is known by the other to be irreplaceable and incomparably valuable. Each sees in the other a unique creation of God with a purpose to serve God and neighbor in and through the family. Each recognizes that the other has chosen to give the gift of his or her life to the marriage, as opposed to some other person or vocation, for the purpose of companionship, partnering, and possibly parenting with the other.

---

10. *Familiaris Consortio*, §64 (*http://www.vatican.va/holy_father/john_paul_ii/apost_exhortations/documents/hf_jp-ii_exh_19811122_familiaris-consortio_en.html*).

The dignity of individual persons within marriage needs to be recognized and respected in a number of ways. Consider, for example, each of the following:

- How should spouses respect and encourage one another's spiritual needs and beliefs?

- How should spouses speak with one another?

- How should spouses respect one another's personal time, relative to the needs and obligations of the family as a whole?

- What kind of employment expectations should spouses have of one another?

- How should members of a family regard and care for extended family and the community at large?

- How should spouses educate their children?

- How should the financial needs and expectations of the family be allocated, especially if one family member seeks or needs an extraordinary expenditure (such as for education or medical treatment)?

These are but a few places to begin thinking about how married persons actively attend to the dignity of themselves, their spouses, and their dependents. I would suggest, however, that the place where respect for the personal dignity of spouses is most evident in married life lies in the care of the physical body. Apart from our bodies, human beings are nothing and can do nothing. It is bodies that people give most obviously to their spouses in marriage: their labor, their presence, their service, and their intimacy. In the gift of one's body in marriage, a person also gives most fundamentally one's sexuality and reproductive potential. To respect one another's dignity means, at a core level, to respect the bodily and sexual dignity of oneself and one's spouse.

DIGNITY OF THE PERSON AND SEXUALITY

Because of the culture that we live in, it is possible to exaggerate the importance of sexuality to the point of obsession. Consider, for example, how much time and energy is devoted to sexual content in films, television programs, media advertisements, billboards, music and video imagery, magazine cover stories, and tabloids. Such a fixation occurs not only in popular culture but in the Catholic Church as well, which has a long history of spirit-matter dualisms.[11] To emphasize sexuality as if it were the single most defining characteristic in human life distorts its true meaning. Sex, like any physical need or activity (eating, exercising, bathing, and so on), should be seen in balance with other needs and functions of our bodies.[12]

On the one hand, it is important to bear in mind the dangers of distorting human sexuality by forcing it to carry more weight and importance than it can reasonably bear. On the other hand, sex and our comfort with our bodies are intimately intertwined with our perceptions and experiences of ourselves as human beings. These perceptions and experiences are

---

11. Because of the spirit-matter dualism that Christian theology inherited from Greek philosophy, sex has been simultaneously demeaned as base and sinful while obsessively discussed and regulated. Beverly Harrison argues this important point in her article, "Misogyny and Homophobia: The Unexplored Connections," in *Making the Connections: Essays in Feminist Social Ethics*, ed. Carol S. Robb (Boston: Beacon Press, 1985), 135–66.

12. William May's article "Four Mischievous Theories of Sex: Demonic, Divine, Casual, and Nuisance" explores four popular conceptions of sex, all of which distort reality by focusing errantly on a single dimension of sexual experience. May expands upon common, contemporary misperceptions and exaggerations of sexuality. The article is found in Kieran Scott and Michael Warren, eds., *Perspectives on Marriage: A Reader*, 3rd ed. (New York and Oxford: Oxford University Press, 2007), 186–95.

likewise intimately intertwined with our experience of marriage.

Evolving models of marriage and human personhood have affected how we understand human sexuality. As already noted, throughout most of Christian history the main purpose for which women and men married was the procreation of children. Today, by contrast, the companionship that emerges from a true communion of persons is recognized as an equal end.[13] The benefits of a revised attitude toward sexuality are numerous. In part driven by the late-twentieth century "sexual revolutions" that transformed traditional attitudes toward gender, homosexuality, birth control, and sexual freedom, today many are less inclined than in previous eras to demonize sex and bodies as wicked or dirty. Although many will argue that we still have a long way to go, in Western society generally we are more comfortable with the human body and recognize that human sexuality is to be celebrated and enjoyed. Sexual companionship in marriage has achieved new possibilities by being an integral part of a truly consummated communion of persons, contributing to openness, vulnerability, compassion, and play.

For better or for worse, one might say that attitudes toward sexuality have become "relaxed." These more relaxed attitudes have affected several dimensions of marriage and family life, with a resulting range of positive and negative outcomes. Consider some of the following data that many believe result from transformed marital and sexual norms over the past several decades:[14]

- People are delaying marriage. Forty years ago, only one in ten American women between the ages of 25 and 29 was single. At the turn of the twenty-first century, 40 percent of women in that age range were unmarried.

- In 1960, only one in twenty children was born outside of marriage. By 2000, one of every three children was born outside of marriage.

- Cohabitation had increased sevenfold from the 1970s to 1999. Cohabiting couples did not necessarily marry even when they became pregnant.

- Heterosexual, same-sex, and elderly couples have steadily increased their rates of cohabitation since the 1960s.

- Since the 1980s, increased numbers of older women and lesbian women have used new reproductive technologies and sperm banks in order to start non-traditional families.

- In 2003, half of all working mothers had children under one year of age, and women with children older than one year had the same rate of employment as women with no children.

These trends reveal a number of cultural shifts. Sexual experience outside of marriage has (within this context) become increasingly socially acceptable. Prolonged dating and engagements, deferral of marriage, or rejection of marriage altogether are natural outcomes to society's acceptance of sexual activity outside of marriage. Accompanying these changes in marriage is a related increase in the birth of children outside of marriage, which has also become more socially acceptable. Non-traditional family structures are now more prevalent, providing options to women especially to engage in and support family life apart from men. The impact on children in this regard remains ambiguous but the

---

13. For Catholics, this sentiment is expressed in Vatican Council II's *Gaudium et Spes*, §50.

14. The following data are taken from Stephanie Coontz, *Marriage: A History; From Obedience to Intimacy, or How Love Conquered Marriage* (New York: Viking Press, 2005), 263–64.

evidence suggests generally negative outcomes, including increases in crime and unemployment.

While it is a benefit to genuine companionship that people expect a joyful sexual relationship with their spouses, it is also quite clear that the more relaxed attitudes toward sexuality have had many questionable impacts on individual persons and society as a whole. Premature sexual encounter, for instance, has a lasting and often damaging impact on teenagers.[15] On the social level, the reality of children born outside of wedlock has far-reaching consequences, placing unique strains on mothers, fathers, children, and the community that contributes to their care.[16] Occurrence of sexually transmitted diseases is rising, affecting not only the afflicted individuals but also the loved ones who suffer with them and the community at large that must bear increasing healthcare costs. There is, furthermore, the negative outcome of sexual violence that is statistically correlated with violent imagery—both real and dramatically enacted—in sexually explicit material.[17] And there is the more subtle but insidious disappointment and damage to self-worth resulting from mismatched levels of commitment in sexual relationships, in both casual and cohabiting situations, in which one partner is more emotionally invested in the relationship than the other.[18] These are but a few of the negative outcomes of contemporary attitudes toward sexuality.

For several decades, the women's movement, the sexual revolution, and other movements have helped people to better understand such issues as gender, sexual biology, psychology, and role stereotyping. In many ways, a positive and liberating development in our understanding of the sexual dimension of human life has occurred. On the other hand, the classic understanding of sexuality as fundamentally oriented toward the procreation of children has been suppressed if not lost altogether. Although interpreting sexuality as oriented exclusively toward procreation is too narrow, today's attitude has erred in nearly the exact opposite fashion by excluding procreation as an end to sexuality at all.

Although human sexuality may have a range of ends associated with it, an inseparable end—from a teleological point of view—is the reproduction of new life. To divorce sexuality from procreation is to distort its primary biological purpose. One need not argue that all sex must be undertaken with the aim of making children in order to respect sexual procreativity; however, a teleological argument holds that no sex should be divorced from the deepest respect for the unique, procreative potential of one's body and the body of one's beloved. Of course, not all individuals are sexually fertile due to a variety of physical conditions, both congenital and acquired. Likewise, sexually inactive persons relationally do not enact their reproductive potential. Nevertheless, every person's reproductive biological characteristics constitute the seat of their sexual, procreative potential. As a result, the sexual physicality of every person's body should

---

15. See, for instance, Pamela Haag, *Voices of a Generation: Teenage Girls on Sex, School, and Self* (New York: Marlowe & Company, 2000) and Thomas Lickona, "The Neglected Heart: The Emotional Dangers of Premature Sexual Involvement," in Kieran Scott and Michael Warren, eds., *Perspectives on Marriage: A Reader*, 3rd ed. (New York and Oxford: Oxford University Press, 2007), 196–206.

16. See Alan Booth, Ann Crouter, and Nancy Landale, *Just Living Together: Implications of Cohabitation on Families, Children, and Social Policy*, Penn State University Family Issues Symposia (Mahwah, NJ: Lawrence Erlbaum, 2002).

17. Catherine Itzin, ed., *Pornography: Women, Violence, and Civil Liberties* (New York: Oxford University Press, 1992). Several articles in this comprehensive volume argue for a causal relationship between pornography and violence, including Liz Kelly, "Pornography and Child Sexual Abuse," 113–23; Ray Wyre, "Pornography and Sexual Violence: Working with Sex Offenders," 236–47; and Diana Russell, "Pornography and Rape: A Causal Model," 310–49.

18. This mismatch in commitment levels is explored in Barbara Dafoe Whitehead's documentary *Marriage: Just a Piece of Paper?* produced and directed by Brian Boyer (Chicago: University of Chicago and WTTW-TV, 2002).

be regarded with the dignity and respect that stems from its creative potential as a reflection of the *imago dei*, the image of God.

Within natural, sexual reproduction, however, human beings find themselves in the unique condition of physically and literally becoming the biological basis of another human being's life. In this sense, human beings act as co-creators with God in the transmission of new life. In particular for women who gestate, bear, and breast-feed children, new life is made possible through the yielding of one's body to processes that are beyond intellectual control. A testimony to the creative force of sexual reproduction is seen in every instance of a mother's gestational months, the life-giving bloodshed of a mother in delivery, and the irreplaceable nourishment that comes in a mother's milk.

It is this creative and consequentially weighty potential of sexuality that is so frequently today unacknowledged in casual and uncommitted attitudes toward sexuality. In the absence of respect for the biological nature of one's sexual partner and the emotional aftermath of sexual encounters, the dignity of the human being is compromised. For, in sexual encounter, two become as one physical being. In fact, they arguably become a single biological organism.[19] The ethical implication that follows is that sexual encounter constitutes a level of interpersonal and biological union that is inherently binding. Alexander Pruss suggests the following anecdote to make this point:

> One can also say that the [sexual] act signifies a depth of love that cannot be impermanent. To engage in the act without the commitment of a permanently and objectively binding union is like the case of a young man who says to a young woman "I love you passionately, wondrously, infinitely. Should you refuse me, I will pine away for the rest of my life in sadness and pain—but

let that not concern you, for I will do this with the consolation that I have loved and that you are happy with another. But, I beg, break not my heart, for without you I cannot live. So, my dearest, my beloved, will you live with me?" while making the mental reservation "until I grow tired of you." This reservation would contradict everything else that was said, making it all into a lie, and were the unfortunate young woman to know about this reservation, she might do very well indeed to slap the liar on the cheek and leave him in disgust. In the same way, a sexual act without the context of objective commitment of a permanent union is an intrinsic contradiction or, worse, a lie. Such a sexual act is like uttering these same lines, with the clause "until we grow tired of each other."[20]

Of course, there are many ways and circumstances in which human beings engage in sex and even produce offspring. Many of them are far from ideal. Children born out of sexual violation, children born out of systemic poverty, children born to hostile partners—these are but a few of the examples of challenging circumstances in which new life can emerge. These kinds of circumstances are important to our discussion because they point out the gulf that can and does exist between the ideal and the flawed conditions of human life. That gulf leads us to ask, what conditions would human beings ideally choose in which to experience sexuality? What conditions surrounding sexual expression would respect the inalienable, personal dignity of sexual partners and their offspring? What conditions of human sexual expression contribute to the flourishing of human society as a whole rather than to its demise?

In what conditions does human flourishing occur such that the dignity of persons as individuals and in society with one another is most manifest? Clearly certain conditions for sexual

---

19. This is the major argument of Alexander Pruss, "Christian Sexual Ethics and Teleological Organicity," *The Thomist* 64 (2007): 71–100. Used by permission.

20. Ibid., 80.

expression and the reproduction of children better ensure dignity and welfare than others. Moreover, when sexuality is inseparably linked to reproductive potential, in addition to companionship and play, certain principles that govern human sexuality begin to emerge.

Questions like these have led Catholic moral theology to place sexual encounter within the boundaries of marital union.[21] Where can human persons maximize the value and purpose of their sexuality? In the stable marital union forged by a covenant of charity and sealed for the communication of grace. When two people work toward realizing a sacramental marriage, that marriage becomes the place where play, companionship, and bodily vulnerability are safe and genuine. Dignity

WHAT ABOUT SAME-SEX MARRIAGE?

One of the most contentious debates in church and state today is the issue of same-sex marriage. Critics of same-sex marriage state a number of objections, primary among them that same-sex marriage cannot achieve the teleological end of biological reproduction. As marriage has historically been undertaken for the primary purpose of reproduction, same-sex marriage challenges classical conceptions of what marriage is and what purposes it serves.

In his discussion of the issue,[22] Stephen Pope evaluates and refutes the teleological and procreative objections to same-sex marriage. Pope contends that human sexuality serves other ends besides the procreation of children, including the enhancement of intimacy and the strengthening of emotional bonds between lovers. Furthermore, as much of human sexual activity is non-procreative (for instance, sex after a woman's menopause), the *telos* of human sexuality ought to be understood as more than the gestation of children. Pope argues that procreativity extends far beyond the biological phase of reproduction since rearing and caring for children lasts well into adulthood. Adoptive, same-sex couples participate in the latter kind of procreativity and hence may also fulfill the procreative end of marriage.

While Pope makes a teleological argument in favor of the possibility of same-sex marriage, other practical concerns often motivate advocates of same-sex marriage. These include such issues as whether same-sex partners can receive employer medical benefits, inherit property and assets from a deceased partner, make medical decisions on behalf of a partner, file joint income taxes, and so on.

From our discussion of marriage in this book, the issue may be seen in terms of the following questions: Can same-sex marriage be a covenant or a sacrament? Can it support human dignity and, specifically, sexual dignity? Can it be a location for Christian charity, both within and outside of the immediacy of the family unity? Can it be a location for justice? Does the historical flexibility of the meaning and form of marriage allow for its present-day extension to same-sex couples?

---

21. The United States Conference of Catholic Bishops makes available online a wide variety of Vatican and papal statements, U.S. bishops' statements, and committee reports on marriage and sexuality. These documents include, among other topics, Catholic Church teachings on marriage, birth control, sexuality, homosexuality, parenting and the education of children, marriage preparation, child sexual abuse, violence against women, gerontology, and cohabitation. The online sources are quite convenient and illuminating, and can be accessed at *http://www.usccb.org/laity/marriage/publications.shtml.*

22. Stephen Pope, "Same-Sex Marriage: Threat or Aspiration," in *Perspectives on Marriage: A Reader*, eds., Kieran Scott and Michael Warren, 3rd ed. (New York and Oxford: Oxford University Press, 2007), 141–46.

ensues in the respect and care for one another's bodies—that is the ideal and goal of sacramental marriage. Celebration of the reproductive potential of oneself and one's beloved opens the way for prayer and reverence of creation, of nature, and of the processes that sustain it.

Sex outside of marriage, by contrast, lacks the stability of the intent toward permanence, if not permanence itself.[23] This leaves one or both partners subject to abandonment, disappointment, and relational demise. Sex divorced from its procreative end is a distortion that objectifies human beings and enables people to treat one another as ends to pleasure rather than as persons with an inherent and inalienable *telos* as creatures in the image of God. Consider the distance between viewing a woman's body as an instance of the image of God and the eroticized portrayal of women pole dancing in music videos. Likewise, consider the way male sexuality is diminished by the endless pills and products marketed for "male enhancement." The full sexual self cannot be reduced to mere anatomy, and the contrast is stark when we consider that the sexual dignity of men and women is rooted in the inalienable dignity and creative potential of the persons as irreplaceable creations of a loving God.

APPLICATION TO FAMILY AND MARRIAGE TODAY

A discussion of sexuality, marriage, and human dignity is not easy; people are highly and personally invested in these matters. Most of us feel that only we know what is best for us and no one should be making our decisions, especially about what occurs in the privacy of our bedrooms. Many argue that the Catholic Church lacks proportionality in its discussion of issues such as abortion and birth control, which makes its teaching seem unreasonably legalistic and strict rather than open and dialogical. Many also feel that the Catholic Church has inadequately considered the needs and dignity of homosexual persons in committed relationships, revealing an underdeveloped understanding of human sexuality.

Another serious problem is the irony that most Catholic teaching on sexual behavior comes historically from a celibate male clergy. Of course, an exclusively male perspective is inadequate to know or discuss human sexuality in its entirety, since sexuality includes and affects both males and females. Moreover, celibates do not have the experience of raising families and do not have regular sexual experiences within the context of marriage. In addition, Church teaching on sexual issues has been compromised by the moral failings of many clergy members and the hierarchy that protected them in the sexual abuse of parishioners, many of them children. These legitimate concerns reveal a need for the Catholic Church to develop its teaching on human sexuality.[24]

A renewed Catholic dialogue on matters of sexual dignity is challenging. Indeed, the broad theological anthropology and its understanding of sexuality need to be revisited in light of our contemporary understandings of human biology, personhood, and gender. Areas of discussion that have been influenced by contemporary anthropology and hence require ongoing dialogue within the Church include: the role of women in leadership positions within society and Church; sexuality outside of the context of marriage;

---

23. This teaching pertains to both heterosexual and homosexual sexual activity outside of marriage. For a Vatican statement on same-sex marriage, consult *Considerations Regarding Proposals to Give Legal Recognitions to Unions Between Homosexual Persons*.

24. Such a development is offered in Todd Salzman and Michael Lawler's recent book *The Sexual Person: Toward a Renewed Catholic Anthropology* (Washington: Georgetown University Press, 2008).

proportional consideration of birth control and abortion; celibacy of the clergy; reproductive technologies; and same-sex relationships. The Church must undertake such discussion if it is to be genuinely responsive to the questions and issues of present and future generations.

While these issues loom large and give us pause in our processing of Catholic Church teaching on sexuality, they should not do so to the point of overshadowing the great wisdom of the teaching on the dignity of the human person and its manifestation in human sexuality. It is far too easy for contemporary persons to fail to see the beauty and power of human reproductivity. Indeed, it is all too common to treat our reproductive capacity as a burden to be suppressed until such a time as we desire to have a baby, and then, to use any reproductive technologies available to ensure conception on demand. Familiarity, knowledge, and cooperation with our bodies and their reproductive capacities are possible for human beings with minimal biological self-knowledge and observation. To understand human bodies is to be empowered. To cooperate with them is to respect the biological seat of human personhood. To respect the reproductive capacity of ourselves and others is to see one another as bearers of the image of God, who carry within us the potential for carrying on the work of creation.

If we viewed ourselves and others in this highly dignified light, casual sexual encounters, premature sexual encounters, and abusive or violent expressions of sexuality would be dramatically reduced. How might the pornography industry be affected if pornographers and consumers alike viewed sexuality as a holy expression of divinely creative potentialities? How might sex among children and adolescents be limited if youth were convinced of the dignity and worth of their bodies by messages that were reinforced in media and education? How might children benefit if they were born within truly sacramental marriages, where communion of persons was modeled and consummated through the life-long sexual companionship of parents? How might marriage as an institution be strengthened if married people authentically treated their marriages as sacramental unions where the dignity of their spouse's body and person was placed ahead of personal desire or need? Finally, how might marriage as an institution gain greater respect and status in the eyes of unmarried people if the ideal were more frequently manifested by married couples?

In conclusion, we return to the concept that opened this chapter. We may choose how to perceive marriage. We may also choose how to perceive human persons and, in particular, the purpose of human sexuality. The Catholic theological tradition argues as it does because, based on its perception of sexuality in nature and its interpretation of the purpose of sexuality through divine revelation, it sees human beings as vessels of God and bearers of God's image. From this viewpoint, moral arguments on sexuality must be made in light of the preservation and celebration of human dignity in sexuality for individuals as well as social welfare. There is ongoing debate as to what conditions best ensure this dignity. However, the stance in favor of human dignity that comes from the Catholic Church today should not be taking lightly insofar as it is a rare perspective in a contemporary era that too often debases and cheapens sexuality for a laugh, a thrill, or a dollar.

Questions for Review and Discussion

1. What does *telos* mean? How does this concept relate to natural law?

2. What does the Catholic Church teach regarding the relationship between natural law and the will of God? What moral implications can be drawn from this teaching?

3. According to Catholic teaching, what two components are necessary for a just society in which human dignity is preserved?

4. Why does Catholic teaching hold that human beings reflect the image of God? How can such a lofty concept be applied to a morally corrupt person, such as a violent criminal?

5. How is marriage a microcosm of society? In general, how might spouses respect the dignity of one another?

6. Is sexual dignity part of our present culture? Develop both a "yes" and "no" response to this question.

7. Marriage is not always a condition in which personal and sexual dignity is experienced. What are some obstacles to dignity in marriage?

8. If there are obstacles to personal and sexual dignity in marriage, are there other contexts in which personal and sexual dignity could meaningfully be lived out?

Resources for Further Reading

Resources for Human Dignity

Robert Kraynak and Glenn Tinder, eds., *In Defense of Human Dignity: Essays for Our Time* (Notre Dame: University of Notre Dame Press, 2003).

Eberhard Schockenhoff, *Natural Law and Human Dignity: Universal Ethics in an Historical World* (Washington: Catholic University of America Press, 2003).

Resources for Sexuality and Marriage

Lisa Sowle Cahill, *Between the Sexes: Foundations for a Christian Ethics of Sexuality* (Philadelphia: Fortress Press, and New York: Paulist Press, 1985).

James M. Childs, Jr., *Faithful Conversation: Christian Perspectives on Homosexuality* (Minneapolis: Fortress Press, 2003).

Kieran Scott and Harold Horell, eds., *Human Sexuality in the Catholic Tradition* (Lanham, MD: Rowman & Littlefield, 2007).

Todd Salzman and Michael Lawler, *The Sexual Person: Toward a Renewed Catholic Anthropology* (Washington: Georgetown University Press, 2008).

Evelyn Eaton Whitehead and James D. Whitehead, *A Sense of Sexuality: Christian Love and Intimacy* (New York: Crossroad, 1989).

CHAPTER 8

CONVERSION, CHARACTER, COMMITMENT

Thus far our discussions have focused on several foundational themes in the Christian theology of marriage, specifically covenant, charity, sacramentality, and dignity, especially as these themes are developed in Roman Catholic thinking. A repeating issue that has surfaced in these discussions is the gulf that can and does exist between the ideal value we seek to place on marriage and the lived reality that often falls radically short of the ideal. Christians have traditionally argued that the reason for this gulf between the ideal and the actual is *sin*. Sin impairs the human ability to realize perfection in our lives individually and collectively. But Christians also believe that people are not bound by sin but can overcome it, to some extent. This is what Christians call *redemption* or *salvation*.

The overcoming of sin through redemption is one of the most important areas of Christian theology. Indeed, the central premise of Christian faith is that people are saved, but the notion of salvation raises many questions. Saved from what? Saved individually or communally? Saved in this world or in an afterlife? How are we

saved? Are we saved by our own actions or are we passive recipients of salvation through a pure gift of grace? In the arena of marriage, different questions arise. What does sin within marriage look like? How is it overcome? How is marriage both a condition of grace and a condition that requires salvation through grace?

Christian theology holds that the struggle against sin is mitigated by the saving effects of Jesus' life. The mitigating work of Jesus, however, does not affect those who are totally passive. Although there is longstanding debate over how much human beings cooperate with God's grace (versus how much God's grace operates upon people independently of their will), most Christians hold that some internal change or transformation on the part of the person is the required outcome of God's saving grace. We call this transformation *conversion*.

Conversion refers to the change of heart people experience when they see error in past behavior and seek to change patterns of thought and behavior. Conversion may begin in a single, dramatic moment, but if it is to be lasting, it is a process that is lived out over a lifetime. The converted person cultivates a particular character that meets life's situations with virtue. A converted Christian manifests certain qualities of character; these qualities define the individual's fundamental orientation and core values, permeating that person's entire life. Within marriage and family, one's character affects not only the life of one's spouse but also the quality of the marriage.

This chapter will consider the relationship between conversion and character in marriage. We begin by establishing a basic framework for thinking about sin and redemption. We move into a discussion of conversion as a core Christian concept, and then consider the development of virtues that result from converted character. We conclude with a consideration of the deep implications of character formation for marriage and family life.

TOOLS

Before discussing character formation, we need to take a fundamental look at the moral challenges people face. Likewise we need to consider the Christian understanding of salvation as that which makes conversion and positive character formation possible. We begin by discussing sin.

Sin can be understood in many ways. We can think of sin as instances of individual bad acts, such as lying, stealing, or assault. Or we can think of sin as situations or conditions of society that affect people collectively, such as slavery, warfare, or poverty.

We also can think of sin in more abstract terms, such as disordered love or values. For example, it is proper for me to love my work. As a teacher, I meet wonderful students, attend professional conferences, and engage in lifelong learning. All of these things are rewarding and help me to grow as a person and in my faith.

However, if I love my work to the point that I neglect my family or take advantage of my colleagues in order to succeed, then my love for my work is a disordered love; I see it not as a means to an end but as an end in itself. As another example, many people fall into the trap of valuing money for the sake of money—not as a means to meeting needs but as an end in itself. This is a classic example of disordered love.

C. S. Lewis colorfully describes this condition of human sinfulness and the challenges of morality in his book *Christian Behavior* in the following passage:

There are two ways in which the human machine goes wrong. One is when human individuals drift apart from one another, or else collide with one another and do one another damage, by cheating or bullying. The other is when things go wrong inside the individual—when the different parts of him (his different faculties and desires and so on) either drift apart or interfere with one another. You can get the idea plain if you think of us as a fleet of ships sailing in formation. The voyage will be a success only, in the first place, if the ships don't collide and get in one another's way; and, secondly, if each ship is seaworthy and has her engines in good order. As a matter of fact, you can't have either of these two things without the other. If the ships keep on having collisions they won't remain seaworthy very long. On the other hand, if their steering gears are out of order they won't be able to avoid collisions. Or, if you like, think of humanity as a band playing a tune. To get a good result, you need two things. Each player's individual instrument must be in tune, and also each must come in at the right moment so as to combine with all the others.

But there is one thing we haven't yet taken into account. We haven't asked where the fleet is trying to get to, or what piece of music the band is trying to play. The instruments might be all in tune and might all come in at the right moment,

AUGUSTINE ON LOVE

Augustine's classic treatise *De Doctrina Christiana* (*Teaching Christianity*, ca. 426–427) is a revered instructional manual for teaching Christian faith and Scripture. Augustine begins by arguing that the key to interpreting Scripture properly is understanding that its final purpose is to instruct people in the love of God, which is expressed in the love of neighbor. Properly ordered love, according to Augustine, values all things, including people, not for their own sake but for God's sake. He says:

> We have been commanded, after all, to love one another; but the question is whether people are to be loved by others for their own sake, or for the sake of something else. If it is for their own sake, then they are things for us to enjoy; if for the sake of something else, they are for us to use. Now it seems to me that they are to be loved for the sake of something else, because if a thing is to be loved for its own sake, it means that it constitutes the life of bliss, which consoles us in this present time with the hope of it, even though it is not yet a reality. "Cursed," however, "is the one who places his hopes in man" (Jer 17:5).
>
> But none of us ought either to find enjoyment in ourselves, if you consider the matter straightforwardly, because we ought not either to love ourselves for our own sakes, but for the sake of the one whom we are to enjoy. Then indeed are people as good as can be, when they aim all their lives long at that unchanging life and cling to it with all their hearts. But if they love themselves for their own sakes, they are not relating themselves to God; rather, in turning to themselves, they are not turning to anything unchangeable. And that is why their enjoyment of themselves is to some extent defective, because they are better when they cleave to the unchangeable good and are tightly bound to

> it, than when they release themselves from it and cling even to themselves.
>
> So if you ought not to love yourself for your own sake, but for the sake of the one to whom your love is most rightly directed as its end, other people must not take offense if you also love them for God's sake and not their own. This, after all, is the rule of love that God has set for us: "You shall love," he says, "your neighbor as yourself; God, however, with your whole heart and your whole soul and your whole mind" (Mark 12:30–31; Lev 19:18; Deut 6:5). Thus all your thoughts and your whole life and all your intelligence should be focused on him from whom you have received the very things you devote to him. Now when he said "with your whole heart, your whole soul, your whole mind," he did not leave out any part of our life, which could be left vacant, so to speak, and leave room for wanting to enjoy something else. Instead, whatever else occurs to you as fit to be loved must be whisked along toward that point to which the whole impetus of your love is hastening.
>
> So all who love their neighbors in the right way ought so to deal with them that they too love God with all their heart, all their soul, all their mind. By loving them, you see, in this way as themselves, they are relating all their love of themselves and of the others to that love of God, which allows no channel to be led off from itself that will diminish its own flow.[1]

What is the error, according to Augustine, in loving oneself for one's own sake and loving another for his or her own sake? What might the risks of disordered love be? How might loving oneself or one's neighbor for God's sake differ in practice from loving for the sake of the person? How might these practical differences be experienced in marriage and family life?

---

1. Augustine, *Teaching Christianity: De Doctrina Christiana*, trans. Edmund Hill, OP (New York: New City Press, 1996), 114–15. Used by permission of New City Press.

but even so the performance wouldn't be a success if they had been engaged to provide dance music and actually played nothing but Dead Marches. And however well the fleet sailed, its voyage would be a failure if it were meant to reach New York and actually arrived at Calcutta.

Morality, then, seems to be concerned with three things. Firstly, with fair play and harmony between individuals. Secondly, with what might be called tidying up or harmonizing the things inside each individual. Thirdly, with the general purpose of human life as a whole: what man was made for: what course the whole fleet ought to be on: what tune the conductor of the band wants it to play.[2]

Human morality, then, has personal (or internal), relational, and teleological challenges. Sin—whether understood as individual acts, social conditions, disordered love, or some combination of all three—has the effect of creating a gulf between what we know would be good and what we actually do as persons and societies. This gulf affects our inner states, our relationships, and the way we understand the meaning of our lives.

Consider how these dimensions of sin affect marriage and family life. At an interior level, sin distorts a person's inner self. Like a fragile instrument, people can be broken by hurts, fears, past events, egotism, self-doubt, anger, jealousy, laziness, cowardice, imprudence, and so on. When we are honest with ourselves, we see our weaknesses quite plainly and know ourselves in ways we would rather mask from others. Personal deficits affect how individuals present themselves to their spouses, children, and extended family both intentionally and unintentionally. An example of an intentional effect would be a verbally cruel outburst of anger against one's spouse over a job loss. An unintentional effect could be a parent unwittingly forcing a child into an activity because the parent excelled at the same activity as a child.

Personal deficits translate into relational dysfunction—when the individuals are out of tune, their relationship goes out of tune. This is especially true when bad patterns of communication and interaction become habit. For example, one spouse may be angry at the other over the use of free time, such as when one partner joins a sports league that requires time, energy, and even a financial commitment. The unhappy spouse may choose to live with unresolved issues related to the sports team but act out frustration over the matter by excessive recreational shopping. Both parties are acting selfishly whether they are aware of it or not, and both are failing to respond constructively to the challenges of managing limited time and money while fostering conditions for personal expression. The result is a breakdown of intimacy, honesty, and harmony.

The breakdown points to an ulterior problem, which is a lack of shared direction and purpose. While each spouse is entitled to some personal time, neither in this scenario has given due consideration to how his or her actions relate to the marriage as a whole. The sports team may in fact take up too much time, while the shopping is an artificial means to fill up the vacuum created by the other spouse's absence. The spouses have not asked themselves whether their actions (including the inaction of not discussing and resolving the situation harmoniously) manifest a true covenant, reflect charity, provide conditions of grace, or make their matrimony truly holy. The one should ask whether the sports team advances the good of the marriage; the other should ask if spending money recreationally interrupts the family's economic stability or ability to give charitably. In the absence of these sorts of reflective questions, both reveal that they have lost sight of the *telos* or goal of their actions in relationship to their marriage. When such situations multiply over the course of years, spouses can lose sight of the purpose and direction of their marriage altogether.

---

2. C. S. Lewis, *Christian Behavior* (New York: Macmillan Company, 1945), 1–2.

Of course, typically people do not enter into marriage intending to behave badly or expecting a bad outcome. People want to do better and strive for more than they seem to be able to do. Christians believe that our frequent failures are the effect of sin. Sin, Christianity teaches, is a defect not only of the will, which cannot adequately govern our actions, but also of the mind or intellect. The inability to *will* what is best is also colored by the inability to *know* what is best.[3] Perfect foreknowledge might allow us to always choose the good. Unfortunately, this is not our situation.

That we not only fail to *do* what is best but also to *know* what is best requires corrective action. Corrective action begins with a personal change of heart and a desire to overcome sinfulness. Such a desire, however, must be bolstered by a long-term commitment to change. To this end, Christian moral theology posits two central concepts that help people to envision and realize how they might redirect themselves and their relationships toward healthier and holier outcomes. These concepts are *conversion* and *character formation*.[4]

CONVERSION

The story of religions, Christianity included, is a story of human beings grappling to overcome estrangement and to re-form patterns of personal and corporate life. I once heard the contemporary theologian David Tracy remark that the one common element he could deduce from his career-long study of religion was that *all* religions share an impulse to overcome the ego. It is selfishness and egotism that lead people to mistreat others and make bad choices. The correction to egotism is overcoming the self. The re-formation of human life toward its proper end is the goal of Christian life. The Christian theological tradition argues that we can in fact be freed from egotism to live out genuine charity, to offer the gift of self to others, and to work toward realizing the image of God within ourselves.

How does this personal re-formation occur? Christians generally believe that it is achieved through the remarkable life of Jesus of Nazareth, whose perfect relationship with God realized in actuality the ideal toward which human beings previously could only strive. Jesus, in his absolute acceptance of God's will, manifests a life of total gift of self in the service of others. Jesus overcomes temptations to selfishness and egotism—even to the point of yielding his life for his vision and ministry—so that others might see how it is possible to submit one's will totally to God.

In the Bible as well as in post-biblical writings, the story of Jesus' followers is not one of immediate or perfect adherence to Jesus' teachings and way of life.[5] We find, rather, stories about

---

3. Frans Jozef van Beeck speaks to the condition of sin in "Part III: Finitude and Fall" of his systematic theology *God Encountered: A Contemporary Catholic Systematic Theology* (Collegeville, MN: Liturgical Press, 1995). Of the impact of sin (which he understands classically as concupiscence) on both will and mind, he says, "Our desires, those of the mind as much as those of the body, are badly scrambled. Natural desire still looks 'only natural,' and so does *propatheia* but both now often positively misdirect our native ability to make responsible choices, both as individuals and as social groups" (p. 15).

4. Van Beeck here comments: "Here also lies the root of the Christian understanding of the resolution of the paralyzing deadlock brought about by sin and evil. The great Tradition places this resolution, not in the stamping out of sin or in its destruction, but in the sinner's *conversion* and *reconciliation* with God. Far from being obliterated, expunged from the record, canceled from memory, or ignored, *sin and its effects are remembered and acknowledged*; mature forgiveness is based not on forgiving but on remembering. Thus sin and its effects become the stuff of conversion and reconciliation, and hence, of the praise of God. . . . Finally we can at least begin to choose freely, and virtue can once again become what it was always meant to be: intrinsically more delightful than vice" (pp. 18–19).

5. For example, the story of Peter's denial of Christ and subsequent shame (Luke 22:54–62) is an example of the struggles and imperfections of even the dearest of Jesus' followers.

strengthened human knowledge and willpower to cooperate with the divine will. We find people able to see for the first time the gulf between what they are and ought to be, and we witness them finding the strength and courage to work toward greater personal humility and service to others. The process by which human beings are able to work toward overcoming sin is enabled by a fundamental shift in outlook, priorities, and sense of purpose in life called *conversion*.

Religious conversion, though quite real, is difficult to quantify.[6] Most accounts of religious conversion are told as first-person stories about dramatic life-shifts, usually recalled decades after the conversion experience took place.[7] In addition, conversion stories are often told as events with a supernatural quality attached to them that defies explanation or understanding, such as when people report hearing God's voice telling them to do something. This leads others to question the nature, authenticity, and repeatability of such events.

Gillespie observes that scholarly studies of religious conversion have historically focused on personal experiences. However, we should not be intimidated by the sudden, supernatural, and extrinsic quality of many personal accounts from considering the more gradual, internal, and intentional dimensions of religiously based conversions. Moreover, conversion need not refer to the transition from an unreligious state or another religion to an entirely new religion—as in a Christian converting to Islam. Conversion can be a transition between states of commitment ideologically and behaviorally. An example of such a conversion might be when a person finally commits to remaining sober after a long battle with addiction punctuated by failed attempts at rehabilitation.

While conversion accounts are interesting to consider as case studies, it is perhaps more helpful to consider first the common threads in religious conversion within the Christian theological tradition. I would suggest that the principle element that Christian conversion stories share is the twofold experience of turning away from one's prior ways and dedicating oneself to a new course of action. Gillespie asserts that this twofold process is rooted in both Old and New Testament accounts of conversion. In the Old Testament, he suggests that conversion involves both a turning from and a turning toward something. "The turning might be from injustice to justice, or from inhumanity to humanity, or from idols to gods. For the Hebrew, conversion was never just the experience of changing, but included a goal of action on the part of the believer where the conception of God's will was being fulfilled in turning around. It was a movement back to knowing God."[8] In the New Testament, conversions likewise suggest a movement toward something new, with passages implying everything from returning home, to changing one's mind, to restoration.[9]

---

6. V. Bailey Gillespie, *The Dynamics of Religious Conversion: Identity and Transformation* (Birmingham, AL: Religious Education Press, 1991).

7. Classic stories of religious conversion abound in Christian literature, from the Bible through modern times. Editors H. Newton Malony and Samuel Southard expertly document religious conversions from comparative religious, sociological, literary, and cultural perspectives in their volume *Handbook of Religious Conversion* (Birmingham, AL: Religious Education Press, 1992). Part 3 of this volume looks at Christian conversion from the perspectives of the Bible, Catholicism, Protestantism, and Evangelicalism. In particular, the discussion of Catholic views of conversion and Catholic converts is helpful in introducing a range of conversion stories from the classic accounts of Saint Paul and Augustine to the more recent stories of Dorothy Day and Thomas Merton (pp. 119–22).

8. Gillespie, *Dynamics of Religious Conversion*, 23.

9. Ibid., 28.

Conversion requires both an admission of error and a focus on new patterns of behavior. C. S. Lewis argues that Christ takes it for granted that people are bad and need saving.[10] This is why Jesus begins his ministry with the challenge to repent in order to be prepared for the kingdom of God. Unless people believe that they need saving, according to Lewis, they will never be able to hear the words of Christ because they will be consumed with their own sense of self-sufficiency. Lewis does not argue this to make his readers feel bad about themselves. Quite the contrary, Lewis argues this because he recognizes that the path to improvement can only begin with an honest assessment of personal shortcomings.

While conversion begins at a personal level, it reaches beyond the individual and touches relationships with others as well as one's orientation to God. To recall our opening comments about conversion, the moral life involves a personal, a relational, and a teleological component. This triple-layered quality of conversion is captured well by twentieth-century theologian Bernard Lonergan:

> Fundamental to religious living is conversion. It is a topic little studied in traditional theology since there remains very little of it when one reaches the universal, the abstract, the static. For conversion occurs in the lives of individuals. It is not merely a change or even a development; rather, it is a radical transformation on which follows, on all levels of living, an interlocked series of changes and developments. What hitherto was

WHAT DOES CONVERSION LOOK LIKE?

Have you ever experienced or witnessed a dramatic change of heart? What was the experience like? Was it difficult, sudden, long in coming, hard to maintain? What precipitated the change? Would you characterize it as religious? What were the effects of this change on the individual as well as on relationships between the individual and others? In general, would you characterize this experience as a "conversion"? Why or why not?

unnoticed becomes vivid and present. What had been of no concern becomes a matter of high import. So great a change in one's apprehensions and one's values accompanies no less a change in oneself, in one's relations to other persons and in one's relations to God.[11]

CONVERSION'S IMPACT ON MARRIAGE

The implications of conversion for spouses and their marriages are far-reaching. Recalling our earlier discussions of covenant, charity, sacrament, and dignity, we can begin to see the ways a married individual is called upon to be converted: as an individual, within the marriage, and as one called to live in the image of God. To be covenanted to one's spouse requires setting aside one's former independent life in order to live in total union with another. The former life of the individual is, in a sense, lost so that the new life as one-with-another within the marriage can begin. The

---

10. C. S. Lewis, *The Problem of Pain* (New York: HarperCollins, 2001), 50–51.

11. Bernard Lonergan, "Theology in Its New Context," in *Conversion: Perspectives on Personal and Social Transformation*, ed. Walter E. Con (New York: Alba House, 1978), 12–13.

steadfast covenant of marriage becomes a locus of new life that requires conversion as a condition of entrance and as a condition of marital success.

Charity, like covenant, requires a turning away from disordered self-love. To be charitable in the sense of loving through giving oneself in service to others is the central, moral response of Jesus to the Father. Conversion experienced as this moral response, in turn, becomes the central challenge of the New Testament to Christians.[12] Conversion to active love reflective of Jesus' values is required of all Christians and is to be lived out in relationship to intimates, to the Christian community, and to all neighbors of every sort. Marriage once again becomes a unique locus for the convert's call to live out active charity, especially as the New Testament charges spouses with this task.[13] Moreover, marriage acts as a locus from which family members are strengthened to show charity for neighbors and non-intimates. In this sense, Christian marriage both requires and enables conversion to charity.

The change of heart that constitutes conversion is both a matter of grace, with which the convert is gifted, as well as a matter of personal response and choice. As mentioned earlier, Christians have long debated the degree to which people are passive recipients or active participants in grace. Even a brief attempt at exploring that debate lies far beyond the reach of this present discussion. However, drawing on previous discussions of the Catholic theology of marriage as a sacrament, we can say that marriage constitutes a state of grace whereby spouses confer grace upon one another. To enter into a genuinely sacramental marriage requires at least the intent to be an occasion of grace for one's spouse. Again, sincerely marrying another

with this intent represents a form of conversion from one's former life toward life with another, with the foremost responsibility of seeing to the other's spiritual and personal well-being. When two people bring to their marriage this intent, the marriage becomes a place both for receiving and participating in sacramental grace.

Finally, the dignity of all human beings may be inalienable, but this dignity is not always easy to see whether in oneself or in others. Particularly when people live together intimately, they frequently lose sight of each other's core dignity because they become familiar to the point of taking one another for granted. Conversion requires renewed sight and a return to seeing in every human being a creature made in the image of God. Marriage and family life provide a special context for negotiating the challenges of respecting, expressing, and fostering the personal dignity of oneself, one's kin, and one's neighbors.

In summation, when people see the dangers of self-aggrandizement and wish to let go of egotistical self-absorption, the process of conversion can begin. Conversion allows people to look outward for ways to serve, rather than ways to be served. Conversion enables people to find the joy in giving their talents, energies, and personhood away and ultimately to experience the ecstasy of finding happiness in others. True covenant, charity, grace, and dignity become possible for the converted heart and are essential to the good of marriage.

CHARACTER

We are mistaken if we believe conversion to be a one-time event. Individuals may and perhaps

---

12. This is the main claim of Charles Curran, "Conversion: The Central Moral Message of Jesus," in *Conversion: Perspectives on Personal and Social Transformation*, ed. Walter E. Con (New York: Alba House, 1978), 225–45.

13. See Eph 5:21–32.

must have powerful moments in their lives when the need for personal change is glaringly obvious. Yet it is also easy to gain some distance from those moments and to forget the great insights that they revealed to us. Conversions may begin with dramatic moments, such as biblical Paul reports, but they are not limited to those kinds of experiences nor are they contained entirely by them. It would be better to say that conversions may begin by dramatic or deeply life-altering events, but they are lasting when they decidedly affect our decision to establish within ourselves a character marked by a transformation of heart, lived out in active expression.

Character development occurs over time through the deliberate cultivation of virtues.[14] The ancient Greeks identified four "cardinal" virtues, so called because the good life hinges on them (*cardo* is Latin for "hinge"). These virtues are justice, fortitude, temperance, and prudence. In the Christian theological tradition, the three "theological" virtues of faith, hope, and charity are coupled with these four cardinal virtues. Altogether, the seven virtues constitute a set of qualities whereby, when habitually demonstrated, a person achieves a virtuous character, able to live out the intentions born of conversion. These virtues play a key role in intimate relationships, moreover, as they constitute core characteristics of persons capable of living marriages as covenants.

At the heart of a system of ethics based on the habituation of virtues lies the notion that true human goodness is determined by a proper end or *telos*. A teleological understanding of virtues posits that some qualities are more truly human than others. To put it another way, one can contrast what a human sometimes is with what

a human ought to be. Joseph Kotva summarizes this situation well:

> Virtue ethics has then a tripartite structure: (1) human-nature-as-it-exists; (2) human-nature-as-it-could-be; and (3) those habits, capacities, interests, inclinations, precepts, injunctions, and prohibitions that will move us from point one to point two. Thus, within a teleological virtue ethic certain kinds of actions, habits, capacities, and inclinations are discouraged because they direct us away from our true nature. Other kinds of actions, habits, capacities, and inclinations are encouraged because they lead us to our true end. Virtue theory deals with the transition from who we are to who we could be. A concern with this transition requires that we also try to discover or uncover our true nature or telos and ascertain our present state or nature.[15]

How do we know what we are and what we ought to be? From a Christian point of view, a human ought to be one who embodies the image of God. How is this achieved? Again the Christian view is that through grace a human being is converted and hence is able both to desire and to work toward manifesting that image through actions. The qualities of justice, fortitude, temperance, prudence, and especially the qualities of faith, hope, and charity determine the actions, habits, inclinations, and capacities that help human beings embody the image of God.

In the New Testament, as we have discussed, charity or love is the ultimate virtue, without which none of the others matters. In classical virtue ethics, charity is best expressed in the discussion of friendship.

Both Aristotle and Thomas Aquinas establish important foundations for Christian thought on

---

14. For an excellent college student's introduction to virtue ethics, see William Mattison III, *Introducing Moral Theology: True Happiness and the Virtues* (Grand Rapids: Brazos, 2008).

15. Joseph Kotva, Jr., *The Christian Case for Virtue Ethics* (Washington: Georgetown University Press, 1996), 17.

friendship.[16] Aristotle evaluates different types of friendship, with the fullest kind oriented toward the teleological good of the other. In full friendship, one is attracted to the other on the grounds of the inherent goodness of the other and seeks to contribute to that goodness through friendship. For Aquinas, this fullest kind of friendship has its optimal expression in the human friendship with God. William Mattison describes friendship with God as the highest form of charity because God is perfect goodness. Analyzing Aquinas, he says, "Charity is loving God above all else, not arbitrarily but because God is goodness, and the source of all that is good. . . . There is no further good to seek above or beyond God. And thus charity is resting in, enjoying God, as supremely good, much as we would appreciate and enjoy a true friend."[17]

Friendship as described here is an important concept for a theology of marriage and family. For friendship between spouses, while many-layered, has its fullest meaning when spouses seek to nurture the inherent goodness of one another. Through their friendship, spouses can encourage this goodness and value, which we might also describe as dignity. And the goal of nurturing one another's goodness is ultimately or teleologically rooted in the love of God.

While we might agree that people are intended to become friends with God through a charity-driven life, we might still wonder how people are to acquire this virtue (let alone the other virtues). Aristotle suggests that people acquire virtues through striving toward excellence or *arete*. The key to achieving excellence in virtues lies in the striving toward it. In other words, the process of becoming virtuous is key to virtue itself. All virtues, according to Aristotle, are acquired by repetition and habituation. A person is not virtuous by being generous one time. Rather one develops a character of generosity by consistently practicing generosity. Over time, it can be said of a person that he or she has a generous character, but no such statement can be made of a person on account of one odd moment of generosity in a lifetime of stinginess. Likewise, a person who consistently acts lazy or irritable demonstrates a lazy or irritable character, while a person who is consistently prompt, studious, and gentle may be said to have a character reflecting these virtues.

According to Aristotle, no character traits are acquired that are not possible or in some sense natural to us. And all character traits are habitual, both virtuous and unvirtuous alike. The key to Aristotle's genius here, and the reason he is important to us in this discussion, is his emphasis on character development as a matter of habitual choice. We choose every time whether we wish to be generous or stingy. When we have a habit of being generous, it becomes consistently easier to be generous. So also when we debase our characters by negative behaviors, we make it easier to scar ourselves and others repeatedly. Habitual practice is how we develop characters, whether for good or bad. We are, as a result, not bound by any behaviors by necessity, yet past performance creates in us predispositions to behave as we have in the past.

From a Christian point of view, this understanding of the acquisition of virtue holds true. Although we have argued at some length that sin interrupts perfect achievement of the characters people might wish to develop, we have also argued that the effects of Jesus' life are liberating in that they bring about a release from bondage to selfishness. The point

---

16. For a clear introduction to Aristotle's virtue ethics, see Anna Lannstrom, *Loving the Fine: Virtue and Happiness in Aristotle's Ethics* (Notre Dame: University of Notre Dame Press, 2006). For Aristotle's discussion of friendship, see *Nichomachean Ethics* in *The Basic Works of Aristotle*, ed. Richard McKeon (New York: Random House, 1941), 927–1112. Also pertinent here is Thomas Aquinas, *Summa Theologiae* II–II 23.

17. Mattison, *Introducing Moral Theology*, 294.

IS CHARACTER LIMITED?

How do you deliberately cultivate a character, and what qualities do you think are desirable in yourself and in others? By what standards do you evaluate character traits? Is it possible to choose how you want to be and then to become it, or do you think people are bound by their nature to behave certain ways? What do you think might be the limits (psychological, physical, spiritual, intellectual, and so on) to the freedom people have to craft themselves?

These questions deal essentially with the scope of human freedom, which in theological terms falls under the rubric of "theological anthropology." From your perspective, is personal character formation a religious or theological concern? Can you make an argument for why certain character traits are ultimately superior to others? What grounds support your claims?

of synthesis between this ancient Greek notion of character and the Christian notion of conversion is that they are both achieved *diachronically*, or over time. The converted charitable character is, to borrow the term, the *arete* or the excellence of the Christian life. It is a turning around within oneself that is always in process of becoming what it intends to be. Even while it is in process, it is realizing the virtues of charity, faith, hope, and the other virtues toward which it strives.

APPLICATION TO FAMILY AND MARRIAGE TODAY

Charity is considered the highest expression of virtue because it has a teleological orientation toward God. Striving toward charity, however, is not authentic if it is conceived as a singular relationship between God and an individual. This is because no individual exists alone in the world. Indeed all human beings exist in varying levels of community with others, from members of one's family to the human community at large. "If anyone says, 'I love God,' but hates his brother, he is a liar; for whoever does not love a brother whom he has seen cannot love God whom he has not seen" (1 John 4:20). Christian character has far-reaching social implications because Christians express their love of God by loving their neighbors, their brothers, their spouses, and their children. The virtues of a properly converted Christian character can be seen in their full significance in the family, because the family both challenges and demands its members to live out communally an active love of God.[18]

In service to one's family, individuals must ultimately decide to instill consistently and habitually within themselves patterns of behavior that are modeled after Christ's example of charity and service. The goal is the development of a character that finds self-giving as natural as breathing. This process, which begins with conversion of heart, is sustained through the intentional development of character. Through this character at the individual level, Christians cultivate a social character that reflects the core values by which they understand and make sense of their lives as individuals and the purpose of their marriage.

Because it is so easy to take advantage of those closest to us, it becomes crucial for spouses

---

18. The social implications of Christian virtue ethics and especially the role that the Christian family plays in both demonstrating and shaping the moral life of society are the subjects of Stanley Hauerwas, *A Community of Character: Toward a Constructive Christian Social Ethic* (Notre Dame and London: University of Notre Dame Press, 1981). Part 3 (pp. 155–74) on the moral value of the family and ethical reflections on the family is particularly useful here.

to bring converted characters to their relationships within family life. This means that spouses must, first and foremost, recognize the potential for disfiguring self-interest that persists in their lives and must regard themselves with humility. A humble character is open and conciliatory, forgiving and accepting, patient, gentle, and kind. It is a character modeled after the characteristics of love described in Paul's First Letter to the Corinthians. Such qualities are not mere platitudes but directives for the character that persons should bring to those whom they claim to love.

When two people having converted characters cooperate to form an open spirit of dialogue and mutual self-giving, the possibility of a new character of the marriage emerges. Like a person, a marriage has a personality and character of its own, and it reflects the habitual and repetitive behaviors of its spouses. If two people consistently build each other up through self-gift, patience, and cooperation, the marriage that results will have an admirable character. It will be enduring and kind within itself, and consequently, it will shine as an example of excellence to others. If, on the other hand, the marriage is afflicted with habitual arguing, name-calling,

and selfish refusal to concede, the marriage will find itself thin, worn, and disfigured.

Marriage ultimately is about choice. People choose whether they will view—and live out—marriage as a sacrament or not. They choose whether to seek to instill within their marriage the character of covenant or not. They choose whether to act in charity through the service of self or not. They choose whether to regard one another with dignity or not. They make choices that become habits that either strengthen or weaken them as individuals and their marriage as a union.

Our choices express the genuineness of personal conversion. Those with whom we share intimate and daily life will feel our choices most keenly. Although we may at times feel trapped by bad patterns or destructive actions, Christianity teaches that people can at any time allow for the grace of conversion to operate within their lives. Although we may have established patterns of behavior that are negative, we can choose to habituate different patterns that over time transform the character of the marriage toward one of true charity. The reality of sin reminds us that our efforts will remain flawed, but the greater reality of redemption reminds us that we are free to strive toward holiness.

Questions for Review and Discussion

1. How would you define different types of sin? Can you think of a situation in which types of sin overlap?

2. What is conversion? What two elements are consistent in Christian conversion stories? How would you personally define conversion?

3. Name and describe the cardinal virtues. Name and describe the theological virtues.

4. How do these virtues relate to a Christian understanding of friendship with God?

5. According to Aristotle, how is a virtuous character formed?

6. Can people change their character deliberately? If so, what does such a change involve?

7. How do conversion and character relate to marriage and family life?

8. What principle challenges do you see within modern marriages that require conversion and character formation?

Resources for Further Reading

Resources for Character, Conversion, and Commitment

V. Bailey Gillespie, *The Dynamics of Religious Conversion: Identity and Transformation* (Birmingham, AL: Religious Education Press, 1991).

Stanley Hauerwas, *A Community of Character: Toward a Constructive Christian Social Ethic* (Notre Dame and London: University of Notre Dame, 1981).

Joseph Kotva, Jr., *The Christian Case for Virtue Ethics* (Washington: Georgetown University Press, 1996).

Vincent MacNamara, *Love, Law and Christian Life: Basic Attitudes of Christian Morality* (Wilmington, DE: Michael Glazier, 1988).

H. Newton Malony and Samuel Southard, ed., *Handbook of Religious Conversion* (Birmingham, AL: Religious Education Press, 1992).

Daniel Statman, ed., *Virtue Ethics: A Critical Reader* (Washington: Georgetown University Press, 1997).

Stan van Hooft, *Understanding Virtue Ethics* (Chesham, UK: Acumen Press, 2006).

JUSTICE AND MARRIAGE

Justice is key to our thinking about a Christian theology of the family; we cannot claim to have love where there is no justice. Marriage and family life are a special context in which questions of love and justice take on a unique significance because of the great potential within marriage both for injustice as well as for Christian love to alleviate injustice. Unfortunately, and perhaps surprisingly, over the ages married life has often put spouses and children in physical jeopardy and been the source of much suffering. Although the family should be among the highest of human goods, procuring both joy and safety for its members, this is sadly not always the case. Even worse, we cannot only blame sinful human individuals within marriages for abuse and suffering; the patriarchal structure of the traditional family, historically endorsed by the churches and society at large, has actually contributed to the possibility of abuse and suffering within marriage.[1]

The twentieth-century theologian Jon Sobrino, in his reflection on contemporary theologies of liberation, argues that the classic definition of theology as "faith seeking understanding" ought to be revised in favor of "faith seeking love."[2] He argues, moreover, that love ought to be understood as action toward justice. Sobrino reminds his readers that when we attend to the world around us, we see a great deal of real and tangible suffering resulting from hunger, poverty, exile, genocide, and physical destruction. If the intent is to love others with the active love of Jesus in the Bible, it becomes critical for Christians to

---

1. Even today the Roman Catholic Church's pronouncement *Gaudium et Spes,* §52, seems to assume a female-homemaker model: "The father's active presence is very important for the children's education; the mother, too, has a central role in the home, for the children, especially the younger children, depend very much upon her; this role must be safeguarded without, however, underrating women's legitimate social advancement." Does this statement imply that some forms of social advancement are not "legitimate" for women? The potentially negative effects of the patriarchal family model will be explored further in this chapter. Used by permission.

2. Jon Sobrino, "Theology in a Suffering World," in *Pluralism and Oppression: Theology in World Perspective*, ed. Paul Knitter (Lanham, MD: University of America Press, 1991), 153–77.

consider what it means to love people who are suffering. To acknowledge suffering, and even to feel moved by it, is not sufficient for Christian love. For Sobrino, loving others means working toward justice for them. This means creating and ensuring conditions of human flourishing. At the heart of the biblical mandate to love lies the concept of justice.[3]

Justice is a societal *and* a theological concern. Justice might at first seem to pertain only to laws or the judicial system, but reflection on justice is also a deep part of the Christian theological tradition. In the modern Western theological context, people have frequently replaced fear over the wrath of God at injustice with a more comfortable emphasis on God's mercy and forgiveness. Nevertheless, much of the Christian story remains a reflection on human sinfulness and the need for correction.[4] Theologians have long recognized that a certain tension exists between God's offer of mercy and God's demand for justice. Nevertheless, all recognize that divine justice must in some way underlie the most fundamental notions of the goodness of God.

When we ask how family life realizes justice, we must consider both the interior and exterior dimensions of family life. In other words, we need to ask (1) what does justice look like within a family—between spouses and between parents and children? and (2) what does justice look like between the family and society? This and the following chapters will deal with these questions.

In this chapter our task is to consider the issue of justice and injustice within the family. We will first lay a theological foundation for thinking about the justice of God. Then we will evaluate the family from a historical perspective with respect to its potential for injustice. We will consider present-day violence and abuse within families to demonstrate the emergency that results from injustice in family life. Finally, we will reflect upon contemporary family life and the ways in which our concepts of covenant, charity, sacrament, and dignity may establish a foundation for true justice within marriage and family life.

TOOLS

In Christian teaching, God's justice is intricately related to God's love. To the extent that justice and love are related, both must be present within the context of marriage and family life if marital love is to mirror God's love.

The relationship between love and justice is the subject of much Christian reflection, both ancient and contemporary. In the Old Testament, God's love is expressed through the covenant with the Israelites. Indeed, the covenant relationship defines both love and justice.[5] As noted before, the covenant is not simply a matter of divine-human relations. It is also very much a matter of relationships between humans. To put it another way, in the Old Testament the human community's justice is governed by God's justice. What does this justice look like? As God entered into the covenant with the people of Israel, God promised to watch, guide, and protect their history. The people in turn were to extend to one another justice that reflected God's providential care of the whole community. Mary Elsbernd

---

3. The emphasis on active and just love pervades the Old Testament notion of covenant, where social justice is inseparably tied to God's justice. For example, the prophet Amos relates God's hatred of feasts and offerings made vain by the absence of justice: "But if you would offer me holocausts, then let justice surge like water, and goodness like an unfailing stream" (5:23–24). Similar sentiments abound in the New Testament, especially in the Johannine literature's explicit emphasis on active love and justice: "Children, let us love not in word or speech but in deed and truth" (1 John 3:18).

4. See the discussion of conversion in chapter 8.

5. For a review of covenant love, see chapter 2.

and Reimund Bieringer express these horizontal and vertical dimensions of God's justice well:

> Faithful adherence to God in the whole of living encompassed patterns in economic, political, and social relationships, as well as ritual expression (Isa 11:1–9; Psalm 72). Economic, political, social, and religious patterns were just when they reflected the community's adherence to God as creator and liberator. The practical denial of this relationship with their creator and liberator was community injustice: rituals without relationship, economic exploitation of the poor, political intrigue, and social abandonment of the widow or orphan (Amos 8:4–6). The prophets proclaimed that these unjust practices destroyed relational patterns reflected in the harmony of Eden's garden and in liberation from Egypt's bondage.
>
> In the covenant context of the Hebrew Scriptures, then, justice is best described as the faithful fulfillment of the demands and obligations flowing from the covenant relationship.[6]

In the New Testament, justice is also intricately related to love. Jesus' love, especially expressed to marginalized people, is at its heart an expression of his concern for human dignity and justice.[7] Again, Elsbernd and Bieringer provide a helpful recapitulation of the scope of Jesus' love in the New Testament by exploring the categories in which his love is expressed. They argue that Jesus' just love requires (1) care for human embodiment (meaning care for the body, mind, and spirit), (2) a focus on relationality, (3) awareness of the social location or context of people to whom one ministers, (4) sensitivity to difference and uniqueness among people, and (5) accountable moral agency.[8]

The love of God in the Bible, while total and salvific, is balanced by an equally strong sense of God's judgment of injustice. In the Old Testament, this judgment is expressed in terms of the punishment of the Israelites through exile, conquest, and land loss.[9] In the New Testament, the notion of God's punishment is expressed in terms of an apocalyptic second coming of Christ and the final judgment of humankind.[10] While both testaments thematically focus on love and salvation, both also acknowledge an inherent connection between God's mercy and God's ultimate concern for justice.

The relationship between God's justice and God's mercy poses a philosophical problem. Does God's love cancel out God's justice? Does God's justice cancel out God's love? The problem achieved a particularly clear articulation in the writing of Anselm, bishop of Canterbury in the eleventh century, in his work *Cur Deus Homo* (*Why God Became Man*). This work, which defined for centuries Christian thinking about

---

6. Mary Elsbernd and Reimund Bieringer, *When Love Is Not Enough: A Theo-Ethic of Justice* (Collegeville, MN: Liturgical Press, 2002), 43.

7. For a review of charity in the New Testament, consult chapter 3.

8. Elsbernd and Bieringer, *When Love Is Not Enough*, 63–72.

9. For example, in the prophet Micah the Lord cries out to the Israelites, condemning them for violence, false speech, criminal hoarding, and rigging their balances so as to overcharge in the marketplace (6:9–11). For these injustices, we read, "Rather I will begin to strike you with devastation because of your sins. You shall sow, yet not reap, tread out the olive, yet pour no oil, and the grapes, yet drink no wine. You shall eat, without being satisfied, food that will leave you empty; what you acquire, you cannot save; what you do save, I will deliver up to the sword. . . . I will deliver you up to ruin, and your citizens to derision; and you shall bear the reproach of the nations" (6:13–16).

10. For example, Matthew 23 describes the injustice and hypocrisies of the scribes and the Pharisees. Matthew 24 follows with Jesus foretelling the destruction of the Temple and the great calamities that will mark the coming of the Son of Man to bring judgment upon the nations for their crimes. "Amen, I say to you, there will not be left here a stone upon another stone that will not be thrown down" (24:2).

how Jesus' death on the cross saves humanity, is helpful in understanding the tension between God's justice and mercy.

Anselm reasoned that on the one hand, if God is merciful, then God would desire to realize peace, happiness, forgiveness, and reconciliation with all of creation. Even in the face of sin and error, God would overlook all insults to the divine will and issue a pardon to all of creation so as to have the full harmony with creation that was God's original intent. If God is all powerful, then forgiveness of error should not be beyond the scope of God's action.

However, if God is just, Anselm reasoned, then God must provide some measure of reward and punishment for human behavior. Some people live meritorious lives of service and uprightness while others are advantage-seeking, injurious, and wicked. To treat both sets of individuals alike would be unfair, and to overlook wickedness altogether by treating bad behaviors as if they were good would be to condone wickedness. Such a course would itself be unjust, and as such, could not be possible to God; God's goodness cannot be arbitrary, such that it is totally opposite of what we deem good. Rather, God's goodness must be the standard and measure of all that we consider good. Therefore, God's justice, as an application of the standards of goodness, is not arbitrary but necessary to God. As a result, God's requirement for justice seems to conflict with God's desire for mercy. Since two contradictory things cannot be simultaneously maintained, a philosophical dilemma arises.

Anselm attempted to solve this problem by reflecting on the saving work of Jesus on the cross. To understand Anselm's argument, we need to understand his thinking on how one determines the seriousness of a crime. For Anselm, sin is measured not simply by the seriousness of the crime committed. (Some crimes are more serious than others—murder is a worse crime than stealing a pack of gum.) Rather, sin is also measured by the status of the person against whom the crime or offense has been committed. To Anselm it would be more serious to tell a lie to one's parents than to one's brother or sister. It is more serious to write graffiti on the principal's office than on the locker of a classmate. By this line of reasoning, any offense against God, no matter what, is infinitely serious because God is infinite; no one enjoys a higher station than God.

For this reason, Anselm argues, human beings are in trouble! We have committed a crime of infinite significance through sin (any and every sin, from the very first act of disobedience through the sins we commit today), and as finite creatures, we are totally unable to rectify the situation. The only one who could pay back for such a crime would be someone who was also infinite, namely God. The problem is that God is not the one who "owes" for the offense of human sins; humans are. Thus we are in a real quandary because we owe something that we will never be able to pay.[11] Anselm concludes that human beings are at last saved by Jesus, who as both God and man is able to repay humanity's debt through the free offering of his life on the cross.

Anselm sheds light on the logical tension between God's mercy and God's justice. It would be unjust for God to treat everyone the same, especially if that meant rewarding the immoral behaviors of the wicked. If God's goodness is

---

11. Anselm solves this problem by arguing that Jesus, as God, has the infinite capacity to make up for humanity's sin and, as man, he is obligated to make up for humanity's sin. The equal and coexisting divine and human natures in Jesus, for Anselm, are the solution to the problem of God's justice reconciling with God's mercy. Because God cannot simply overlook injustice, God in God's mercy creates the solution through Jesus' Incarnation and crucifixion to grace human beings with forgiveness while meting out God's demand for justice. Jesus, as the mediator for human beings, takes on punishment for sin and, through his total obedience to the will of God, overcomes sin.

THE TENSION BETWEEN MERCY AND JUSTICE

Consider your own experience of the tension between mercy and justice. We all cringe at stories of murder, rape, abduction, and other crimes that go unpunished. We rebel when we learn of people losing their retirements and pensions from companies whose executives continue to earn record-high bonuses and salaries. We revolt inside at such injustice not merely because we want vengeance but because it is manifestly wrong for someone to get away with such acts and to think he was entitled to violate another person.

Why do we generally feel that it is important that people acknowledge their wrongdoing, and perhaps make some amends, before we can comfortably receive them back into regular company? If wrongs go unpunished and unacknowledged, why do we feel deeply unsatisfied? Why do we typically desire recompense for evil, if not in this life then in some ultimate form of justice? If we seek genuine conversion and correction on the part of those who commit wrongs, not because we like to see their sorrow, but because only in true repentance can genuine restitution begin, then we are responding to the tension between a desire for mercy and a requirement for justice.

anything other than totally arbitrary, then God's justice must somehow reward and punish fairly.

The point of considering the relationship between mercy and justice here is to show that these twin aspects of love cannot be separated, according to Christian theology. Within the context of marriage and family life, mercy (or forgiveness) and justice are central to authentic love. Both the biblical and theological traditions insist that genuine love, the kind that reflects divine love, cannot exist apart from justice.

Consider what it means to love a child. Love involves discipline and guidance, sometimes punishment and reward. Generally, we do not involve ourselves in the behaviors of other people's children whom we do not know. We refrain from doing so because it would exceed the boundaries of responsibility and good judgment to discipline other people's children. Our own children, however, we must manage a great deal because their future success as human beings depends upon proper rearing and guidance. To love means to be willing to provide discipline, structure, and even punishment, balancing mercy with justice for the good of the child.

Because Christians believe that the life of Jesus effects some transformation in human beings, the fear of God's boundless wrath can be replaced by the trust in God's desire for reconciliation. However, this reconciliation is not possible so long as human beings willfully remain in an openly hostile refusal to love and be loved by God. Only through the human pursuit of justice and reconciliation among ourselves do we love one another and God. From a theological point of view, then, the divine love of justice is central to an understanding of who God is and how God operates in the life of Jesus.

CONSIDERATIONS ON MARRIAGE AND (IN)JUSTICE

Justice is central to our understanding God's love; therefore it should be at the forefront of our minds when we consider such concepts as covenant, charity, sacraments, and human dignity. Bearing in mind how important justice is from a theological perspective in general, it is only appropriate to explore more fully how justice intersects with marriage and family life. We might assume that, based on our previous discussions, justice would be a primary aim of marriage and family life. But if we address the question from a historical point of view, we find that genuine justice has often been absent from family life.

In previous chapters, we looked at marriage in its historical development. One dimension of marriage that emerges prominently from any historical analysis is its thoroughly patriarchal character throughout most of Western history.[12] The patriarchal family structure, seen from the biblical era throughout most of the twentieth century, has historically distorted relationships within the family in ways that run contrary to the full human dignity of men, women, and children. Although certainly not all patriarchal marriages were or are loveless, they nevertheless represent a relationship of imbalanced power and access that overwhelmingly favored and continues to favor men. Because the patriarchal structure of the family has historically reflected a broader patriarchal structure in both church and society, women have found little recourse in dealing with their diminished personal power and status.

One might here argue that a Christian should not care too much about power and status, as service and self-gift are the principle moral requirements laid out by Jesus. It is useful here to remember, however, that service and self-gift, if they are not to be exploitative, must be voluntary. To the extent that women have historically had no choice in the matter of their status, diminished social access within family, church, and society becomes a state of forced oppression. In concrete terms, this state has provided women few legal protections from abuse, rape, and arbitrary divorce, while it simultaneously has established harsh penalties for real or imagined crimes against male spouses. It has denied women legal, civic, and religious status, which has restricted their ability to do such things as initiate divorce, own property, or earn and retain personal income. Women have had to endure polygamy and concubinage, while being required to meet the highest standards of chastity and sexual exclusivity and to suffer the harshest penalties at real or perceived failures to meet these standards.

Women's historically diminished status in marriage (and church and society) has had a corollary in the distortion of men's roles in relationship to women and children. Men have been responsible for the external and public dimensions of family life, which has forced a sense of competition, financial responsibility, and emotional distance from intimate relationships. In particular, while women have typically been in a position to foster intimate relationships with their children, men have had historically fewer opportunities for intimacy and involvement in their children's lives. Much as women have lacked full access to participation in social spheres beyond the home, men have lacked full participation within that same home. This reality is humanly distorting for both women and men.[13]

---

12. For a review of patriarchal marriage structures, see chapters 4 and 6.

13. Christine Gudorf makes this argument in her article "Western Religion and the Patriarchal Family," in *Perspectives on Marriage: A Reader,* 2nd ed., eds. Kieran Scott and Michael Warren (New York: Oxford University Press, 2000), 285–304. Also, consider J. Michael Clark, "Faludi, Fight Club, and Phallic Masculinity: Exploring the Emasculating Economics of Patriarchy," in *The Journal of Men's Studies* 11, no. 1 (September 22, 2002): 65–77, and Susan Faludi, *Stiffed: The Betrayal of the American Man* (New York: HarperCollins, 2000).

Along with their parents, children have also experienced distortion in the patriarchal family structure in the way they come to perceive their own gender roles, especially with respect to power and authority. The male represents ultimate power, a stereotype boys learn to emulate and girls to fear. The female represents warmth and nurture, which over time becomes alien to males and overly defining for females. Neither boys nor girls experience balanced power and relational dynamics with either parent. This experience ultimately skews the adult child's future self-concept and relationship potential.[14]

The distortion of all parties wrought by the patriarchal family structure and reinforced by church and society has undermined the possibility of true covenant, charity, sacrament, and dignity within marriage. I would argue this is the case primarily because the humanity of both men and women has been caricatured by the forced expectations and limitations of the roles assigned to men and women within marriage.[15] The image of God in human beings becomes distorted. When the image of God within the human is marred, so too are the conditions of just, covenantal love to which Christians are called. The result is the grave potential for violations of the marriage covenant, that is, marital injustice. While this injustice takes many forms, domestic violence is among the most painful examples of how unjust and unchecked structures within marriage can go terribly awry.

Within the patriarchal structures of church, society, and family, women have historically lacked the right to vote, own property, earn an income, sue, initiate divorce, retain custody of children in the case of divorce, or seek legal action against their spouses for physical abuse. In fact, the legal coverage of a woman's identity by her husband (including the custom of a woman's taking on her husband's name), called *coverture*,[16] ensured that the husband, who would be held responsible for his wife's actions, was entitled to chastise her. The right of chastisement meant that husbands had the legal right to physically reprimand their wives. This practice of English law carried over into colonial America and was recognized and supported by both law courts and Christian churches throughout the end of the nineteenth century.[17] The impact can be seen in such measures as the "rule of thumb," which attempted to restrict the amount of damage a man could do to his wife by limiting to a thumb's width the size of the object with which a husband could beat his wife. Such measures were not meant to end wife-beating but to limit the damage done by it.[18]

The very real mortal danger that women faced in marriages, even Christian marriages, throughout most of history came to be radically challenged in the nineteenth century in the United States by the women reformers, more commonly known for their work to win women's

---

14. Gudorf also describes these impacts on children in her discussion of patriarchal marriage.

15. Here gender analysis studies are of the utmost importance, as they explore the issues surrounding biological propensities and sociological formation of men and women in the construction of gender. This chapter cannot take up this question, but a helpful resource in this regard is Michelle Lazar, *Feminist Critical Discourse Analysis: Gender, Power, and Ideology* (Basingstoke, UK and New York: Palgrave Macmillan, 2008).

16. Harvard Business School makes available an online publication called *Women, Enterprise, & Society*, which provides online texts pertaining to women and the law. For documents on nineteenth century American coverture practice, consult *http://www.library.hbs.edu/hc/wes/collections/women_law/marriage_coverture/*.

17. William G. Bailey, *The Encyclopedia of Police Science*, 2nd ed. (New York: Garland, 1995), 225.

18. For a fuller account of women's historical experience of domestic violence as captured here, see Gloria Durka's article "Domestic Violence: The Long Sad Silence," in *Perspectives on Marriage: A Reader*, eds. Kieran Scott and Michael Warren, 2nd ed. (New York: Oxford University Press, 2000), 254–63.

suffrage and to abolish slavery. The efforts of reformers such as Susan B. Anthony and Elizabeth Cady Stanton proved victorious through the passage of the 19th amendment in 1920, which gave women legal enfranchisement. However, it is chilling to remember that this change in women's legal status is not even one century removed from our present-day experience. What is more, although women now enjoy, within an American context, greater constitutional freedom, statistics reveal that women remain vulnerable to their intimate partners and are frequent victims of physical abuse in marriage. A sampling of statistics from the United States Department of Justice's Bureau of Justice Statistics on reported incidents of domestic violence from 2001–2005 is staggering:[19]

- Of female victims of homicide, 30.1 percent were killed by an intimate; 11.7 percent were killed by another family member. Of male victims of homicide, 5.3 percent were killed by an intimate and 6.7 percent by another family member.

- Women between the ages of 20–24 were at the highest risk of all non-fatal intimate partner violence.

- Married women separated from their spouses were at the highest risk of intimate partner violence in a comparison of married, divorced, and widowed women.

- Most intimate partner violence occurs between spouses as opposed to between boyfriends and girlfriends.

- While females in every income level are at greater risk of intimate partner violence than males, females in households with lower annual incomes experienced the highest annual rates of domestic violence incidents.

- Female victim households with children were slightly over 17 percent more likely to experience intimate partner violence than male victim households with children.

- Female victim households are five times more prevalent than male victim households.

- One third of all female murder victims are killed by an intimate compared with 3 percent of male murder victims. The percentage of females killed by an intimate is increasing, while the percentage of males killed by an intimate is decreasing.

- Girlfriends are more likely to be killed by an intimate than any other group of intimates.

Statistically, then, women are still very vulnerable within marriage and intimate relationships. Lenient state laws or insufficient resources[20] concerning the punishment of batterers and sexual offenders are vestigial reminders of the previous centuries' outright condoning of the marital chastisement of women and the regarding of women's bodies, especially their sexuality, as male property. When we realize how vulnerable women are to intimate partner violence, we can begin to understand that violence against women is a pervasive legacy of patriarchal culture, including the patriarchal culture of family and church. That culture continues to devalue and demean women's bodies and persons even while it relies upon women for its continued existence.[21]

---

19. *http://www.ojp/usdoj.gov/bjs/intimate/victims.*

20. The National Coalition Against Domestic Violence provides online information on domestic violence statistics, laws, and support resources on a state-by-state basis at *www.ncadv.org.*

21. See also Lenore Walker, "The Battered Woman: Myths and Reality," in *Perspectives on Marriage: A Reader*, eds. Kieran Scott and Michael Warren, 3rd ed. (Oxford and New York: Oxford University Press, 2007), 276–92, for a careful look at common misperceptions and truths regarding the reality of domestic violence.

The prevalence of domestic violence merits our attention, but there are other forms of injustice within marriage and family life that we might also note:

- Adultery and abandonment
- Child abuse
- Sexual assault of spouse or children
- Elder abuse
- Verbal battery
- Abuse or separation of a spouse from finances, material property, or information and access to shared assets
- Refusal to bear or sire children
- Excessive expectations for reproduction of children
- Neglect in physical or mental sickness or end-of-life care

All forms of marital and family injustice stem from fundamental failures to recognize one's marriage as a covenant, based on charity, intended to be a state of grace, to be lived out in respect for the dignity of one another. These failures result both from a corresponding failure of individual conversion to proper characters within marriage and from social failures to dismantle power inequities that contribute to injustice. From a Christian perspective, one of the great tragedies of marital injustice is that churches have not historically taken a counter-cultural posture against prejudicial thought and action against women in any sphere, including their own. As such, a constructive response is needed that can delineate for family, church, and society at least minimum conditions for justice in sexuality and marriage. In the absence of such conditions, Christians reveal a deep blindness to the relationship between God's mercy and God's love. For love that does not strive toward justice is not love at all.

CONDITIONS FOR JUSTICE IN SEXUALITY AND MARRIAGE

Margaret Farley's work *A Framework for Christian Sexual Ethics*[22] attempts to provide a framework for thinking about the conditions for justice within sexual and marital relationships. She is careful to note, along with other marriage commentators such as Rosemary Radford Ruether and Nancy Cotts, that any discussion of marriage cannot today responsibly presume a particular family structure as normative, nor can it resolve every issue pertaining to marriage and family justice. There are many types of families, including single-parent households, multigenerational households, ethnically and religiously mixed households, adoptive households, foster households, intensive care-giving households, intact families separated by great geographical distances, and divorced and remarried households. To these models, moreover, can be added households with cohabitants and children, non-kin living cooperatives, and same-sex partners with or without children, all of whom may also describe themselves as families. Contemporary family structures, then, exceed the nuclear family model of mother, father, and biological offspring.

Having thus qualified "family," Farley suggests certain parameters outside of which conditions for justice in love are dangerously lacking. In terms of norms for justice in sexual relationships, Farley argues that couples must experience the minimum conditions of no unjust harm, free consent of partners, mutuality, equality, commitment, fruitfulness, and social justice. These norms are based on the following principles:

---

22. Margaret Farley, *A Framework for Christian Sexual Ethics* (New York and London: Continuum, 2006).

Respect for the autonomy and relationality that characterize persons as ends in themselves, and hence respect for their well-being

Respect for autonomy

Respect for relationality

Respect for persons as sexual beings in society[23]

One should note that these characteristics of just sexual love do not specify a context of marriage. For this discussion, Farley reviews classically held conditions for just love within marriage. These have historically been monogamy, sexual exclusivity, and permanence. She argues that while these conditions are necessary as a social framework for just love within marriage, they are insufficient; other qualities are needed in order to protect spouses from abusive and exploitative relationships. Monogamy, sexual exclusivity, and permanence can become conditions for justice when they are further conditioned by free choice,

mutuality, equality, commitment, fruitfulness, and responsibility to the wider world.[24] We might add further insights from the broader dialogue on the ethics of just love. Elsbernd's and Bieringer's emphases on participation, hospitality, and a respect for difference also provide direction for thinking about how one should articulate the attitudes and values that most richly contribute to justice within marriage.

When guided by these thoughtful conditions, Christianity provides abundant resources for correcting injustice within marriage as well as guiding its just expressions. We noted at the beginning of this chapter that divine justice is an aspect of divine love. In the context of marriage, we see well how divine justice must be a part of love. At the very minimum, we might ask what could the mandate to love one another in active charity mean if it does not at least involve a total rejection of physical violation of human bodies. What could a covenant of intimate communion of persons mean if not, at the very minimum, preservation of each other's bodies? What could recognition of the dignity of the human person mean if not respect for the dignity of one's physical person first and foremost? The implications of physical care are self-evident if genuine covenant, charity, and dignity are genuinely sought.

Despite some of its historical shortcomings regarding the status of women,[25] the Catholic Church in particular upholds the dignity of human bodies and the dignity of sexuality in a way that is absolutely

THINK ABOUT IT

Farley suggests several criteria for justice in sexual relationships as well as justice in marriage. Do you agree with these criteria? Are they sufficient? Would you add more to the list or refine it in any way? To put it another way, what minimal conditions do you see as necessary for justice in intimate relationships?

---

23. Ibid., 231.

24. Ibid., 265.

25. For instance, some would argue that the Church assigns questionable value to the dignity of a woman's body relative to the dignity of a child in the womb. Some contend that Catholic teaching accords dignity to the fetus disproportionate to the value accorded a woman's health, a woman's dignity in the face of rape or abuse, and the many economic, social, and other issues that factor into the dignity with which a woman can raise a child. The debate over proportionality and abortion is helpfully explored in Vincent Genovesi, "The Principle of Proportionality," in *In Pursuit of Love: Catholic Morality and Human Sexuality*, 2nd ed. (Collegeville, MN: Liturgical Press, 1996), 374–95.

uncompromising in its teleological vision. Stemming from this vision, the principles of charity, covenant, sacrament, and dignity remain prophetic concepts in the Catholic (and indeed the whole Christian) treasury, waiting for the day in which they will be fully understood and realized. These concepts call everyone, and especially spouses, to a reform that realizes in human relationships authentic, nonviolent, and just communion of persons. Patriarchal culture, incidences of abuse, and marital injustice of whatever kind are incompatible with divine justice. While God's mercy invites us to conversion, God's justice demands it. Justice and mercy, twin aspects of God's love, move us toward correction of injustice and help us to shape better patterns of human community.

WHEN DOMESTIC VIOLENCE OCCURS

What should a person do in a situation of domestic violence? The National Domestic Violence Hotline provides extensive resources for understanding abuse and seeking help. Among the active steps it cites, the hotline recommends that a person suffering abuse and preparing to leave an abusive situation should:

1. Request a police escort
2. Plan for a quick escape
3. Set aside emergency money
4. Set aside an extra set of car keys
5. Pack clothing for oneself and one's children
6. Collect and bring with oneself important documents, medications, credit cards, and telephone numbers
7. Plan for a false trail at least six hours away from the intended place of relocation

From the National Domestic Violence Hotline, *http://www.ndvh.org*.

APPLICATION TO FAMILY AND MARRIAGE TODAY

All injustice within family life must be rejected. Abuse—whether of children, a male spouse, a female spouse, an elderly relative, or a family pet—is intolerable and incompatible with the principles of covenant, charity, sacrament, and human dignity. No human can or should assume the right to inflict harm on the body of another for the alleged aim of the other's moral correction or improvement. Such a corrective measure is spurious at best, but even if a case could be made that it is a divine prerogative to use such measures, no such case can be made that a corresponding human prerogative exists.

Any argument that would condone marital or family violence as redemptive or tolerable flies in the face of the spirit of Christian faith. Within contemporary family life, it is again necessary to remember that what people make of marriages is a matter of choice. Christian marriage is not a guarantee against sexual, physical, or emotional abuse, nor is Christian marriage a justification to tolerate sexual, physical, or emotional abuse. Many people cite their religious faith as a primary reason to endure violence, arguing that their tradition does not permit divorce, that they feel responsible for their partner's salvation, or that suffering is noble. We must remember that it is precisely the violation of persons that Jesus' work sought to redress, and the healing of bodies became the mechanism Jesus used to heal spirits. Abuse is not divinely ordered for any human being. Physical, bodily safety is the primary concern of justice in marriage. Spiritual, moral, and existential concerns must be addressed only after safety and cessation of abuse have been achieved.

Christians committed to covenant, charity, sacramentality, and dignity should talk openly about and attempt to live the principles of a just foundation in marriage. They should reflect openly in dialogue about the way in which justice is both present and absent within their families. Where justice is present, it should be nurtured. Where justice is lacking, genuine conversion is requisite. Only then can one's commitment to covenant, charity, sacramentality, and dignity in the character of individual persons and their relationships within the family begin to be realized.

Questions for Review and Discussion

1. Describe how God's love and God's justice are related in the Bible.

2. What is the philosophical tension between God's love and justice? How does Anselm try to solve this tension?

3. What contemporary examples can you think of that reveal a tension even within yourself over the competing values of justice and mercy?

4. How has the patriarchal structure of the family distorted the relationship between men and women in marriage? How has this distortion contributed to the possibility of domestic violence, especially against women?

5. Beyond domestic violence, what other forms of marital or family injustice come to mind for you?

6. Recount and explain Farley's suggestions for parameters for thinking about marital and sexual justice. Would you consider any other conditions necessary for just love?

7. Do you think modern-day marriage structures are more or less just than in the past? How might marriages become more just?

8. What external influences contribute to the presence or lack of justice within marriages today?

Resources for Further Reading

Resources for Just Love

Mary Elsbernd and Reimund Bieringer, *When Love Is Not Enough: A Theo-Ethic of Justice* (Collegeville, MN: Liturgical Press, 2002).

Kenneth Himes, OFM, ed., *Modern Catholic Social Teaching: Commentaries and Interpretations* (Washington: Georgetown University Press, 2005).

Thomas Schubeck, *Love That Does Justice* (Maryknoll, NY: Orbis 2007).

Resources for Justice in Marriage

Raquel Kennedy Bergen, ed., *Issues in Intimate Violence* (Thousand Oaks, CA: Sage Publications, 1998).

Albert Cardarelli, ed., *Violence Between Intimate Partners: Patterns, Causes, and Effects* (Boston: Allyn and Becon, 1997).

Emmanuel Clapsis, ed., *Violence and Christian Spirituality: An Ecumenical Conversation* (Brookline, MA: Holy Cross Orthodox Press, 2007).

Helen Conway, *Domestic Violence and the Church* (Carlisle: Paternoster Press, 1998).

Anne Weatherholt, *Breaking the Silence: The Church Responds to Domestic Violence* (Harrisburg, PA: Morehouse Publishing 2008).

CHAPTER 10

DOMESTIC CHURCH

In the previous chapter, we considered the theme of justice within marriage. Here we consider the theme of justice between the family unit and the greater society to which it belongs. Justice issues pertain not only to the relationships between husbands, wives, and their children but also to the relationships between families and society as a whole. On the one hand, society has an obligation to create just structures so that family life can flourish. On the other hand, the family has an obligation to participate within society *as a family* to ensure justice for others outside of itself.

We have seen how justice within marriage can be distorted. By the same token, justice issues between the family and society are also vulnerable to distortion. In particular, charity in marriage often leads to an idolization of the family. Because of the deep attachment people feel to their spouse, children, and parents, it is possible to privilege familial relationships above all others, forgetting that as individuals and as members of families we have responsibilities to serve others outside of the family.

A Christian theological perspective on family and marriage recognizes that loving service must extend beyond one's family members and reach out toward others in the world around us. As a vocation, marriage and family life are intended to strengthen people for this outreach, just as they are intended to strengthen people internally and intimately. The New Testament record of Jesus and the early Christians reflects this attitude that Christians must serve the community. This requirement is not limited to celibate Christians or Christians without family obligations, but rather falls to all Christians, including Christians with families.

The requirement to serve the community has been addressed through the Christian commitment to social justice, which is today one of the great strengths of the Roman Catholic Church. The Church has argued eloquently that families have a special charge and obligation to act as domestic churches toward the end of serving the community in their unique capacity as families. In this chapter we consider what it means to call the family a *domestic church*. What are the cultural obstacles to viewing the family this way? What is the Roman Catholic Church's social teaching and its teaching on domestic church? How might this teaching be applied to contemporary family life?

TOOLS

Two key obstacles to social justice are individualism and consumerism. With respect to the first, the twenty-first century American context may be characterized by many descriptors, but few will disagree that one of them is individualism.[1] Our culture is fixated on meeting individual, personal needs and wishes. In previous eras, individuals saw themselves as belonging to families and communities. Although individuals have presumably always had personal wishes, desires, talents, and interests, historically people recognized that personal desires often needed to be subordinated to the good of families and communities. Indeed, this sort of mentality underlay arranged marriages. Whether an arranged marriage reflected personal desire or not, people yielded to the needs of their families and communities because it was through the common strength of families and communities that individuals might prosper in good times and survive in bad.[2]

While today people may benefit from a higher valuation of individual needs and interests, family and community reliance are as important as ever. Anyone who has experienced a personal disaster, such as a house fire, or a natural disaster, such as a flood, will attest to the role that family and community play in helping us over such hurdles.[3] However, modern lifestyles and contemporary technologies have gone a long way to making individuals and individual family units much more independent from one another than in previous eras. Several decades ago in Western European and American contexts, the large, multigenerational household was replaced by the smaller, nuclear family. Even now, the nuclear model of family is considered normative and other forms of family organization are seen as deviant. In the nuclear family model, often adult children, parents, grandparents, and extended kin live great distances from one another. People are more isolated from neighbors, and families generally keep more to themselves.[4]

Underlying these changes is a sense of personal, individual importance. Modern lifestyles enable us to explore a range of options for our lives, but often personal preferences undermine a sense of belonging, commitment, duty, and responsibility to society. A basic tension exists between the individual's sense of opportunity and

---

1. For a scholarly treatment of individualism as a predominant theme of Western ideology, consult Louis Dumont, *Essays on Individualism: Modern Ideologies in Anthropological Perspective* (Chicago: University of Chicago Press, 1992).

2. For example, Mary Elsbernd and Reimund Bieringer note, "Given the lived situation of the Hebrew people some three thousand years ago, the survival of individuals depended on the survival of the community. The just community structured around patterns of right relationships meant life for all its members." *When Love Is Not Enough: A Theo-Ethic of Justice* (Collegeville, MN: Liturgical Press, 2002), 42.

3. Conversely, the community at large bears a large share of blame for failing to prepare New Orleans for Hurricane Katrina in 2005. Now the community needs to help displaced victims to recover their lives, property, and livelihood. Interventions at every level from the family to the federal government have been crucial to meeting at least the minimal needs of those affected by this natural (and human) disaster.

4. Stephanie Coontz explores the decade from roughly 1950–1960 in the United States and Western Europe, in which the modern nuclear family emerged as the normative model of family organization to the exclusion of all others. Anyone who did not conform to this family model, which implicitly assumed a love-based match headed by a male breadwinner, was considered deeply troubled. Coontz investigates the history and mythology of this "traditional" family structure in her chapter "The Era of Ozzie and Harriet: The Long Decade of 'Traditional' Marriage," in *Marriage: A History* (New York: Viking Press, 2005), 229–46.

desire and the individual's obligation to others. The Second Vatican Council's *Pastoral Constitution on the Church in the Modern World* captures well this tension in its statement on humanity's deeper questions:

> The dichotomy affecting the modern world is, in fact, a symptom of the deeper dichotomy that is rooted in humanity itself. It is the meeting point of many conflicting forces. As created beings, people are subject to many limitations, but they feel unlimited in their desires and their sense of being destined for a higher life. They feel the pull of many attractions and are compelled to choose between them and reject some among them. Worse still, feeble and sinful as they are, they often do the very thing they hate and do not do what they want. And so they feel themselves divided, and the result is a host of discords in social life.[5]

The tensions of individualism are felt keenly in marriage and family life, which is affected somewhat ironically in two related but competing ways. On the one hand, we look to marriage as the place where we ought to find personal satisfaction. We seek from marriage happiness and fulfillment ranging from the home we live in, to the vacations we take, to the gifts we receive, to sexual satisfaction. Whereas people formerly brought a sense of duty, role fulfillment, and personal responsibility *to* marriage, people now seek to derive pleasure and personal satisfaction *from* family life.

On the other hand, singular focus on marriage and family life as a *thing* that ought to do or accomplish something *for us* individually can lead to great disappointment when the expectations are too great. When marriages fail to meet a desired sense of personal growth and happiness, people may simply walk away from them. This mixture of a lack of personal accountability and extraordinarily high expectations reveals a deep desire to be served rather than to serve. Peter Marin speaks eloquently to this reality in the following passage:

> What I hear, everywhere around me, are complaints, descriptions of unmet demands, disappointments—that someone has failed them, let them down, is not what they ought to be. This is the strain that runs through much that I have heard as a therapist, teacher, or friend when men and women talk about one another (though men are less articulate, feel less justified than women in their public complaints). Many of these complaints are accurate, of course—we do fail one another. But their accuracy cannot hide the fact that the expectations have less to do with the world as it is or people as they are than with mistaken, preconceived, borrowed or inherited notions about what men and women ought to be or can be. The tone of all this is not merely one of sadness or unanswered yearning; more often than not it is a tone of judgment, impatience, even contempt. It is as if every lover is also an enemy, as if every companion is less an invited guest than an unwanted intruder.[6]

Within the context of marriage, this state is in essence what we mean by the term *individualism*.

Coupled with a generally individualistic attitude within our culture is a comparably widespread *consumerist* mentality.[7] Not only do we seek out satisfaction in material possessions but we also feel a sense of entitlement to

---

5. *Gaudium et Spes*, §10. Used by permission.

6. Peter Marin, "A Revolution's Broken Promises," in *Perspectives on Marriage: A Reader*, eds. Kieran Scott and Michael Warren, 3rd ed. (New York and Oxford: Oxford University Press, 2007), 174.

7. For a lucid discussion of the corrupting and, if left unchecked, ultimately devastating effects of consumerism consult Benjamin Barber's *Consumed: How Markets Corrupt Children, Infantilize Adults, and Swallow Citizens Whole* (New York and London: W. W. Norton & Company, 2007).

our satisfaction by what we consume. After all, the customer is always right. As a customer, one expects a certain level of service. If I do not receive what I want in the fashion I want, I can take my business elsewhere. Among the various dimensions of life that are affected by this attitude, personal relationships are among the most marred by it.

Consider how consumerism works within the wedding industry, as couples seek to buy a wedding rather than to prepare for a marriage. In the past several decades, an entire industry has sprung up around weddings. Couples spend months and even years laboriously deciding what flowers to have, what veil to wear, what cake to serve, what party favors to present, what video and photographic artifacts to create, and so on. Shockingly, the average wedding cost in 2005 was $26,327.[8]

Weddings, of course, are joyous events that are not to be disparaged. However, it is worth considering how the sheer investment of hours that a couple will put into their wedding plans greatly exceeds the hours a couple will invest in actual marriage preparation with a counselor or pastor. The former can only be judged in months, while the latter is usually accomplished (often begrudgingly) in an afternoon or weekend at most.[9]

The wedding industry promotes the illusion that happiness in a relationship can be purchased by creating a fairy tale wedding that brings to life every dream for romance, love, and commitment. Much is invested in the details of the wedding, while too often little is invested in preparation for the marriage. To the great demise of marital stability, the consumerist attitude toward marriage radically under-prepares one for the reality of married life and, fueled by individualism, results all too often in divorce.[10] In her spirited text *The Meaning of Wife*, Anne Kingston comments on the impact consumerism has on weddings and marriage:

> If the modern wife is an enigma, the modern bride is a no-brainer. She's pure fairy tale, transmitting hope, purity, and primal desire. Within the marketplace, her ephemeral status only ramps up her appeal: with a shelf life of less than a day, she's ever fresh. Becoming a one-day bride, rather than a lifetime wife, is presented by marketers as the ultimate female fantasy, yet another one-size-fits-all fiction. . . . Most often the bride is featured in serene isolation, implying that the ideal wedding tableau is a solo female fantasy. This too is useful from an advertising perspective. The bride alone, no groom in sight, communicates a flawless ideal separate from the messy, complicated, often prosaic reality of marriage. A self-satisfied solo bride spooning ice cream into her mouth appeared in a print ad for Haagen-Dazs that ran in 2001. "They can start without you," reads the copy. The pitch is brilliant, combining the seductive appeal of the bride with the luscious dairy fat substituting for the groom. It's a telling snapshot of the romantic perception of contemporary marriage—an institution that promises intimacy and total self-indulgence.[11]

---

8. Grace Wong, "Ka-ching: Wedding Price Tag Nears 30K," CNN Money.com, at *http://money.cnn.com/2005/05/20/pf/weddings/* (accessed July 17, 2009).

9. As an example, the Roman Catholic Church requires a period of time, usually no shorter than six months prior to the wedding, during which time a couple makes wedding preparations with a priest. The formal pre-marital counseling is called "Pre-Cana," at which a couple will meet with group leaders to discuss matters such as intimacy, finances, substance use, spirituality, and so on. The content is covered in a number of hours, which are completed over a weekend, an afternoon, or in several weekly sessions.

10. Stephen Post's discussion on individualism and divorce is helpful here in *More Lasting Unions: Christianity, the Family, and Society* (Grand Rapids: Eerdmans, 2000), 18. See also Barbara Dafoe Whitehead, *The Divorce Culture: Rethinking Our Commitments to Marriage and Family* (New York: Vintage Press, 1996).

11. Anne Kingston, *The Meaning of Wife* (New York: Farrar, Strauss and Giroux, 2004), 27–28.

THE PUSH TO CONSUME

Describe your own experiences and observations of consumerism. How are you personally affected by the push to consume? How do you think society is affected by consumerism? In what ways do you think marriages and families might be affected by consumerism? In your responses, consider such aspects as personal debt, conflict over what to consume and when to consume it, environmental impact of consumption, and governmental impact of consumption. Do you consider consumerism to be a spiritual or religious concern as well as a family and marital concern? Why or why not?

Consumerism impacts not only how contemporary people are trained to view marriage but also how we behave within marriage. People continue to build happiness, or at least the illusion of happiness, by acquisition. We work for things: homes, cars, appliances, vacations, toys, jewelry. Many of the things we work for are necessary, but many are not. The debate over which things to acquire and when to acquire them often leads couples into financial struggles, and these are compounded when both marriage partners seek their own desires instead of what is good for or needed most by the family as a whole. When couples are preoccupied negotiating acquisitions and expenditures, the family's responsibility to those outside the family unit becomes a luxury of time and money that few can afford.

CASE STUDY: *THE GODFATHER*

A brief reflection on a popular movie will help to clarify our discussion, if perhaps by its exaggeration. In the classic movie *The Godfather* by Francis Ford Coppola (1972), the audience watches the transformation of a young man who initially rejects a life of crime but eventually embraces it. The character, Michael Corleone (Al Pacino), is an army man, whom we see at the start of the film on a visit to his home for the occasion of his sister's wedding. His girlfriend is astounded by the lavish wedding, and Michael explains to her that it is financed by the criminal endeavors of his father. When Michael's father falls victim to a shooting, Michael deems no one in his father's entourage strong enough to protect his father or avenge him, and takes up arms for the sake of his dad. He kills the men who are trying to kill his father, and, because he was prompted to do so by love, feels justified in his actions.

This points Michael down a criminal path, and in this life he is very successful. Eventually he marries and has children, whom he loves deeply. He continues in a life of crime, which has become his business, not out of love of money or murderous rage but out of love for his family. Of course the criminal lifestyle eventually tears his family apart, which pains Michael at the core of his being because he feels that whatever he has done, he has done for the love and care of his wife and children. In fact, his dream is ultimately to legitimize the family businesses so as to bring the family full circle into affluent society. The irony of the film is that Michael loses his family by trying to provide for them in this way. In trying to be a father and a husband through illegitimate means, he loses his family's confidence, trust, and respect. In trying to protect them, he leads them into harm. Had he chosen to be a painter, a small business owner, a merchant, or a city employee, his family might not have had wealth and luxuries but they would have kept their husband and father.

WHAT WENT WRONG?

Though the film exaggerates the human tendency to place immediate family over the good of others, it captures the essence of wrongful idolization of kin. Michael serves his family, but he does not care what happens to others so long as his family is well off. It is easy to make the same mistake, although obviously most of us do not go to the extremes Michael does.

Clearly it is necessary to place one's family's immediate needs foremost in thought and deed much, or even most, of the time. Indeed, it serves the community as a whole if I provide for my family and look after my children, because it means that I am not placing a burden on others for their care.[12] However, there must be a balance between the time and resources I dedicate to my immediate family and the time and resources I dedicate to others, my extended human family.

If my church, for example, is raising money for needy families in my community, and I refuse to give what I can while I spend lavishly on toys for my own children, I have rejected a genuine need of others, which I could have met, instead indulging my own children. Indeed, I have given my children even less by giving them yet another toy, because I have not modeled the charity that would have guided them beyond individualism and consumerism. In order to avoid idolatry, family life must be evaluated in the light of the common good, the family good, and the individual good. These goods, furthermore, must be kept in harmony.

The obstacles of consumerism and individualism press us to rethink the purpose of the Christian family.[13] Family life should be a location for personal satisfaction, happiness, and individual growth. But it must also be a location for service, duty, responsibility, and work. From a Christian theological point of view, family life must make us more aware of the communal nature of human existence and, as a result, more committed to social welfare in all of its needs and dimensions. The challenge is to balance one's commitments to family with one's obligations as human beings to others in the world. Stephen Post summarizes this challenge to the Christian family:

> So how shall we balance love for those who are near and dear with love for strangers? The first sphere of love is the one where our natural sympathies lie. The moral life does not require that we trample on these sympathies. On the contrary, it must build on them. Theology does this by telling the story of familial love writ large under a God whose love is parental toward everyone and who makes us all brothers and sisters in sibling solicitude. To love the stranger is an act of filial love as well. The chief task of ethics and all higher religions is to extend human sympathy and solicitude to the stranger.[14]

CATHOLIC SOCIAL TEACHING

Catholic social teaching is useful in sorting through the competing needs and obligations that all human beings must negotiate. According to Catholic social teaching, human beings ought to be guided in decisions about how to balance competing needs by remembering the two poles that constitute human society.[15] On the one hand, there is the individual human being. Catholic

---

12. This is the distinction made in ethics between personal or special relations and impersonal relations.

13. *Familiaris Consortio*, §17 cites the four basic tasks of the Christian family. These include (1) forming a community of persons, (2) serving life, (3) participating in the development of society, and (4) sharing in the life and mission of the Church.

14. Stephen Post, *Spheres of Love: Toward a New Ethics of the Family* (Dallas: Southern Methodist University Press, 1994), 146.

15. Recall the discussion on human dignity in chapter 7.

theology recognizes that each person is a unique creation of God, made in the divine image and likeness, and destined for eternal fellowship with the holy Trinity. Nothing can be deemed moral or tolerable that interrupts basic human dignity and freedom. In this way Catholic thought upholds without question the importance of the individual in society. At the same time, however, Catholic theology recognizes that individuals are not islands but fundamentally interdependent and interrelated. Human society can only protect the dignity and rights of the individual if it functions to protect *all* human rights and dignity.

The good of society—the common good—is a state of peace and justice in which human life, dignity, and freedom are met across all strata, from the richest to the poorest. It is not limited to a sense of good as the greatest good for the greatest number of people; rather, good refers fundamentally to the creation of conditions of flourishing for the most vulnerable in society. Seven basic principles of Catholic social teaching have been articulated by the United States Conference of Catholic Bishops that help clarify the major concerns of Catholic teaching about the good of individuals in relationship to the good of society.[16]

1. **The dignity and life of every human being.** From the most vulnerable to the most powerful, from the criminal on death row to the genuinely righteous, from a baby in the womb to the aged in a nursing home, the Catholic Church teaches that each individual is inherently dignified and has an inalienable right to his or her life, given by God.

2. **The right of individuals to meaningful participation in family and community life.** It is not enough to recognize the rights of the individual to life. That life must be given proper space to exist within and meaningfully contribute to society, whether through family life or other means.

3. **Rights and responsibilities.** This means, as with the first theme, that the Church clarifies the meaning of human dignity by recognizing that human beings are entitled to at least a minimum quality of life, in which access to food, water, healthcare, clothing, shelter, employment, education, a fair wage, and political participation are possible. Human beings have these rights individually as well as the responsibility to ensure them for others socially.

4. **Dignity of work.** The Church also recognizes that labor is one of the ways in which people are able to participate meaningfully in society. In the absence of dignity of work, people find themselves exploited through inadequate wages, violence, hostile working conditions, and obstacles to unionization. The Church sides with workers in their struggles to secure minimum standards of fairness and safety in the work environment.

5. **Option for the poor.** The Church recognizes that the essence of Jesus' ministry was his care for the socially marginalized and oppressed. Indeed, marginalization and victimization by the state characterizes Jesus' own life, for he died by capital punishment at the hands of the state. Any authentic expression of Christianity will look to the neediest in society to determine how well or poorly they are surviving. In its assessment of social welfare, it will ask with Jesus, "How have you treated the least of my brothers?"

---

16. The following list is excerpted from the USCCB statement, "Themes of Catholic Social Teaching," *www.usccb.org/sdwp/projects/socialteaching/excerpt.shtml* (accessed April 16, 2009). These seven themes are derived from the fuller USCCB document *Sharing Catholic Social Teaching: Challenges and Directions* (2005).

BALANCING NEEDS

Catholic social teaching offers seven basic principles that help to define what the relationship between the individual and society should be. These principles are helpful tools for negotiating the competing interests that sometimes arise between individuals and the community. These competing interests, for example, might be seen in instances when a minority concern is weighed against or factored into public policy that affects the broader community. Such an instance might be the question on the part of a school board over whether to eliminate peanut products from school lunches so as to protect the few students who have severe peanut allergies.

From family life, to local politics, to global concerns, a good society needs to balance individual needs with those of the broader community. What criteria do you think are necessary for balancing individual and social needs? Specifically, what criteria are necessary within the context of marriage to protect individual family members as well as the welfare and stability of the family as a unit? Additionally, what criteria should govern individual family concerns and rights vis-à-vis the society as a whole?

6. **Solidarity.** This commitment means that the Church not only sees the poorest and most marginalized in society but that it recognizes a responsibility to stand with them in their needs. To be present to those in need in their struggle; to raise awareness on the part of the poor to their own dignity and rights; to empower them to work for the realization of their rights; to stand with them in their successes and failures—these are the marks of solidarity with the poor.

7. **Care and protection of the natural world.** This commitment recognizes that not only human beings but all of creation is dignified and created with the loving purpose of God. As it is linked with other human beings, human society is indelibly linked with the welfare of the environment and the natural world. If the planetary health of air, water, and land is compromised by abusive human behavior (pollution, overpopulation, climate change, deforestation, desertification, and extinction of species),

we will find ourselves undercutting the very possibility of life altogether.

As we have said, dignity is the key interpretive principle of Catholic social teaching, simultaneously governing individual rights and the common welfare. This teaching comes from the faith assertion that human persons are the willed creation of God, and that we bear as individuals and as communities the image of God. Human dignity is, therefore, attached to the inalienable quality of our humanness. It is not, consequently, a result of anything else—such as the prestige of our work, physical beauty, intellectual acumen, financial security, or social prowess. As the U.S. bishops' pastoral letter on war and peace, *The Challenge of Peace* (15), reminds us, "The human person is the clearest reflection of God's presence in the world; all of the Church's work in pursuit of both justice and peace is designed to protect and promote the dignity of every human person. For each person not only reflects God, but is the expression of God's creative work and the meaning of Christ's redemptive ministry."

DOMESTIC CHURCH

Juxtaposed with our previous discussion of distorted commitments to family life fueled by individualism and consumerism, Catholic social teaching asks people to consider carefully whether families promote or obstruct common welfare. This consideration invites Catholics to undertake a meaningful assessment of the way in which they personally balance individual, family, and social needs and goods. In balancing family needs and the needs of others in the community, Catholics can be guided by considering the family as a *domestic church*. In its Second Vatican Council document on the nature of the Church, *Lumen Gentium*, the Church teaches that marriage is a holy state and that spouses with their children constitute an integral dimension of the universal Church. The relevant segment on marriage as domestic church reads as follows:

> Finally, Christian spouses, in virtue of the sacrament of Matrimony, whereby they signify and partake of the mystery of that unity and fruitful love which exists between Christ and His Church, help each other to attain to holiness in their married life and in the rearing and education of their children. By reason of their state and rank in life they have their own special gift among the people of God. From the wedlock of Christians there comes the family, in which new citizens of human society are born, who by the grace of the Holy Spirit received in baptism are made children of God, thus perpetuating the people of God through the centuries. The family is, so to speak, the domestic church. In it parents should, by their word and example, be the first preachers of the faith to their children; they should encourage them in the vocation which is proper to each of them, fostering with special care vocation to a sacred state.

> Fortified by so many and such powerful means of salvation, all the faithful, whatever their condition or state, are called by the Lord, each in his own way, to that perfect holiness whereby the Father Himself is perfect.[17]

This section affirms several things about married persons. First, it recognizes that married life is holy in its manifestation of Christ's love for the Church. Second, it recognizes that holiness is a component of rearing children. Third, it recognizes that married life provides people with a special and unique gift, which is the procreation of children and hence the continuation of human society. As the first preachers of faith to their children, parents have a deeply important role in fostering not only the holiness of one another as spouses but also of their children as parents. As such the family has an obligation to be church to its members. However, the family has obligations to recognize its interdependence with others in society as well.

The Church affirms the interdependence of all persons in its *Constitution on the Church in the Modern World* (*Gaudium et Spes*) in which it states the following about the relationship between individuals and society:

> One of the most striking features of today's world, and one due in no small measure to modern progress, is the very great increase in mutual interdependence between people. Genuine sororal and fraternal dialogue is not advanced by progress of this sort, however, but takes place at a deeper level in a community of persons which calls for mutual respect for each one's full spiritual dignity. Christian revelation greatly fosters the establishment of such communion and at the same time promotes deeper understanding of the laws of social living which the creator has inscribed in people's spiritual and moral nature.

---

17. *Lumen Gentium*, §11. Used by permission.

Some recent pronouncements of the church's teaching authority have dealt at length with Christian teaching on human society. The council, therefore, proposes to repeat only a few of the more important truths and to outline the basis of these truths in the light of revelation. Later, it will deal with some of their implications which have social importance for our day.

God, who has a parent's care for all of us, desired that all men and women should form one family and deal with each other as brothers and sisters. All, in fact, are destined to the very same end, namely God himself, since they have been created in the likeness of God, who "made from one every nation of humankind who live on all the face of the earth" (Acts 17:26). Love of God and of one's neighbor, then, is the first and greatest commandment. Scripture teaches us that love of God cannot be separated from love of one's neighbor: "Any other commandment [is] summed up in this sentence: 'You shall love your neighbor as yourself. . . . ' therefore love is the fulfilling of the law" (Rom 13:9–10; see 1 Jn 4:20). It goes without saying that this is a matter of the utmost importance to people who are coming to rely more and more on each other and to a world which is becoming more unified every day.

Furthermore, the Lord Jesus, when praying to the Father "that they may all be one, even as we are one" (Jn 17:21–22), has opened up new horizons closed to human reason by indicating that there is certain similarity between the union existing among the divine persons and the union of God's children in truth and love. It follows, then, that if human beings are the only creatures on earth that God has wanted for their own sake, they can fully discover their true selves only in sincere self-giving.

The fact that human beings are social by nature indicates that the betterment of the person and the improvement of society depend on each other. Insofar as humanity by its very nature stands completely in need of life in society, it is and it ought to be the beginning, the subject, and the object of every social organization. Life in society is not something accessory to humanity: through their dealings with others, through mutual service, and through fraternal and sororal dialogue, men and women develop all their talents and become able to rise to their destiny.[18]

The family may be thought of as a corporate identity: one body comprised of several individuals. As a corporate identity, it must look after the individual people who comprise it, but it must at the same time function as a contributor to society such that it seeks *as a family* to open itself to the greater society as a whole. For a family's strength and sustainability simultaneously derive from and contribute to the strength and stability of society. Just as the person and the advance of society depend upon one another, families, like persons, also contribute to and depend upon the advance of society.[19]

A domestic church is church at the family level. This means everything that a church provides at the social level, a family provides to its members at the family level. If we remember that the spouses are the ministers of the sacrament of matrimony to one another—that they are the priests of their marriage—it becomes clearer that marriage partners have a religious vocation in their life as spouses and parents. In their religious vocation, spouses act as a microcosm of the Church. We might then ask, what does the Church do? It strives to meet the spiritual needs of its members, to spread the good news to

---

18. *Gaudium et Spes*, §23–25. Used by permission.

19. The Vatican document *Charter of the Rights of the Family* (1983) is key in explicating both the freedoms and responsibilities of the Catholic family.

others, to meet the needs of the poor and under-privileged, to be a moral exemplar to human society, and to be a faithful pilgrim in this world in preparation for the fullness of the kingdom of God. To these tasks, families are called as domestic churches.

In fact, when we begin to consider families as domestic churches, we can see very clearly that there is no substantive separation between the family as church and the gathering of the Christian community as the universal church on any given Sunday. For church is not comprised of walls and buildings but of people. The moral life of the church is not comprised of dusty textbooks but of the lives of human beings striving to live out their faith despite struggles, limitations, and imperfections. When we remember that the earliest Christian churches were in fact house churches—there were, of course, no actual church buildings when Christians first began worshipping together—it becomes clear that the Church does not make the people but rather that the people make the Church. Families, when they strive to become sacred covenants of love and commitment both in themselves and in their relationships with others, are the Church in the daily interactions of human beings.

APPLICATION TO FAMILY AND MARRIAGE TODAY

To be a domestic church in the contemporary culture is to be countercultural. It is to go against the tide of consumerism and individualism in favor of solidarity with the human community. It is to see one's family not myopically as a source of personal satisfaction but as a unit within society that has a responsibility to society as well as rights within society. The family unit is affected dramatically by a range of laws that govern taxes, welfare, education, healthcare, reproductive technologies, and more. As such, families have an enormous stake in society. Families need to cooperate with one another in ensuring laws that make it possible for families and individual family members to flourish. Moreover, the Church has an obligation to support families in their quest for justice, peace, and social welfare by its support of people in their respective roles as spouses, parents, children, and caregivers.

When trying to determine if one's family acts as a domestic church, the following questions might prove helpful. While they may be most relevant to Catholics who identify with the notion of family as domestic church, they may prove useful for anyone seeking to analyze the social awareness of his or her own family experience.

- Does my family act as the domestic church through sharing the gospel message with others in my community?

WHAT MODEL FOR FAMILY STRUCTURE?

The Roman Catholic Church is patriarchal and hierarchal. Given that the Church asserts that families should be domestic churches, we may well ask whether the family structure should model the patriarchal and hierarchal structure of the Catholic Church. Alternatively, should the Church in its official structure reflect families, and if so, which family structures should it reflect?

Given that all analogies have strengths and weaknesses, what might Catholics consider to be the strengths and weaknesses of considering the family the domestic church? Where does the analogy hold and in what ways does it break down?

- Does my family share private resources (including time and labor) with our community?

- Is my family a location for the personal, and particularly spiritual, flourishing of each of our members? Does it make me myopically inward-focused, or does it support my work as a Christian?

- Does my family help to meet the needs of all its members, such as aged or lonely relatives and extended family in financial straits?

- What specifically has my family, as a family, done to support the vulnerable members in our community?

- What specifically has my family done to care for environmental welfare?

- Are the habits of consumption of my family excessive or abusive? Why and how might I or we correct them?

- Is my work or employment consistent with the values of Catholic social teaching? Is the education of the children in my family consistent with these principles?

- Does my family work collaboratively with other families in the Church or in the community at large?

- Does my family actively seek to manifest covenant love and dignity?

- Do we model sacramental love as spouses and parents for others in our community?

If the Church is the people of God, then the Church is wherever the people are and in whatever circumstances they are. As with every other dimension of family life, it is up to the family itself to claim its rights and responsibilities to be a domestic church just as it is possible to ignore these rights and responsibilities. Naming one's family a "domestic church" is an invitation to realize the fullness of a marriage's spiritual potential, both within the marriage and as an agent within society. The choice remains with the couple to strive toward this realization or to yield to more commonplace models of modern marriage, which demand little vision but reward even less.

Questions for Review and Discussion

1. Describe your understanding of individualism. Can you think of practical ways in which individualism has personally affected your experience of family life?

2. What is consumerism? How does it affect family structures? How might people resist the impulses to consumerism in the world today?

3. What does it mean to say we can make an "idol" out of our families? Can you think of other examples, real or fictitious, in which people idolize their families at the cost of other people?

4. Describe the two poles of human dignity. How does the family represent the integration of these two poles?

5. Name the seven principles of Catholic social teaching. Do you find any of these problematic or unreasonable?

6. Describe your understanding of the domestic church. How does the domestic church interact with the formal church community?

7. In a personal statement, describe your sense of how one's obligations to family members should relate to broader care for others in society. What is realistic and what is overly idealistic?

Resources for Further Reading

Resources for Individualism and Consumerism

Louis Dumont, *Essays on Individualism: Modern Ideologies in Anthropological Perspective* (Chicago: University of Chicago Press, 1992).

Benjamin Barber, *Consumed: How Markets Corrupt Children, Infantilize Adults, and Swallow Citizens Whole* (New York and London: Norton, 2007).

Resources for the Domestic Church

Florence Caffrey Bourg, *Where Two or Three Are Gathered: Christian Families as Domestic Churches* (Notre Dame: University of Notre Dame Press, 2004).

Lisa Sowle Cahill, *Family: A Christian Social Perspective* (Minneapolis: Augsburg Fortress Press, 2000).

Mitch Finley and Kathy Finley, *Christian Families in the Real World: Reflections on a Spirituality for the Domestic Church* (Chicago: Thomas Moore, 1984).

Richard Gaillardetz, *A Daring Promise: A Spirituality of Christian Marriage* (Liguori, MO: Liguori/Triumph, 2007).

Stephen Post, *Spheres of Love: Toward a New Ethics of the Family* (Dallas: Southern Methodist University Press, 1994).

DIVORCE AND FORGIVENESS

Despite people's best efforts, sometimes marriages do not work. Some people come to understand commitment or responsibility too late in a relationship to repair the damages wrought early on. Sometimes one individual in a marriage finds the other unwilling to work on building or sustaining a true partnership. Sometimes people discover that they were too young to marry, that they did not know themselves well enough to make a permanent commitment to another person. Sometimes people find themselves victimized by injustice or violence within marriage that simply needs to be ended.

People do not fall into a sacramental marriage by luck, nor do they move into marriage as if it were a house. Rather, marriage is a relationship between living, changing, growing, aging, developing persons, and it tasks all dimensions of the individuals involved. Sometimes people meet the challenges of marriage with grace and ease, sometimes with frustration and frailty. The success of marriage lies in how well couples negotiate its myriad demands.

Catholic teaching is that the sacrament of marriage is indissoluble. Yet, Catholic marriages, and Christian marriages in general, remain vulnerable to the failings of human beings and sometimes end in divorce. This reality raises the question of how we are to make sense of marriages that are understood to be sacramental and yet sometimes fall apart.

In this chapter we will first consider marriage dissolution. Then we will look at the biblical instruction on divorce, followed by the Catholic Church's teaching on civil divorce and ecclesial annulment. We will further ground these considerations in the fundamental needs for forgiveness and reconciliation, two foundational concepts of Christian theology and anthropology. We will conclude with a consideration of forgiveness and the pastoral care of divorced persons.

TOOLS

The culture of individualism and consumerism, considered in the previous chapter, has made a significant impact on how persons see their commitment to marriage and family life. On the one hand, individuals no longer feel bound to stay in a marriage that is unhappy or abusive. This is a positive outcome of contemporary culture, because it means that people are free to leave situations in which they are threatened or violated. Especially as women have come into greater economic and political freedom, women as a whole are less tolerant of inequity, abuse, or exploitation within marriage. As Marilyn Yalom notes:

> Young women today, marrying on average around twenty-five, often have at least some college education and work experience behind them when they become wives. They enter into marriage on a relatively equal footing with their husbands, and expect to maintain this parity for the rest of their lives. The old ideal of companionate marriage has been reformulated under such new labels as egalitarian marriage, equal partnership, and marital equality.[1]

On the other hand, the culture of individualism and consumerism has over-emphasized individual, personal happiness. When married couples experience unmet needs, spouses often blame their marriages and their marriage partners, and seek happiness and fulfillment elsewhere.[2]

Models of marriages, and consequently expectations about what marriage is supposed to provide, have been in transition for the past several decades. The patriarchal family model has recently been replaced by a more democratic one, where children and parents see one another as equals with equal access, needs, and rights. This new democratic model reduces certain kinds of abuses of power, but it also leaves us with dramatic questions about role, status, and structure.

Who has final authority in a family when conflict arises, and how is conflict to be settled? How has the shift from a male breadwinner to a female breadwinner model affected the identity and feeling of usefulness of a father? How do women juggle the double burden of work and family? How should family and household responsibilities be divided among members of a household? The demise of the patriarchal model may be a good thing, but in its absence people have struggled mightily to arrive at workable alternatives that meet needs and expectations.[3]

Whether a factor of relaxed divorce laws, or changing attitudes toward marriage, or modern individualism and consumerism, or some combination of factors, divorce affects nearly 50 percent of today's American families.[4] The prevalence of divorce should not be regarded lightly, because

---

1. Marilyn Yalom, *A History of the Wife* (New York: HarperCollins, 2001), 394. Copyright © 2001 by Marilyn Yalom. Reprinted by permission of HarperCollins Publishers.

2. In 1970, California attempted to address marital unhappiness by passing a no-fault divorce law, whereby individuals did not have to sue for divorce on the grounds of some wrong action, such as adultery or abandonment. The no-fault divorce model quickly spread throughout the United States, making it easy for either partner to end the marriage based simply on personal preference expressed in the form of "irreconcilable differences."

3. As Stephanie Coontz comments in her chapter on modern marriage, "Uncharted Territory," "Like it or not, today we are all pioneers, picking our way through uncharted and unstable territory. The old rules are no longer reliable guides to work out modern gender roles and build a secure foundation for marriage. Wherever it is that people want to end up in their family relations today, even if they are totally committed to creating a so-called traditional marriage, they have to get there by a different route from the past." In *Marriage: A History* (New York: Viking Press, 2005), 282–83.

4. Rosemary Radford Ruether speaks to this sobering reality: "Almost half of all American marriages dissolve in divorce at some point. Almost 40 percent of those end within the first four years, particularly among those who marry in their late teens and early twenties. Another 40 percent of divorcing couples are in their thirties or early forties, and some 20 percent in their late forties and beyond. For American women [and men], divorce may thus occur at several stages in their life cycle: after a few years of marriage, usually without children; at mid-career, with children who are still dependent; or at a point when children are completing college and/or about to become independent." In *Christianity and the Making of the Modern Family* (Boston: Beacon Press, 2000), 186.

divorce devastates those who experience it. The impact is especially harsh for women and children, as Marilyn Yalom again tells:

> When couples divorce, it is almost always the ex-wife who loses out financially. According to the latest statistics, divorce produces a 27 percent decline in women's standard of living and 10 percent increase in that of men. This represents an almost 40 percent gap between what ex-wives and what ex-husbands experience financially in the aftermath of a divorce. Part of this difference is attributable to the fact that the mothers, in the great majority of cases, are granted custody of the children. Even when the mother is awarded child support, it is frequently insufficient and not always forthcoming. Another factor is the lower earning power of women on the whole—75 percent of what men earn. Many women are still segregated in low-paying jobs and hindered in advancement by home and childcare responsibilities, as well as by the sacrifices they have made promoting their husbands' careers rather than their own.

In addition to the disadvantageous financial consequences of divorce for many women and their children, the emotional distress is often deep and long-lasting. While no-fault divorce, first instituted in California in 1970 and subsequently adopted in most of the United States, was intended to remove the blame and acrimony from prolonged adversarial litigation, today's divorces are still often as bitter as those of the past. Divorce continues to be a major family disruption with prolonged consequences for the spouses, their offspring, and extended kin.[5]

Divorce affects many areas of life: employment, household, financial stability, psycho-social stability, physical health, extended family relationships, child welfare, child custody, relationships of persons to their faith communities, and community welfare. Perhaps most devastating is the long-term effect of divorce on children. When no-fault divorces were first promoted, the rationale was that people would be happier and more successful if they were free to leave bad or unhappy marriages behind. Shockingly, the negative impacts of divorce, especially on children, were neither studied nor anticipated when divorce laws changed, as researcher Judith Wallerstein uncovered in her longitudinal studies of children from divorced families. Although divorced persons are typically able to recover from the trauma of divorce after several years of healing and rebuilding, Wallerstein's research revealed that children are permanently affected by their parents' divorce—throughout adulthood and into their own marriages and parenting relationships.

In particular, Wallerstein discovered that children of divorce experience short-term problems with school, self-esteem, peer-socialization, and anxiety disorders. Into adulthood they experience long-term difficulties with intimate relationships, trust, substance dependencies, emotional and psychological disorders, criminal violence, and suicide risk. Moreover, children of divorce, and those who have witnessed divorce among their peers' families, become increasingly suspicious of marriage and any happiness in general as they live with the unshakeable fear of the "other shoe dropping." Many young people who have experienced or witnessed divorce fear that it is the inevitable outcome of marriage. They consequently elect either to delay marriage or not to marry at all.[6]

---

5. Yalom, *History of the Wife*, 394–95.

6. Wallerstein's research, begun in the 1970s, tracked children of divorce at intervals throughout their lives, beginning with the months immediately following the divorce and continuing with meetings every few years. As of 2000, Wallerstein was still in contact with roughly 80 percent of her research group. These people, whom she met as children, are now adults in mid-life. Wallerstein's work reveals that regardless of age, these individuals identify themselves as "children of divorce," and almost to a person

The impact of divorce on children has a rippling effect throughout the culture. For instance, because marriage is being delayed or rejected altogether, pre-marital or non-marital sex is increasingly normative. This reality increases risk of abandonment, parenthood out of wedlock, relational infidelity, and disease. Couples who are not married, even those with children, separate more frequently than couples who are married. The result is that children born to unmarried parents are at greater risk of living in broken homes than children born to wed parents. Even more disturbing, a high percentage of fathers who do not live with their children frequently do not see their children at all. This puts fathers, mothers, and children at financial and psychosocial risk. Finally, couples who cohabit and subsequently marry are more likely to divorce than couples who marry and then live together. In effect, couples who live together before marriage as a sort of "trial" actually put their future marital relationship at greater risk for divorce.[7]

By any measure, divorce is widely damaging and has ramifications that reach far beyond the husband and wife. It is fair to say that the prevalence of divorce creates a context in which divorce is more likely to occur. Although divorce can be the best option to end a hostile, dangerous, or abusive marriage, any serious assessment of divorce outcomes will reveal the widespread phenomenon of modern divorce as destructive to persons, to families, and to the broad stability of community and society.

BIBLICAL TEACHING ON DIVORCE

The biblical teaching on divorce can be confusing. For one thing, the Old and New Testaments do not agree. For another, the New Testament passages sometimes disagree with each other and are difficult to interpret. This scriptural ambiguity makes it difficult to speak of an absolute "biblical position" on divorce.[8] Moreover, we should note that many conditions that warrant consideration for divorce are not discussed in the Scriptures in that context, including domestic violence, sexual abuse of spouse or children, substance abuse, and psychological disorder. Nevertheless, as the Bible is the foundational and primary source of Christian faith, it is important to have some understanding of what the Bible says about divorce, even if it is incomplete or unclear at points.

In the Old Testament, there seem to be a number of socially accepted conditions for divorce. Although the references to divorce and the possibility of remarriage outnumber what

---

describe the end of their childhood as the day when their parents divorced. Her compassionate study synthesizes the experiences of these adult children, revealing the profound impact of divorce on such dimensions of human development as: moral agency, responsibility, intimacy, faith, psychological health, adult sexuality, premature sexual experience, sense of purpose, marital stability, parenting styles, choice of marriage partner, and self-worth. Her most recent findings are published in *The Unexpected Legacy of Divorce*, coauthored with Julia Lewis and Sandra Blakeslee (New York: Hyperion, 2000).

7. These outcomes, among others, are explored in Barbara Dafoe Whitehead's documentary *Marriage: Just a Piece of Paper?* produced and directed by Brian Boyer (Chicago: University of Chicago and WTTW-TV, 2002).

8. "The Old and New Testament refer in a few places to divorce. But it must be stated at once that the meaning of these passages is not clear. If it were, there would never have developed differences of opinion on this question, and no synod or council would have felt it necessary to make official pronouncements on the problem. . . . As we shall see, an analysis of the pertinent texts from the Old and New Testaments does not lead us to any unequivocal decision. From the fact that the Fathers were not able to arrive at a unanimous opinion of the meaning of the relevant Scripture passages, and that Christians of the East and of the West are divided today on this score, we must infer that it will always be impossible to settle the problem by reference to holy scripture alone." Victor Pospishil, *Divorce and Remarriage: Towards a New Catholic Teaching* (New York: Herder & Herder, 1967), 19–20.

can be cited here, the conditions for permissible divorce in the Old Testament include a husband's disapproval of his wife, the marriage of a Jew to a non-Jew (Ezra 10:3), and adultery.[9] In Hebraic custom the husband issued a writ of divorce to his wife (called a *get*) and returned her to her father's household (Deut 24:1–4). A woman, however, could neither issue a *get* nor initiate divorce. She was also not protected against divorce unless her husband had violated her before the marriage (Deut 22:28–29) or had falsely accused her of not being a virgin at the time of the marriage, of which crime she was later acquitted (Deut 22:13–19). Victor Pospishil notes that the Mosaic Law seems primarily to comment on what was permitted in divorce and what was commanded, with two conditions pertaining to each. A husband was *permitted* to dismiss his wife, and a dismissed woman was *permitted* to remarry another man so long as he was not a priest. A husband dismissing his wife was *commanded* to issue her a writ of divorce, and the Law *commanded* that a dismissed woman could not return to her former husband.[10]

The New Testament teachings on divorce must be understood in light of the Hebrew context as well as the needs of the developing Christian community. This is especially the case as women were particularly vulnerable to unjust divorce, and Jesus directed much of his ministry to vulnerable populations, including women.[11] There are several strong injunctions against divorce in the Gospels (Matt 5:31–32, 19:1–12; Mark 10:1–12; Luke 16:18). Mark and Luke absolutely prohibit divorce, whereas Matthew allows that only in the case of *porneia*, sexual transgression, can a husband legitimately leave his wife. The meaning of *porneia*, however, is ambiguous and much disputed. *Porneia* is frequently interpreted to mean "adultery," but translations of the term vary; Protestant versions favor "adultery," while Catholic versions prefer "unless the marriage is unlawful" (NAB) or equivalent. There is no scholarly consensus about the historical context of the term or why it occurs only in Matthew's Gospel.[12] The passage in Matthew concludes with Jesus' teaching that if a man abandons his wife unlawfully, and she subsequently marries another, she has essentially been forced to commit adultery. Why is this adultery? Because she is still lawfully married to her first husband!

Additional New Testament passages further confuse any absolutist reading of the biblical teaching. For example, in 1 Corinthians 7:1–15, Paul instructs the church in Corinth on the matter of marriage. He states that husbands and wives should not separate, but if they do, they either should remain unmarried or they should reunite. However, since many of the people in the Corinthian Church were new converts to the Christian faith, it is not difficult to imagine that there were frequently instances where a new convert was married to a person who chose not to convert. Paul suggests that people should not divorce their spouses, even if they were unbelievers, so long as the unbelievers wanted to stay in their marriages. However, if the unbelieving spouse wanted a divorce, the Christian partner

---

9. It should be noted that the typical punishment for adultery was death by stoning. For the female, violation through rape was considered a form of adultery if it took place within city walls, where it was supposed that the female could have cried out for help and merely chose not to do so. See Deut 22:22–27.

10. Pospishil, *Divorce and Remarriage*, 25.

11. See also the discussion of charity in chapter 3.

12. Pierre Hegy, "Disputed Biblical Interpretations about Marriage and Divorce," in *Catholic Divorce: The Deception of Annulments*, eds. Pierre Hegy and Joseph Martos (New York: Continuum, 2000), 65.

was not bound to stay in the marriage. Paul tells us he is offering his own opinion, not that of Jesus, which leaves us to determine whether his opinion is binding or not.[13] If we accept it as binding, then the New Testament permits divorce when a Christian seeks separation from a non-Christian spouse. This echoes the Old Testament mandate of divorce between Jews and non-Jews.

Many fine scholars who have studied the biblical teachings on divorce find them ultimately inconclusive on the matter. At best we infer that the Bible recognizes marriage as a sacred and binding bond. Although the exact nature of *porneia* is disputed, the New Testament attributes to Jesus' teaching this condition alone as a permissible cause for divorce. The spirit of the New Testament teachings considered together is that divorce is a serious matter, not to be recognized as licit for any but the most serious of sexual infractions. Remarriage that occurs when a marriage is still lawfully binding is, as a result, not considered remarriage at all but in fact adultery.

We need to remember, of course, that any application of biblical teaching to today's marriages requires a historical-critical awareness of the nature of the Bible and a responsible and intentional methodology for reading and interpreting the text.[14] While it is misguided and often dangerous to apply biblical teaching point-by-point to all situations, it is fair to conclude that as a general rule Scripture, and particularly the New Testament, argues for the binding quality of marriage and seeks to restrict severely the conditions for permissible divorce.

CATHOLIC TEACHING ON DIVORCE AND ANNULMENT

Given the deleterious outcomes of divorce, the biblical injunctions against divorce and remarriage, and Catholic theology of marriage as a sacrament, it is not surprising that the Catholic Church rejects divorce as moral or permissible under every circumstance. This teaching is one of the most confusing aspects of Catholic theology, and consequently it requires quite a bit of unpacking.

To begin, we must recall that the Catholic Church recognizes marriage to be one of the seven great sacraments.[15] It sees marriage as a holy vocation to which people are called by God, for service to one another, their children, and the community at large. It understands marriages to be the proper context for the transmission of human life. It furthermore recognizes that marriage, as the first place where children will encounter instruction about God, should act as a domestic church. Joined to the parents, children also become participants in the domestic church, where they learn how to strive for value-rich service to others in their communities.

Like the relationship between Christ and church, marriages are considered sacred and indissoluble. Since marriages are created by the grace of God, they cannot be undercut or undone by human power. Once two baptized Christians enter into marriage, the union becomes permanent and binding for the whole of their lives. Even when personal sinfulness and error would threaten the union, the Catholic Church holds

---

13. Here one might revisit the discussion in chapter 5 of Petrine and Pauline Privilege, which constitute the two ancient conditions, unrelated to sexual infractions, under which a marriage could be dissolved between a Christian and a non-Christian.

14. Hegy's article is an excellent example of critical biblical scholarship on the New Testament teaching on divorce. Decidedly against the Catholic reading of the New Testament as definitively prohibiting divorce, except in the cases of Pauline and Petrine Privilege, this article articulates the ambiguities of the New Testament teaching in matters ranging from original source material to modern translations of the text.

15. Marriage as a sacrament is discussed in chapter 5.

that the grace of the sacrament of marriage will help married people overcome their struggles. As Hosea and Gomer overcame radical estrangement, as God's love for Israel endured every human shortcoming, so too are all marriages infused with the quality of indissolubility.

At this point any attentive reader will be thinking that while this may be fine theology, it is not realistic—nor is it the case that Catholics never divorce. How can the Catholic Church hold that divorced Catholics are still living in sacramental marriages? To answer this question, we need to distinguish between different types of marital bonds. Michael Lawler, a contemporary theologian of marriage and family issues, has argued that marriage involves several types of bonds. Understanding these bonds is helpful in grasping the Church's teaching.[16]

First, Lawler describes the natural bond between people, which is characterized by affection, love, desire, and so on. Even before people marry, strong feelings of affection and love lead them to make commitments to one another. Whether any representative of the Church or state is there to proclaim or recognize it, the commitment people freely make to one another is real.

When the bond of love or affection is such that people seek to have it sanctioned and recognized as a legal entity, they may opt to enter into civil marriage. The legal or civil bond of marriage is a second type of bond, which holds people together in intimate relationship. As Lawler says, "marital commitment adds to the already-existing interpersonal commitment and bond of love a legal commitment and bond of law."[17] Certain laws govern whose natural bonds can be recognized as legally binding marital unions. For instance, in the United States persons already legally bound to one marriage cannot enter

simultaneously into a second legal marriage. Consanguinous marriages—marriages between close relatives—are also legally prohibited. Marriage between minors is legally prohibited as well.

To say that something is legal simply means that it is permitted by the governing laws of the state. It says nothing of the quality (or even presence) of love between people; people who love one another not a whit can marry so long as they are legally free to do so. The point of civil marriage is that it creates a legal entity, namely a marriage, which consequently has certain binding rights and responsibilities. These include rights for spouses to inherit property from the other, to make healthcare decisions on behalf of the other, and to file income taxes together.

A third bond in marriage, states Lawler, is the spiritual bond between people that is recognized by their religious community. This is the bond recognized by the Catholic Church. Just as a couple, bound naturally by love, seeks to have their union established as the *legal* entity of civil marriage, they may also elect to have their marriages established as an *ecclesial* entity. When the Catholic Church recognizes a marriage, it sees that marriage as a sacramental reality that has been called forth by the spouses, who are in fact responding to a calling by God to the marriage. Like civil marriage, which has legal obligations and rewards, a sacramental marriage has ecclesial obligations and rewards. These include the support and blessing of the Church, the call to service on behalf of the Church, and the opportunity to baptize and rear children within the Church.

In each case, the bonds of marriage intend to strengthen and reinforce the couple to create a permanent union. Even while one bond of marriage may be stressed over others from time to time, those other bonds remain to keep the

---

16. Michael Lawler, *Marriage and the Catholic Church: Disputed Questions* (Collegeville, MN: Liturgical Press, 2002), 66–91.

17. Ibid., 73.

marriage intact. To illustrate this point, consider the example of a couple bound by love alone. When life's hardships stress the affection the two lovers share for each other, it is perhaps logical to break off the commitment. Breaking the commitment becomes significantly more difficult when the two people are united in a civil marriage, for they have to file for civil divorce. The matter is further complicated if they have declared before God, in a religious marriage, that their intent in uniting is to create a permanent communion of their lives and persons. Like concentric circles, the bonds of marriage create strata of personal, legal, and spiritual obligations. Lawler describes these obligations:

> [The mutual love of Christians] binds them together in an interpersonal relationship, which is a bond and obligation of love. Their wedding binds them together in a civil relationship, which is a bond and obligation of law. Their marriage as a sacrament binds them together in a religious relationship, which is a bond and obligation of divine grace.[18]

It is, of course, possible for people to fall out of love, and as a result to break the first bond. Likewise, it is possible for people to end their marriages through divorce, much as it is possible for a corporation to dissolve. As for the ecclesial bond, however, the Catholic Church holds that this most sacred union, designed and achieved by God's grace, is indissoluble. Although people may fall out of love and the law may permit a divorce, the Catholic Church holds that truly sacramental marriages between baptized Christians can never be undone. Even though a couple may have a divorce, which is governed by the state, the Catholic Church still sees an ecclesial bond as permanent. Since the Catholic Church still sees the couple as married by virtue of their ecclesial bond, it will not recognize any subsequent marriage by either party as lawful or moral.

So, then, how does the Catholic Church deal with the reality of civil divorce and remarriage? It allows for people who have experienced civil divorce to petition for a declaration of nullity. This is what is commonly referred to as an "annulment." By seeking an annulment, people can ask the Catholic Church to declare that although a wedding took place, a sacramental marriage was never in fact contracted.

In order to understand the Catholic Church's rationale in granting annulments, it is helpful to consider that since the Church holds marriage to be indissoluble, it makes sense that the Church would also have vested interest in defining what actually constitutes a sacramental marriage in the first place. One can think of instances where a marriage may only appear to have taken place. For example, two teenagers may solicit a celebrant and present false documentation about their age; then despite the celebration of a church wedding in the presence of a priest, a sacramental marriage may never have taken place. Or, a woman, pregnant out of wedlock and forced to marry by her parents, in fact may not be entering into a sacramental union at all.

Indeed, the Catholic Church establishes from the outset certain fundamental impediments to marriage, which include:[19]

1. **Non-age**—unions between a couple in which either is underage, with the female being considered underage below 14 and the male below 16

2. **Impotence**—when the marriage is not consummated sexually

---

18. Ibid., 74.

19. These impediments are helpfully indexed in Geoffrey Robinson, *Marriage, Divorce and Nullity: A Guide to the Annulment Process in the Catholic Church* (Oakville, ON: Novalis Press and Collegeville, MN: Liturgical Press, 1984), 80–81.

3. **Previous bond**—when one or both parties were formerly married, the marriage was not annulled, and the previous spouse is still living

4. **Disparity of cult**—marriage between a Christian and a non-Christian that has not received a proper dispensation from one's bishop

5. **Sacred orders**—an ordained priest cannot be married

6. **Public vows**—a vowed religious brother or nun cannot be married unless he or she receives a dispensation from the vow of celibacy

7. **Abduction**—a person cannot be abducted and forced to marry

8. **Crime**—if one murders his or her spouse to enable a new marriage, the new marriage is not valid

9. **Consanguinity**—marriage between close relatives is not valid

10. **Affinity**—one cannot marry his or her deceased spouse's parent or child

11. **De facto relatives**—people who live together cannot later marry the parent or child of the cohabiting partner

12. **Adoption**—one cannot marry an adopted child or sibling

Impediments to marriage are not the only causes for a marriage to be declared null from the outset. A marriage may also be declared null if it has an improper *form* or if the *consent*, by which the marriage is created in the first place, is somehow defective. The *form* refers to the formal, public nature of a wedding. For Catholics, a bishop, priest, or deacon needs to preside over the wedding in order for the marriage to be valid. If two people on a whim declare to one another that they are married, or if they seek marriage

before an improper celebrant without a dispensation, the marriage would be declared null on the grounds of improper form. The Catholic Church will recognize marriage between two non-Catholic Christians as valid and sacramental, however, so long as they had a proper public ceremony before a civil or religious celebrant.[20]

Marriages may also be declared null on the grounds of defective *consent*. The priest, bishop, or deacon who celebrates a marriage in the Catholic Church is only a witness to the proceedings. The marriage is actually formed by the consent of the couple getting married. As such, the consent is all-important in the formation of a sacramental union, and if it is somehow impaired so also is the validity of the marriage. There are six major categories under which consent in marriage may be considered defective, warranting a declaration of nullity if sought. These include:[21]

1. **Force or fear**—by which a person is compelled to marry against his or her free will

2. **Deceit**—by which a person conceals something about himself or herself, the nature of which affects the whole of the marriage

3. **Intentions against marriage**—including a failure of intention to be faithful, to marry permanently, to bear children, or to share life with another

4. **Insanity**—such that a person is incapable of freely consenting to marriage

5. **Lack of canonical discretion**—which refers to deep psychological unpreparedness to enter into marriage in earnest

6. **Incapacity**—which is a basic acknowledgment that an individual is simply and utterly incapable of fulfilling the obligations and duties of marriage and that a spouse cannot be sacramentally bound to an individual so unfit for marriage

20. Ibid., 82.
21. Ibid., 82–84.

Although annulments are granted for defects in form and other impediments, it can be difficult to grasp how an annulment based on a defect of consent may be granted. Since a wedding obviously occurred, which is often followed by years of married life as well as by children, one might wonder what kind of information could yield the conclusion that a sacramental marriage never occurred. An example may help.

Let's imagine that Mary has had a strained relationship with her parents throughout her teenage years. She wants very much to leave her home but is not sure how to go about it. Her high school boyfriend, Timothy, suggests that they marry. Although she has apprehensions about going through with it, she marries Tim and even has a child with him. Three years into the marriage, however, Mary leaves the marriage to go to graduate school. She and Tim divorce. Five years later, Timothy has fallen in love with another woman whom he wishes to marry. According to the Catholic Church, his marriage to Mary is still binding and hence he cannot be remarried with the Church's blessing. Although nothing is preventing Timothy from remarrying civilly, if he wants his new marriage to be recognized as licit by the Church, he needs to seek an annulment—a declaration of nullity—of the first marriage.

THE ANNULMENT PROCESS

Persons seeking an annulment need to contact the marriage tribunal in their diocese. They do this usually by first speaking with a parish priest who helps to initiate the process. The marriage tribunal is a court. Evidence is required, witnesses are heard, and there are judges, but it is not like a courtroom setting as shown on television. Marriage tribunals intend to help people rather than to determine punishments or assign blame for a failed marriage.

Before seeking an annulment, a civil divorce is required. The person petitioning for an annulment needs to provide evidence both of the marriage and of the civil divorce before the process moves forward. The petitioner is also required to provide witnesses who can support his or her case that an annulment should be granted. The petitioner will provide a statement in the form of an interview. Witnesses and the former spouse will also be invited to provide testimony in the form of an interview. Former spouses do not face off, nor is either party subject to a cross-examination in a courtroom setting.

The marriage tribunal consists of judges, who rule on the case; advocates, who are trained to advise persons seeking an annulment; a defender of the bond, who advocates for the marriage and thus opposes the advocates; and notaries, who maintain detailed written accounts of the proceedings. Once a marriage tribunal rules on a case, its decision is reviewed by an appeal tribunal. The judgment is final once the second tribunal confirms the decision of the first.

Once a petition for annulment is filed, the Church proceeds with the process. This is true even when situations that complicate the process arise. Such situations might include uncooperative or unavailable witnesses; an uncooperative or unavailable former spouse; and even civil remarriage during the annulment process. The costs of a marriage tribunal are subsidized by the Church, but persons seeking an annulment are asked to pay a portion. Persons pay according to their ability, and no one is ever denied an annulment hearing on the grounds that he or she cannot pay for the process. The process varies in terms of costs and time, and no party is ever guaranteed an outcome either in favor of or against a declaration of nullity.

The Catholic Church assumes that Timothy and Mary initially married with the intention to create a sacramental union. Without Timothy's petition for an annulment, the Church would have no reason to believe otherwise or to investigate the legitimacy of his marriage to Mary. This is why a hearing on the part of the Church is necessary. The Church convenes a marriage tribunal, which is a court established by the Church to evaluate petitions for annulment. The marriage tribunal interviews Mary's friends from the time, who report that she married not with the intention of creating a lifelong union with Timothy but rather as a means to leave home. The Church finds that Timothy's free consent was faulty because he was not actually aware of what he was consenting to, just as Mary's consent was not entirely free because she was reacting immaturely to parental pressures. Although a wedding and a civil marriage took place, the tribunal concludes that a sacrament of marriage was absent from the beginning. Hence, the marriage is declared null. The ecclesial bond is not broken because it was found to never have existed.[22]

THE PRACTICAL PROS AND CONS OF THE CHURCH'S POSITION

The annulment process has its critics. Some object that the Church is being legalistic on this point. They argue that the Church's court has no legal authority over people, and the mere requirement of the annulment process poses a time-consuming, costly, and emotional burden that penalizes people who have already suffered the pains of divorce. Some assert that the Catholic Church is hypocritical in its refusal to acknowledge divorce as permissible even while sanctioning divorce in a back-door manner by granting annulments.

The pastoral and logical concerns over the annulment process are valid and require exploration. In Timothy's case, for example, he seems to have been doubly wronged by first a loveless marriage and then by the Catholic Church's initial refusal to permit his loving marriage without prior benefit of the annulment process. Moreover, had the tribunal concluded that his first marriage was still ecclesially binding, Timothy would have been asked to refrain from receiving the Eucharist because his current marriage would be considered technically an instance of adultery.

Such issues have garnered much attention in the past several decades by theologians and pastors who understand the deep pains and feelings of rejection that divorced Catholics frequently experience. Divorce recovery ministries are now quite common in parishes. Careful attention is now also paid to working with couples who have experienced divorce, the difficulties of which are compounded by subsequent estrangement from their worship community. As yet, pastoral gentleness, creative theology on marriage, and community support during the annulment process remain the best hopes for divorced and remarried Catholics, because the Church has not altered, nor is likely to alter soon, its teaching that marriage is indissoluble.[23]

From one perspective, the challenges of the annulment process are indisputably legalistic. The process itself can cause financial hardship and emotional duress for divorced Catholics. If an

---

22. Two resources that explain further the Church's teaching and practice regarding annulments with particular discussion of the function and process of marriage tribunals are Ronald Smith, *Annulment: A Step by Step Guide For Divorced Catholics* (Chicago: ACTA Publications, 1995) and Michael Smith Foster, *Annulment: The Wedding That Was; How the Church Can Declare a Marriage Null* (Mahwah, NJ: Paulist Press, 1999).

23. Two articles, both contributions to Kieran Scott and Michael Warren, eds., *Perspectives on Marriage: A Reader* (New York and Oxford: Oxford University Press, 2007), that explore the special pastoral needs of divorced and remarried Catholics are James Young, "Remarried Catholics: Searching for Church Belonging," pp. 367–73, and Michael Lawler, "Divorce and Remarriage in the Catholic Church," pp. 374–88.

annulment is not granted and a Catholic remarries civilly, true and lasting estrangement from the Church can and does occur. From another perspective, however, the Church's teaching presents an optimal view of what is possible for human life and marriage. It is idealistic, but at a time when marital decay is so prevalent, many argue that the Church's teaching is a prophetic reminder of what marriage should and can be.

The dialogue between cultural attitudes in general and the Church's position on marriage can be mutually fruitful. The more the human sciences discover about human personhood, identity, sexuality, and gender, the more information people have to bring to their marriages and families. Enhancing this knowledge are insights drawn from lived experience and communicated by an ever-broadening body of marriage theology, much of it produced by lay theologians, many of them married with children. The Catholic Church is thus challenged to articulate its teachings on marriage, family, and sexuality in ways that meaningfully address modern understandings and concerns.

Conversely, the Church remains an authority for Catholics in matters of faith and morals; its teachings transcend the fluctuating cultural trends and practices of any given historical moment. The Church intends to speak to eternal truths according to its best understanding of Christian revelation. Consequently, its task is to promote, teach, and support all aspects of the sacrament of marriage so that people grasp its sense of what marriage is ideally intended to be. Together, contemporary insights and Church teaching mutually help people arrive at best case practices and understandings of modern Catholic marriages.

APPLICATION TO FAMILY AND MARRIAGE TODAY

In every human endeavor, error is inevitable and failure is possible. This is why the Christian faith believes that human beings require salvation. Humans are not perfect. We cause damage; sometimes we hurt others even when that is not our intent. It is no surprise that marriages, with their potential to bring about the greatest happiness, can also be the source of grave disappointment and loss, for people invest tremendously in them. When marriages end in divorce, it is not because this is an easy or desirable option, but rather because other options seem to have run out. People enduring divorce require compassionate understanding, the ministry of presence from families and friends, and the gentle ministrations of their religious communities. They require both forgiveness and reconciliation for others and for themselves.

HELP FOR TROUBLED MARRIAGES

The Catholic Church attempts to aid married persons contemplating separation or divorce through parish and diocesan support groups, marriage enrichment programs, and ministerial counseling efforts. One of its most successful initiatives has been the Retrouvaille Program.

Considered by some a last resort for troubled marriages, Retrouvaille involves a weekend immersion followed by six to twelve weeks of support sessions. In Retrouvaille, couples gain skills for communication and self-disclosure that help them to reconnect and repair hurt and damage. While the program is Catholic, it is open to couples of all faiths as well as to those without faith commitments. It is heralded as widely successful, and while it is not a counseling program in itself, it is frequently recommended to couples by marriage counselors. More information about the history, process, and outcomes of the Retrouvaille Program may be found online at *http://www.retrouvaille.org*.

People who are considering or who have experienced divorce understand their personal shortcomings intimately. They often carry both shame and blame for their errors and their losses. Forgiveness and reconciliation are critical to people overcoming the hurt of divorce and to those dealing with the complexities of remarriage after an annulment or civil remarriage without the benefit of annulment. Both forgiveness and reconciliation are necessary to encourage these individuals to reintegrate into social and church activities as singles or as single parents, and to recover a sense of hope and well-being. Both forgiveness and reconciliation, moreover, are crucial to the welfare of children of divorce, who already bear the deep and lasting impact of divorce throughout adulthood.

So, then, how do we forgive? What is forgiveness? Forgiveness means letting go of the past. It does not mean that we forget the past, nor does it mean that we ought to endure misdeeds without defending ourselves. It means, rather, that in the aftermath of wrongs done to us, we have the power to end or mitigate the influence such wrongs continue to have over us. Forgiveness is not necessarily an emotional or sentimental leap of healing or amnesia in the human psyche, such that we simply stop caring about what happened. Forgiveness is a choice made, sometimes against emotional instinct, to limit the effect some past hurt will have over the present.

I often ask my students to think about who benefits from forgiveness. Although they recognize that forgiveness benefits the person forgiven, they always argue that it is ultimately a benefit to the one who is doing the forgiving. Sometimes, the person we need to forgive is no longer even living, yet we still need to forgive in order to move on.

Reconciliation is the effort to restore damage or heal conflict in a relationship. All intimate and long-term relationships require reconciliation from time to time. The need for restoration of relationships is expressed in the Catholic sacrament of reconciliation, whereby the grace of healing is found. Just as anointing is a sacrament of healing for physical ailment, reconciliation is a sacrament for healing spiritual ailments that would separate a person from the Catholic Church.[24] The very fact that there is a sacrament that recognizes that grace is needed to heal relationships reveals something critical about human persons: people both need and are capable of reconciliation. Even when a relationship cannot be restored to its former status, spiritual health requires that people forgive one another and seek reconciliation.

As in all areas of its teaching and ministry, the Catholic Church is obliged to regard divorced Catholics and Christians with compassion and forgiveness. The adequacy of the annulment process and the pastoral care of divorced persons can be judged by whether divorced Catholics feel that they have been treated with forgiveness or whether they feel judged and castigated by marriage failure. Has the Church been reconciled to them, as well as divorced persons to the Church? The Church would benefit by erring on the side of forgiveness in its care for divorced and remarried persons. In instances where holding fast to any legalistic dimension of the annulment process would result in estrangement from the Church, a posture of forgiveness would be pastorally and spiritually more effective than a rigid, legal one. As Michael Lawler argues:

> There is strong support in every sector of the Church for reassessment of the pastoral practice related to divorce and remarriage, especially among women who know that women frequently suffer most from divorce. The theological question for assessment can be clearly stated. Can the Catholic Church continue to claim fidelity to the total economy revealed by the compassionate and merciful God and continue to permit one element of that economy, its reading of Jesus' words on divorce and remarriage, to override all others? The question does not admit of an easy answer.

---

24. James Dallen offers a fine treatment of the sacrament of reconciliation in his work *The Reconciling Community* (Collegeville, MN: Liturgical Press, 1991).

But a Church faithful to the Gospel, and to the Spirit who continues to reveal its meanings in contemporary context, can face it secure in the belief that the Spirit will lead it into the truth of God as surely today as at any time in the past.[25]

The reality of divorce reminds all of us of our humanness. In this way, divorce, just as sickness or death, can be a great teacher that instructs us to be humble as we attempt marriage. Even marriages that most sincerely intend to be permanent sometimes end in divorce. True permanence is a matter of God's authorship, which calls us to itself even while it evades us either by death or divorce. We are in the end reminded that sacramental marriage is ultimately an eschatological reality, to consideration of which we now turn.

Questions for Review and Discussion

1. Describe divorce in today's world. Whom does it affect? What are the effects of divorce? How serious a problem is it?

2. Name some of the specific impacts of divorce on children. What ongoing impacts surface when children of divorce grow up?

3. Describe the Old Testament teaching on divorce.

4. Describe the New Testament teaching on divorce.

5. If there is scriptural ambiguity on the matter of divorce, to what spiritual resources can Christians turn for guidance in thinking about whether to divorce or not?

6. What is the Catholic Church's teaching on divorce and remarriage? How does the Catholic Church deal with the reality of divorced Catholics?

7. State the types of impediments to marriage that could be considered grounds for a declaration of nullity.

8. On what grounds do you think divorce is legitimate or warranted, if any? How might reconciliation and forgiveness help to heal the wounds of divorce?

Resources for Further Reading

Resources for Divorce

Christy Buchanan, Eleanor Maccoby, and Sanford Dornbusch, *Adolescents after Divorce* (Cambridge, MA, and London: Harvard University Press, 1996).

William Roberts, *Divorce and Remarriage: Religious and Psychological Perspectives* (Kansas City, MO: Sheed & Ward, 1990).

Judith Wallerstein, Julia Lewis, and Sandra Blakeslee, *The Unexpected Legacy of Divorce: A 25 Year Landmark Study* (New York: Hyperion, 2000).

Resources for Catholic Teaching on Reconciliation, Divorce, and Annulment

James Dallen, *The Reconciling Community: The Rite of Penance* (Collegeville, MN: Liturgical Press, 1986).

Michael Smith Foster, *Annulment: The Wedding That Was; How the Church Can Declare a Marriage Null* (New York: Paulist Press, 1999).

Pierre Hegy and Joseph Martos, eds., *Catholic Divorce: The Deception of Annulments* (New York and London: Continuum, 2000).

Theodore Mackin, SJ, *Divorce and Remarriage: Marriage in the Catholic Church* (New York: Paulist Press, 1984).

Geoffrey Robinson, *Marriage, Divorce and Nullity: A Guide to the Annulment Process in the Catholic Church* (Collegeville, MN: Liturgical Press, 1996).

---

25. Lawler, *Marriage and the Catholic Church*, 113.

CHAPTER 12

MARRIAGE AND THE FUTURE

As we conclude this book, we reflect on the future of marriage and of the theology of marriage. We have considered many aspects of marriage, including: marriage as a covenant, the nature of love or charity within marriage, the sacramental nature of marriage, the historical/developmental nature of marriage, the dignity of human persons as a foundation for sexuality within marriage, justice as a requirement within marriage, marriage as domestic church, the realities of divorce and annulment, and the need for forgiveness and reconciliation in marriage. Much of what we have said so far is idealistic, which may lead one to wonder, why do marriages seem to be so much in jeopardy if marriage is so wonderful? Can this idealistic theology sustain us and make sense into the future, or does the reality of marriage differ too starkly from this theology to leave much reason for hope?

The questions are fair. Indeed, a Catholic theology of marriage is idealistic and by being idealistic runs the risk of being removed from the reality of lived marriage. For example, Catholic theology posits an ideal of what marriage should look like structurally, assigning responsibilities to men and women based on the presumption that gender carries with it essential qualities. Pope John Paul II, in his apostolic letter *On The Dignity and Vocation of Women*, states:

In our times the question of "women's rights" has taken on new significance in the broad context of the rights of the human person. *The biblical and evangelical message* sheds light on this cause, which is the object of much attention today, *by safeguarding the truth about the "unity" of the "two",* that is to say the truth about that dignity and vocation that result from the specific diversity and personal originality of man and woman. Consequently, even the rightful opposition of women to what is expressed in the biblical words "He shall rule over you" (Gen 3:16) must not under any condition lead to the "masculinization" of women. In the name of liberation from male "domination," women must not appropriate to themselves male characteristics contrary to their own feminine "originality." There is a well-founded fear that if they take this path, women will not "reach fulfillment," but instead will *deform and lose what constitutes their essential richness*. It is indeed an enormous richness. In the biblical description, the words of the first man at the sight of the woman who had been created are words of admiration and enchantment, words which fill the whole history of man on earth.[1]

Contemporary critics of the Church's teaching dispute this gender-role typing, arguing that it is constricting and potentially inequitable.

In a broader, and I would argue healthier, way, however, the Church's teaching on marriage is idealistic in the way it champions marriage as holy, dignified, and the fundamental cornerstone of human social flourishing.

In an era in which marriage is compromised by a boundless array of damaging social factors and detractors, the Church continues to affirm marriage as a holy and sacramental union comparable only to the very love between the Creator and the cosmos. This bold affirmation is heightened by the fact of Catholic divorces and the difficulties that the Catholic Church raises for itself by not simply yielding to the pressure to relax its understanding of marriage. The Church maintains that marriage is a holy vocation and that the family is a domestic church. These ideas so genuinely contrast with societal norms that their oddity merits real consideration. Either it's a false ideal or prophetic wisdom.

Church teaching receives much criticism because it is presumed, often accurately, to have originated with ordained clergy who have no direct experience of marriage beyond that of their parents. That presumption, however, must now shift to accommodate the myriad new voices in theology that come from an increasing population of lay theologians and ministers. These voices often speak out of experience and help us to arrive at a more honest and successful theological understanding of marriage. In particular, recently many theologians on family and marriage have suggested that we consider marriage as an eschatological reality. It is this concept and its applications that we now address.

TOOLS

Eschatology is a branch of theology concerned with the last things: death and judgment, heaven and hell, the end of the world, and so on. The word's Greek roots are *eschaton* for the "end" and *logos* for "study of" or "word." Eschatology is, then, the study of the end.[2] Some theologians distinguish between the study of the *eschata* (the final things) and the study of the *eschaton* (the final event).

From the outset, we should note a curiosity in the idea of eschatology: it suggests that one can make a formal study of something that has not yet occurred, including the culmination of the world's history. Given that no one can know precisely how the end will come, we might argue that there is a fair amount of presumption in the notion of eschatology.

And yet, an eschatological perspective is really central to the Christian faith. Jesus preached the kingdom of God, a reality not yet at hand. Jesus taught what the kingdom of God was like, and he called upon people to repent because he believed its advent was near. Even though the kingdom of God was a future reality, according to Jesus, it was to shape and define his

---

1. *Mulieris Dignitatem*, §10 (italics original).

2. Students interested in eschatology should consult Jerry Walls, ed., *The Oxford Handbook of Eschatology* (New York: Oxford University Press, 2007), in which the subject is explored from perspectives ranging from the biblical to contemporary culture.

followers in the present. The values of this coming kingdom were to be lived out in this world, even though these values radically countered usual assumptions. As Richard McBrien notes:

> At the heart and center of Jesus' message of salvation was his proclamation of the coming of the Kingdom of God as a reality open to everyone, including the destitute poor, the sick and the crippled, and tax collectors, sinners, and prostitutes. . . . To speak of the Kingdom of God is to speak of the exercise of divine power on our behalf. The Kingdom is an apocalyptic symbol referring to God's final act of redemption at the end of the world, and so it is a symbol filled with hope. God, acting as King, visits and redeems his people as a loving father—a father who rejoices over regaining his lost children (e.g., Luke 15:1–32). This is the central theme of Jesus' preaching.[3]

While people value money, fame, and high social esteem in this world, charity, compassion, and service are most valued in the kingdom of God. While social barriers separate people from those outside their racial or socio-economic class in this world, all such barriers will be erased in the kingdom of God. While people are alienated from society because of deformity, disease, and difference in this world, all will be loved and received equally in the kingdom of God. While power rules in this world, humility carries the day in the kingdom of God.

Christians at the time of Jesus and today continue to look to Jesus' revolutionary values to shape their own. Yet anyone can see that the values of the kingdom of God do not today overcome worldly values, just as they did not overcome worldly values in Jesus' day. War and violence then as now afflict every sector of the planet. People continue to suffer abuse and humiliation both as individuals and as subgroups within society. Although Christians believe that Jesus' Resurrection promises new life beyond death, in the present world death remains the inevitable outcome for everyone.

In no way, then, can anyone rightly argue that God's kingdom has been realized on Earth. At best Christians can say that the values of the kingdom of God are emergent in the world, begun by the work of Jesus and carried on by the people of God. But no one can argue that the end has been achieved. The end, which one might call the full realization of God's will for creation, is *in process*. This is the crux of eschatology. Christianity teaches that humans have the example and vision of Jesus as a guide for what should and could become of people individually and collectively. As truly free people, Christians have the power, however imperfect, to attempt to realize the vision first offered by Jesus. Christians remain pilgrims on a journey, who go with faith and hope toward their destination, even while stumbling and getting lost along the way.

From this perspective, eschatology and theology are one and the same. All that Christians may say about God, Scripture, tradition, church, morality, and so on may be termed a pilgrim's progress and process, just as all life everywhere is characterized by progress and process. In its *Dogmatic Constitution on the Church*, the Catholic Church speaks poignantly to this pilgrim's process:

> The church, to which we are all called in Christ Jesus, and in which by the grace of God we attain holiness, will receive its perfection only in the glory of heaven, when the time for renewal of all things will have come (Acts 3:21). At that time,

---

3. McBrien, *Catholicism*, 449–450. McBrien also here suggests that while there is some disagreement as to how to interpret Jesus' kingdom sayings, New Testament scholarship tends to agree that there are four sayings historically attributable to Jesus. These are Matt 11:12; Mark 1:15; Luke 11:20, 17:20–21.

together with the human race, the universe itself, which is closely related to humanity and which through it attains its destiny, will be perfectly established in Christ (see Eph 1:10; Col 1:20; 2 Pet 3:10–13).[4]

Some theologians use the phrase "already but not yet" to describe the eschatological perspective. Everything partakes of this perspective. Examples drawn from everyday life help illustrate this point. Take, for instance, the fertilized egg in the womb. From the perspective of the egg, an impossible journey lies ahead before it can become a self-sustaining human being. From the perspective of a human being in her nineties, it cannot be said that she once was not the fertilized egg. For everything she is now was possible within the egg's future trajectory of progress and process. In an even broader perspective, this ninety-year-old woman was also in a latent but undeniable form already present as a possibility-to-be-realized in her mother's ovum, and in her grandmother's before her.

Consider the experience of a college education. As eighteen-year-olds recently graduated from high school, students are asked to declare a major, although they as yet know little about the fields they will pursue; such knowledge is acquired only gradually, as students progress in their chosen fields. The end of becoming a professional is implied in the process of discovering what the end actually entails. And yet it can be said of the accomplished physician—to cite one example—that the possibility of her becoming a physician was already present within her as a toddler in preschool.

Understood as a study of future possibilities, an eschatological perspective can become a source of hope, strength, and vision that gives life purpose and direction. If I have an eschatological perspective about my course of study, I will realize that the hardships of preparing for a final exam, for example, fit within the larger scheme of my professional preparation. I can see my process for what it is and celebrate the steps toward my becoming competent in my field. Professional preparation is but one example of how people implicitly employ an eschatological perspective in their day-to-day activities. Not all fields of study turn out to be the right ones. Even in the process of self-correction, such as in switching majors, one can employ an eschatological perspective that places our actions within the context of their greater life's significance.

The accomplishment of goals does not produce a happy and joyful person if the goals are detached from an ultimate framework of meaning. Even an overtly successful person might not experience inner contentment if his or her successes are merely pearls strung randomly on a string with no eschatological design or purpose. The design, the purpose, gives meaning not only to the process of my becoming an educator but to my choice to become an educator at all. How does my choosing this profession fit with how I understand the ultimate value and purpose of my life? How, in my limited span of time on this earth, does this choice help me to realize my unique gifts, to live out my faith, and to serve and love? Am I doing this because of greed, or fear, or pressure from my family? Or am I doing this because it gives me opportunities to serve, to be my most authentic self, and to love?

An eschatological perspective is ultimately a theological perspective because it forces people to consider the ultimate purpose and value of their choices. To return to our opening comments, it forces us to "study" or think about the "end" even while we are at the beginning or in the middle of things. The end that we do not know in full is nevertheless what calls us and helps us to shape our life's choices.

---

4. *Lumen Gentium*, §48. Used by permission.

From a Christian perspective, when we talk about the kingdom of God, we are talking about an idea that stands as a sharp alternative to the world as it is. Still, the very idea of the kingdom of God helps Christians to operate in the world as if the kingdom of God already existed in its totality. The end that Christians hope for, which is latently possible from the very beginning, is curiously what gives them strength to live so that their free choices align in such a way as to bring it about.

MARRIAGE IN ESCHATOLOGICAL PERSPECTIVE

As with all things in life, marriage can be ultimately satisfying and ultimately "designed" if we bring to it an eschatological perspective.[5] Like every other long-term endeavor, marriage is a work in progress and human beings living within marriages are human beings in progress. We are often tempted to think of marriage as something we enter into, something that is sealed and completed upon delivery, something that—once a wedding has taken place—exists in the past tense. This thinking fosters the illusion that marriage is static and unchanging. It fails to grasp the more vital reality of marriage as a dynamic relationship between living and changing persons.

When marriage is understood to be a vital and dynamic relational process, one can begin to see it as always a present yet future reality. To use eschatological terms, marriage becomes already what one's relationship to a spouse is even while it is not yet fully realized. To speak personally, I am already married to my spouse, but I am always

in the process of becoming one body with him, learning how to live with him, discovering how to find peace with him, and enacting my love for him. This all occurs while I am in the process of becoming myself, realizing my gifts, and learning how to serve others both within and beyond my immediate relations. Marriage is, in this sense, a goal for my relationship with my spouse. I am married to him, yes, but I am always striving to realize fully the love and unity that our marriage was from the beginning intended to bring about.

Even this goal for marriage becomes murky if it stands alone and detached from a deeper, indeed a final, set of values and goals that orient one's total human existence. In this way marriage can finally be understood as a religious vocation. If by "religious" we mean those ideas that characterize our finest notions of a higher power and the best of human ability, then marriage as a religious vocation is a call to live for one another ultimately and fully. Moreover, marriage becomes a context in which I live out my life as fully as possible. It is the context in which my unique gifts, talents, and goals as a human being can best be realized.

It is not a given that simply by being married one's human potential and that of one's spouse will be realized. Marriage is very much like every other long-term goal. You begin it with a certain hope and expectation for what you want your marriage to be ultimately. As Michael Lawler summarizes:

> [Marriage] has an essentially eschatological dimension. Eschatological is a grand theological word for [a] simple and constant human reality, namely, the experience of having to admit "already, but not yet." Already mutual love, but not yet steadfast; already mutual service, but not yet

---

5. An excellent teaching aid for understanding the eschatological perspective on marriage is Bernard Cooke's lecture, "Indissolubility: Guiding Ideal or Existential Reality," in the video recorded series *Marriage in the Catholic Church* (Kansas City, MO: Sheed & Ward, 1988), pt. 2.

without the desire to control; already one body, but not yet one person; already indissoluble in hope and expectation; but not yet in full human reality; already prophetic representation of the covenant union between Christ and his church; but not yet totally adequate representation. For authentic Christian spouses, Christian marriage is always a challenge to which they are called to respond as followers of the Christ who is for them the prophetic symbol of God.[6]

A SYSTEMATIC THEOLOGY OF MARRIAGE

Everything we have considered about marriage falls into place when we think of marriage in an eschatological perspective. From a biblical point of view, the notion of covenant is, at the very least, a lofty ideal. If marriages always had to be covenants all the time, people would often feel like failures. Yet, from an eschatological perspective, a marriage covenant is a goal toward which marriage strives. Marriages are not guaranteed covenants but they may become covenants through commitment and effort. Likewise, charity within marriage is sometimes difficult to realize, but even when spouses miss the mark, the goal of self-giving love remains as a corrective and a challenge to try again.

Sacraments, as the Catholic Church teaches, are signs of grace. The grace of sacraments is witnessed in their effects. What is the effect of the sacrament of marriage, and when does the sacrament take place? From an eschatological perspective, the sacrament of marriage is always in the process of becoming and of gracing spouses with its hopes and possibilities and blessings. The union of a couple, indeed

the consummation of a couple, happens over a committed lifetime of two people intending to become fully one while learning how in their oneness to be most authentically themselves. Their indissolubility as a wedded couple deepens as their marriage more and more becomes covenant and sacrament.

Throughout life people strive to find dignity, to understand the value of all human life, and to enact love as a requirement of authentic justice. Those who achieve a character marked by these qualities are rare and sublime, and for all but true prophets, these qualities exceed most of us much of the time. Nevertheless, dignity and justice for all persons remain the criteria that define goodness and excellent human society, even while they evade our grasp. From an eschatological perspective, people can and should strive toward dignity, honoring ourselves and others and forgiving one another our shames. Within marriage a couple can struggle to be a domestic church, even as they debate the boundaries and competing needs that exist in the tension between societal and familial obligations.

From an eschatological perspective, even marriage failure can be forgiven. Sometimes human beings fail, even while striving toward a noble goal, and even when strengthened by grace. Christians can find solace in the notion that Christ came to save sinners, that is, imperfect people who are in process. Catholics can take solace in the Church's own pilgrim journey, as it strives in all-too-human form to become the vanguard for kingdom values on earth. In an eschatological perspective, self-righteousness is replaced by the humble acknowledgement that all people can do better. A marriage undertaken in good faith may lack the requisite eschatological vision to sustain it into a fully realized union

---

6. Michael Lawler, "Marriage in the Bible," in *Perspectives on Marriage: A Reader*, eds. Kieran Scott and Michael Warren, 3rd ed. (New York and Oxford: Oxford University Press, 2007), 19.

of persons, but forgiveness and reconciliation remain as healing balms that enable former spouses and their children to move on.

In conclusion, an eschatological perspective on marriage is a human perspective just as it is a theological perspective. From a theological perspective, it is concerned with the ultimate goals and purpose of marriage: what marriage is to be, what it is to do, how it will define the total story and final value of two human lives. From a human perspective, it is concerned with the process of living and becoming as we actually exist; that is, in the tension of already-but-not-yet, already married but always becoming married in new and fuller dimensions. An eschatological perspective on marriage reminds us that process and progress are essential to experiencing not only permanence but also transcendent purpose in the journey together.

THE FUTURE OF MARRIAGE

From many accounts, marriage is in crisis. Poverty threatens families throughout the world, and the most vulnerable families are those in which marriage is not even present, that is, single-parent households. Teenage pregnancy is rising and becoming more socially acceptable, even while it puts children and their children at risk. It is increasingly common for couples to choose to live together before marriage, which statistically puts them at higher risk of divorce after marriage. The combined figures for divorces among first and second marriages results in a twenty-first-century divorce rate of nearly 50 percent in the United States. Couples marry later in life than ever before, and many cohabiting couples choose not to marry. Culturally relaxed attitudes toward pre-marital, extra-marital, and non-marital sex suggest that people will delay marriage if they marry at all. One in four households is unsafe due to domestic violence.

Changing economic realities give couples, and particularly women, more freedom in marriage than ever before. People no longer have to stay in bad marriages because of financial need. Moreover, changing understandings of personhood, driven by new studies in gender, psychology, biology, and philosophy, have uprooted the traditional, patriarchal model of family life. Men and women eschew classic molds and expectations of family life, even while they search for meaningful, functional, and ever-evasive alternatives. Non-traditional models of family life are explored, particularly by same-sex couples seeking legal marriage as both an option and a legal right.

All this change has resulted in an upheaval of marriage and its dependability as a social reality. People ask themselves why they should marry, especially when marriage so often appears to be a liability to personal freedom, safety, and happiness. Persons denied marriage, such as same-sex couples, see the inability to marry legally as discrimination, as they view marriage as the ultimate gateway to full social recognition and participation.

In helping to negotiate such questions and crises facing contemporary marriages, it is helpful to remember that the future of marriage as a function of society may also be viewed from an eschatological perspective. Thinking of marriage in this way invites a number of questions about the long-term goals and purposes of marriage today and into the future. What role does marriage play in societal human flourishing? What role does marriage play in the realization of social justice, human dignity, authentic charity, and freedom within society as a whole? One's view of the good of marriage and laws that surround marriage should be formed in relationship to an understanding of marriage as it relates to the common welfare. Is marriage an integral part of society? Should it be? How should it be? Why? Does it reflect the values of the kingdom of God? Can I define my understanding of these values and place marriage within them?

Consider the following questions, based on the above discussion:

- How does the openness or restriction of marriage licenses benefit society? How do both options reflect kingdom values, charity, dignity, justice?
- What does it take to make a covenant? How do covenants build up society? Whose covenants build up society? Do some covenants not build up society at all?
- How do laws define and enforce punishment for domestic violence? Is combating domestic violence a priority of your state? Why or why not?
- How does access to or restriction from legal divorce bolster good marriage?
- How do custody and child support laws contribute to the common welfare?
- What access to reproductive technologies is appropriate? How do these technologies affect marriage?
- How difficult or easy is it in your state to adopt? How does this reflect your state's view of marriage and family?
- How difficult or easy is it in your state to obtain an abortion? What laws surround it?

Who has abortions? Why do people choose to have abortions?

The point of this text is to establish a theological foundation for thinking about marriage, not to settle all questions. It is up to you, the reader, to think through these issues from a theological point of view. I would argue that unreflective marriage benefits no one. The passion of sexual attraction wears off over time, and the daily tasks of laundry, dishes, work, and diapers can become boring if not hated. Hostility, frustration, and a general sense of "I could have done better" can lead people into marital decline, complete with feelings of powerlessness and suffocation.

On the other hand, reflective marriage, seen from an eschatological perspective, is a gift and opportunity. Such a marriage is lived deliberately and is attached to the deepest sense of one's purpose and personal value. Marriage that strives to be covenant and sacrament, marriage that strives to realize dignity and justice, marriage that manifests itself in charity and holy union, marriage that transmits life to children and kin and neighbor is a prophetic stance against all the worst in society and an affirmation of all that is possible in human relationships. Such a marriage represents the possibility of the real becoming the ideal.

Questions for Review and Discussion

1. What is eschatology? Elaborate on the phrase "already but not yet."

2. How is Jesus' teaching about the kingdom of God eschatological?

3. How is marriage an eschatological reality? Does thinking about marriage from this perspective change your understanding of marriage as an institution?

4. Do process and progress define all human endeavors? Explain.

5. Does an eschatological perspective affect thinking about marriage from a broad social point of view? Explain.

6. What is the future of marriage? What are some of the difficulties today's marriages

continued

Questions for Review and Discussion

continued

face, and how would you respond to these dangers individually and collectively?

7. Can the Catholic theology of marriage, in all its idealism, be realized? Is it a viable guide for people entering into marriages today? What are its strengths and weaknesses? Does a Catholic theology of marriage have value for those who are not Catholic? Explain.

8. What is your personal theology of marriage and family life?

Resources for Further Reading

Resources for Eschatology

Carl Braaten and Robert Jensen, eds., *The Last Things: Biblical and Theological Perspectives on Eschatology* (Grand Rapids, MI: Eerdmans, 2002).

Zachary Hayes, *Visions of a Future: A Study of Christian Eschatology* (Collegeville, MN: Liturgical Press, 1990).

Resources for Marriage Today and Tomorrow

Marvin Ellison, *Same-Sex Marriage? A Christian Ethical Analysis* (Cleveland, OH: Pilgrim Press, 2004).

Margaret Farley, *A Framework for Christian Sexual Ethics* (New York and London: Continuum, 2006).

Michael Lawler, *Family: American and Christian* (Chicago: Loyola Press, 1998).

Kieran Scott and Michael Warren, eds., *Perspectives on Marriage: A Reader* (New York: Oxford University Press, 2007).

INDEX

An 'f' following a page number indicates a figure. An 's' indicates a sidebar.

A

abandonment, 109, 128, 130
abduction, 134
Abogunrin, Samuel Oyin, 22
abortions, 24, 86, 147
abuse. *see also* domestic violence
    child/elder, 109
    dignity and, 86
    justice and, 110, 111
    morality and, 111–12
    patriarchy and, 101
    sexual, 85, 108
    what to do, 111s
Acts, Book of, 20–21, 31, 51
Adam and Eve. *see* creation stories
adoption, 84, 134, 147
adultery. *see also* infidelity
    annulments and, 136
    Augustine on, 43
    divorce and, 28, 130
    injustice and, 109
    Leviticus and, 13
    remarriage and, 131
    Roman Empire and, 38
affection, 19, 132
affinity, 134
agape, 30
age at marriage, 81, 146
Age of Reason, 66–67
annulments, 57, 65, 133–37
Anselm, 103–4
anthropology, theological, 85, 98s
apostolic succession, 40

a priori principles, 78
Aquinas, Thomas, 44, 75, 96–97
arete, 97
Aristotle, 44, 60, 96, 97
arranged marriages, 43, 45, 52, 67, 114
asceticism, 41
atonement, 76
attraction, 19
Augustine, 42–43, 56, 64–65, 75, 90s
authority, 43–44, 107, 127, 137

B

Babylon, 7–8, 15
banns of marriage, 61s
baptism, 54, 64, 132
Benedict XVI, 19–20
bias, 6
Bible, The, 7s, 75, 129. *see also* New Testament; Old Testament
Bieringer, Reimund, 103, 110
biological kinship, 27
birth control, 86
bishop of Rome, 63
bishops, 40, 41, 63. *see also* United States Conference of Catholic Bishops
Black Death (bubonic plague), 60
bodies. *see also* sexuality
    Catholic Church and, 110
    dignity and, 80

    Greeks and, 41
    image of God and, 85
    Jesus', 50–51
    justice and, 111
    love and, 103
    motherhood and, 83
    patriarchy and, 108
    sacramentality and, 50
body of Christ, 26–30, 51
Bonaventure, 44
bonds of marriage, 132–33, 134
bride price, 38
bubonic plague (Black Death), 60

C

Cahill, Lisa Sowle, 27
canonization, 7, 40
canon law, 44, 53
Catholic Church. *see* Roman Catholic Church
Catholic Epistles, 21
Catholicism (McBrien), 56
Catholic Reformation, 63
Catholic social teaching, 118–20
celibacy
    basics, 41
    contemporary culture and, 86
    medieval period, 65
    Protestant Reformation and, 64
    remarriage and, 134
    sexuality and, 85
    spirituality and, 66

superiority of, 45
ceremonies, wedding, 1, 15, 44, 57, 61, 116, 134
Challenge of Peace, The (U.S. Bishops), 120
challenges to marriage, 72
change, 34–35, 45, 68s, 93, 94, 144. *see also* conversion
character, 89, 95–98, 145
charity
    bodies and, 110
    conversion and, 95
    covenant, 52, 54
    eschatology and, 145
    God and, 97, 98
    justice and, 113
    marriage and, 30–31
    patriarchy and, 107
    virtues and, 96
Charlemagne, 43, 44
chastisement, right of, 107, 108
child abuse. *see* abuse
childbearing
    Protestant Reformation and, 65
children. *see also* motherhood
    Augustine on, 42
    birth of, 54
    born-out-of-marriage, 81, 82, 129
    charity and, 118
    contemporary culture and, 72
    dignity and, 80
    divorce and, 128–29, 138
    Hebrews and, 24
    Jesus and, 28
    justice and, 104
    non-traditional family structures and, 81–82
    patriarchy and, 29, 107
    Protestant Reformation and, 65
    Renaissance and, 63
    Roman Empire and, 22–23
    Second Vatican Council on, 121
    sexuality and, 86
    spirituality and, 55
choice. *see* freedom
Christ. *see also* Jesus
    charity and, 98

church and, 29–30
    indissolubility and, 56
    Roman Catholic Church and, 53
Christian Behavior (Lewis), 89
Christian marriage, 57
Church in the Modern World, The (Second Vatican Council), 56
Church law, 61
church marriages, 44
classes, social
    Catholic social teaching and, 119, 120
    18th–20th centuries and, 68
    kingdom of God and, 25, 142
    love and, 79
    polygamy and, 45
    Reformation and, 64
    violence and, 108
    women and, 70
clergy
    basics, 35
    Church teaching and, 141
    early, 41, 43, 45
    Reformation and, 64, 65
    sexuality and, 85, 86
Code of Canon Law (Roman Catholic Church), 53, 56
cohabitation, 81, 82, 128, 134, 146
commitment, 83, 93, 109, 132
common good (welfare). *see also* service
    charity and, 52
    dignity and, 77–79, 120
    divorce and, 128
    eschatology and, 146–47
    family and, 118, 121, 123
    Jesus and, 119
    New Testament and, 24
    sexuality and, 83–84
communication, 72, 80, 91
Communion (Eucharist), 54, 55s, 64
communities. *see also* common good (welfare)
    adultery and, 13
    attitudes toward sexuality and, 82

charity and, 98
Church and, 56
dignity and, 80
divorce and, 128, 129, 136
families and, 118, 120s
individualism and, 114
justice and, 103
Paul and, 21
companionship, 71, 77, 81
compassion, 30
Confessions, The (Augustine), 42
confirmation, 54
consanguinity, 61, 132, 134
consent, 44, 57, 62, 109, 134, 135
Constantine, 40
Constitution on the Church in the Modern World (*Gaudium et Spes*) (Catholic Church), 121
consumerism, 115–17, 118, 123, 126–27. *see also* money
consummation, 44, 53, 57, 133, 145
context, 7, 34–46, 47, 60, 83, 103, 109. *see also specific contexts*
contraception, 24
contracts, 17
convents/nuns, 41, 63, 64, 65
conversion, 88–89, 92–96, 99, 111, 130–31
Coontz, Stephanie, 67
Corinthians, First Letter to (Paul), 31, 56, 99, 130
corporeality, 41
corrective actions, 92
Cotts, Nancy, 109
councils, ecumenical, 40, 43, 53, 61s, 63, 66. *see also* Second Vatican Council
counseling, 116, 136, 137s
Counter-Reformation, 63
covenants
    basics, 5–17
    bodies and, 110
    charity and, 52, 54
    Christian, 32
    eschatology and, 145
    fertility and, 11
    indissolubility of, 17
    justice and, 102–3

law and, 12
love and, 52–53
marriage and, 13, 16–17, 52, 94
meaning and, 15
New Testament, 20
Old Testament, 9, 10–12, 14, 15, 16, 102–3
patriarchy and, 107
coverture, 107
creation, 49–51, 52, 77–78. *see also* natural world
creation stories, 10–11, 30, 48–49, 141
crime, 82, 134
Crusades, 44
culture. *see* context
Cur Deus Homo (*Why God Became Man*) (Anselm), 103–4

D

Damian, Peter, 53
daughters, 24
death, 54, 142
deceit, 134
declaration of nullity, 57, 135. *see also* annulments
De Doctrina Christiana (*Teaching Christianity*) (Augustine), 90s
de factor relatives, 134
democracy, 64, 66, 68, 127
denominationalism, 64
dignity
basics, 75, 77–85, 119, 120
bodies and, 110
Catholic Church and, 110–11
contemporary applications, 85–86
conversion and, 95
eschatology and, 145
friendship and, 97
interdependence and, 121
patriarchy and, 107
women and, 140–41
disease, 82, 128
dismissals, 130
disparity of cult, 134

diversity, 2, 64
divine, the, 17
divorce. *see also* indissolubility; remarriage
abuse and, 111
Augustine on, 43
Babylonian spouses and, 8
basics, 137–38
canon law and, 44
consumerism and, 116
contemporary culture and, 72
domestic violence and, 31–32
early church and, 38
Enlightenment and, 67
fall of Rome and, 43
Hebrews and, 24
indissolubility and, 57
Jesus and, 28, 131
medieval period and, 45
Protestant Reformation and, 65
rate, 1, 127–28, 146
reasons for, 126
recovery ministries, 136
Renaissance and, 61–62
Dogmatic Constitution on the Church (Catholic Church), 142
domestic church, 121–24, 145
domestic roles, 62–63
domestic violence, 31–32, 107, 111s, 146, 147. *see also* abuse
dowry, 38

E

early Christians, 31, 37–41
ecclesial marriage, 42, 45, 55, 56, 61, 132, 133, 136
ecclesial reform, 63
ecclesiastic leaders, 42
ecclesiology, 36
economic activity, 62–63, 69–71, 80, 127, 128, 146
ecumenical councils, 40, 43, 53, 61, 63, 66. *see also* Second Vatican Council
education
dignity and, 119

modern world and, 69, 71
reformation and, 63, 64
Renaissance and, 60–61
sexuality and, 86
women and, 41, 61
ego, 92, 95
Egypt, 11–12
18th-20th centuries, 67–69, 107–8
elder abuse. *see* abuse
Elsbernd, Mary, 102–3, 110
emotions
cohabitation and, 82
divorce and, 128
Enlightenment and, 67
forgiveness and, 138
love and, 17
patriarchy and, 106
respect and, 83
sin and, 91
ends, 78
enemies, 30
enfranchisement, 68
Enlightenment, 64, 66–67, 68, 71
Ephesians, Letter to, 28–29
Epistles, 21
equality, 39, 109
eros, 30
eschatology, 141–45
Eucharist (Communion), 54, 55, 64
European revolutions, 68
evolutionary biology, 69
excellence, 97, 145
exclusivity, 110
Exodus, 11–12, 13s
expectations, 115, 127, 144
experience
Catholic Church and, 137
covenants and, 9
divine, of, 17
God, of, 2
moral theology and, 75
a prior principles and, 78
theology and, 4, 5, 141
extra-marital sex, 85
Ezra, 7s, 8

F

failures, marriage, 57, 91–92, 115, 138, 145
faith
    contemporary culture and, 71
    early marriages and, 38
    family and, 27
    grace and, 51
    love and, 31
    social context and, 35–36
    theology and, 4
faithfulness (fidelity), 8, 16, 17. *see also* infidelity
fallenness, 76
families, 109, 114, 123s. *see also* domestic church; *specific family members*
Family: A Christian Social Perspective (Cahill), 27
Farley, Margaret, 109, 110
fathers, 128
fathers, church, 40
fear or force, 134
feminism (women's movements), 69–71, 82, 108, 140–41
fertility, 11
fidelity. *see* faithfulness
fidelity (faithfulness), 8, 16, 17. *see also* infidelity
finances, 117
force or fear, 134
forgiveness, 14–15, 54, 104, 126, 137–38, 145, 146
form of marriage, 134
foundations, 1, 2
A Framework for Christian Sexual Ethics (Farley), 109, 110
freedom. *see also* individualism
    Enlightenment and, 66
    future and, 142
    God and, 49, 77
    human nature and, 98s
    justice and, 110
    kingdom of God and, 144
    sin and, 76, 92
    successful marriages and, 99
    women and, 69–71

freedom of religion, 34
friendship, 17, 96–97
"From Yoke Mates to Soul Mates," 67
fruitfulness, 54, 109, 110
future, 37, 40, 140–47

G

Gaudium et Spes (*Constitution on the Church in the Modern World*) (Catholic Church), 121
gender, 25, 140–41. *see also* men; women
Genesis, 10–11, 64. *see also* creation stories
Gentiles, 37
Germanic influences, 42, 43, 44
get, 130
Gillespie, V. Bailey, 93
Gnostic Christians, 39s
God. *see also* image of God
    Catholic Church on, 122
    charity and, 98
    conversion and, 104
    friendship with, 97
    human likeness to, 77–78, 122
    justice and, 102–5, 111
    love and, 19–20, 30–31, 90s, 118
    meaning and, 2
    Old Testament and, 10, 12, 16
    sacramentality and, 47–50
    will of, 75–76, 78, 92
Godfather, The (Coppola), 117–18
Gomer, 14, 17, 52, 132
goodness, 104, 145
Good Samaritan, 30
Gospels, 20, 22. *see also specific Gospels*
governments, 34, 43–44, 66–67. *see also* laws; legal marriages
grace
    Catholic Church and, 51, 77
    conversion and, 88, 95
    creation and, 49s
    Jesus and, 50

    marriage and, 45, 52–55, 53, 54, 99
    natural world and, 50
    Protestant churches and, 64
    sacramentality and, 49, 74
    sacramentals and, 55
    sacraments and, 51s
    salvation and, 76
    sin and, 77
    spouses and, 57
Gratian, Francis, 44
Greco-Roman world, 40–41, 62
Greek influences, 40–41, 60, 96, 98
guilds, 62

H

habit, 97, 99
happiness, 95, 115, 116, 117, 127, 128, 143
healing, 51, 111, 138
Healing, Sacraments of, 54
Hebrew Bible. *see* Old Testament
Hebrews, 24, 25. *see also* Old Testament
heterosexual cohabitation, 81
hierarchy, 123s. *see also* patriarchy
historical context, 34–46, 47, 60, 83, 103, 109. *see also specific contexts*
holy orders of matrimony, 54–55
Holy Spirit, 37, 51, 121, 139
homes, 63
homicides, 108
homosexuality, 13. *see also* same-sex couples
hope, 31
Hosea, 14–15, 17, 52, 132
hospitality, 110
housework, 63
humanism, 60–61, 62, 64
human nature, 96, 98s, 121
humility, 99, 139, 145
husbands. *see also* men; spouses
    contemporary culture and, 72
    duties of, 29–30, 38
    Genesis, in, 10

love and, 79
modern roles, 59
patriarchy and, 107
Renaissance and, 62, 63
spirituality and, 55

I

ideals
  achievement of, 147
  annulments and, 137
  Catholic Church and, 57, 77,
    141
  sexuality and, 83
  sin and, 88
  struggles for, 92–93
  theology and, 140
identity, 8, 9, 15, 17, 71, 122, 131
idolatry, 118
image of God (*imago dei*)
  Catholic social teaching and,
    120
  conversion and, 92
  dignity and, 78, 79, 83
  patriarchy and, 107
  reproduction and, 86
  sexuality and, 85
  spouses and, 95
  virtues and, 96
imperfection, 57, 137, 145
impotence (sexual), 133
incapacity, 134
Incarnation, 50
independence, 48, 114
indissolubility, 17, 43, 56, 61–62,
  65, 131–32, 145. *see also* annulments; divorce
individualism, 77, 114–15, 118,
  123, 126–27
individuality, 27, 79, 89, 94, 103,
  118–20. *see also* personhood
infidelity, 13, 14, 15, 128. *see also*
  adultery
Initiation, Sacraments of, 54
injustice, 101–9, 117. *see also*
  justice
insanity, 134

institutional Christianity, 22, 35,
  40, 61, 74
intentions, 134
interdependence, 48, 78, 79, 119,
  121, 122
interpretation, 7–8, 8–9, 31–32,
  39s, 78, 131
intrinsic value of the human
  person, 77
Islam, 44, 60, 93
Israel, 10f, 14, 15
Israelites, 7–8, 10–11, 12, 17, 19,
  20, 103

J

Jeremiah, 7–8
Jesus. *see also* Christ; New Testament; salvation
  basics, 22–25
  churches and, 37–38, 42,
    53–54
  conversion and, 92, 95
  divorce and, 28, 131
  family and, 26–28
  grace and, 50
  justice and, 101–2, 103, 105
  kingdom of God and, 141–42
  love and, 19–20
  marginalized people and, 23
  marriage, on, 28
  sacramentality and, 50–51
  service and, 113
  sin and, 76–77, 88
  social classes and, 119
  virtues and, 97
  women and, 24–25, 28, 130
Jesus movement, 33, 51
John, First Letter of, 30–31
John, Gospel of, 19–20
  marriage, on, 52
John Paul II, 79, 140–41
John the Baptist, 22
Joseph, 11–12
Judah, 14, 15
Judaism, 5, 38, 130. *see also* Old
  Testament

justice. *see also* domestic church;
  injustice; social justice
  basics, 77
  charity and, 30
  contemporary applications,
    111–12
  Enlightenment and, 67
  eschatology and, 145
  families and, 105–9
  God's mercy and, 103–5
  kingdom of God and, 26
  love and, 31, 101, 102–3, 110
  women and, 71

K

kingdom of God, 25–26, 28,
  141–42, 144, 145, 146–47
Kingston, Anne, 116
kisses, 55
knowledge, 4, 5, 61, 92. *see also*
  truth
Kotva, Joseph, 96

L

lack of canonical discretion, 134
Law, Mosaic, 28, 30, 37, 130
Lawler, Michael, 132, 138–39, 144
laws, 10–14, 133
lay people, 35
leadership, 39, 40, 42. *see also*
  patriarchy
legal marriages, 44, 56, 61, 67, 130,
  132, 133
Leo III, 43
Leviticus, 12–13
Lewis, C.S., 2, 89, 94
licenses, 147
literacy, 60, 61, 63, 71
literary genres, 8
Liturgy of the Word, 55
Lombard, Peter, 44, 53
Lonergan, Bernard, 94
loss, 15, 137, 138
love. *see also* charity

attraction *vs.*, 19
Augustine on, 90s
body of Christ and, 29
bond, as, 133
character and, 99
contemporary culture and, 1, 71
early marriages and, 38
Enlightenment and, 67
families and, 27, 32
God and, 111, 122
grace and, 52
justice and, 96, 101, 102–4, 109, 110, 117
legal marriages and, 132
Old Testament and, 15–16, 17
sacramentals and, 55
Second Vatican Council on, 121
sexual intercourse and, 83
sin and, 89
Luke, Gospel of, 20–21, 25s, 28, 39, 130
Lumen Gentium (Second Vatican Council), 121
lust, 64–65. *see also* sexuality

M

marginalized people, 23, 103
Marin, Peter, 115
Mark, Gospel of, 28, 39, 130
Marriage Amendment, Federal, 34
marriage tribunals, 57s, 135
Martha (sister of Mary), 24–25
martyrs, 40
Mary (sister of Martha), 25
Mary Magdalene, 39
Mass, 55
Matthew, Gospel of, 25s, 27, 28, 130
Mattison, William, 97
McBrien, Richard, 56, 142
McFague, Sallie, 70s
meaning of existence, 2, 15, 49, 78, 79, 119, 143
meaning of marriage, 47, 52, 57, 59, 67, 144
Meaning of Wife, The (Kingston), 116

Medici family, 60
medieval period, 43–44, 53, 64
men. *see also* gender; husbands; patriarchy; *individual men*
children and, 81–82
contemporary culture and, 71, 146
Enlightenment and, 67
Genesis, in, 10
patriarchy and, 106
Renaissance and, 60, 62
sexuality and, 24, 85
violence and, 108
mercy, 102, 103–5, 104, 111
middle class, 63. *see also* classes, social
miracles, 12, 66
missionaries, 21
modernization, 67–69
monasteries/monks, 41, 42, 44, 65
money, 89, 117. *see also* classes, social; consumerism
monks/monasteries, 41, 42, 44, 65
monogamy, 110
morality. *see also* virtues
abuse and, 111–12
Catholics and, 91
conversion and, 94
dignity and, 75–76
domestic church and, 123
love and, 103, 118
teleological models and, 90
theology and, 119
moral theology, 74–75, 84, 92
Mosaic Law, 28, 30, 37, 130
Moses, 12, 28
motherhood, 70, 71, 81, 83
Muslims, 44
mutuality, 79, 109
mysteries, sacred, 42

N

natural law, 75–76
natural world, 48, 49–50, 75, 120. *see also* creation
neighborliness, 30

New Testament. *see also individual authors; individual personages; specific books*
Augustine on, 90s
basics, 20–25, 37
canonization and, 40
conversion and, 93, 95
covenants and, 16
divorce and, 129, 130–31
justice and, 103
marriage and family, on, 26–32
virtues and, 96
women and, 39s
non-age impediment, 133
non-Catholic marriages, 134
non-traditional families, 81, 146
nuclear families, 114
nuns/convents, 41, 63, 64, 65

O

Old Testament, 5–17, 52, 93, 129–30, 141. *see also* Israelites; Mosaic Law; prophets; *specific books*
On The Dignity and Vocation of Women (John Paul II), 140–41
On the Family (John Paul II), 79
On the Good of Marriage (Augustine), 42
option for the poor, 119
Origin of Species (Darwin), 69
orthodoxy, 40, 42
Osiek, Carolyn, 24
Ozment, Steven, 64, 65

P

pagan converts, 37
pantheism, 48–49
parents, 128, 137–38. *see also* spouses
participation, 110
Pastoral Constitution on the Church in the Modern World (Second Vatican Council), 115